Team Sports Marketing

Pè

Team Sports Marketing

Kirk L. Wakefield

AMSTERDAM • BOSTON • HEIDELBERG • LONDON
NEW YORK • OXFORD • PARIS • SAN DIEGO
SAN FRANCISCO • SINGAPORE • SYDNEY • TOKYO

Butterworth-Heinemann is an imprint of Elsevier

Butterworth–Heinemann is an imprint of Elsevier
30 Corporate Drive, Suite 400, Burlington, MA 01803, USA
Linacre House, Jordan Hill, Oxford OX2 8DP, UK

 Recognizing the importance of preserving what has been written, Elsevier prints
its books on acid-free paper whenever possible.

Library of Congress Cataloging-in-Publication Data
Application submitted

British Library Cataloguing-in-Publication Data
A catalogue record for this book is available from the British Library.

ISBN 13: 978-0-7506-7979-4
ISBN 10: 0-7506-7979-4

For information on all Butterworth–Heinemann publications visit our Web site at
www.books.elsevier.com

Printed in China

06 07 08 09 10   10 9 8 7 6 5 4 3 2 1

Contents

Preface

Team Sports Marketing is different from any other book you have read on the subject of sports marketing—and maybe different from any other book on any subject that has been authored by an academic. This book is different in three ways. First, it contains frequent attempts at humor. The time-tested true practice of academic writers has been to force readers to learn without enjoying it. Evidence of this fact is that Steven Levitt's *Freakenomics* is a *NY Times* Bestseller and he's taken his show on the road to speak to concert-hall audiences—just because someone finally succeeded in making economics interesting. Thankfully, sports marketing is interesting in its own right and offers plenty of opportunities to inject humorous anecdotes and otherwise superfluous remarks that will probably be the only thing that students will remember when it comes test time. Second, this book differs from other sports marketing books in its framework and content. A review of most other sports marketing texts and a principles of marketing text reveals pretty much the same subject matter—only in the sports marketing books they write about sports rather than other goods and services. This text, then, goes beyond principles of marketing. Yes, principles of marketing still work in sports, but there's more to sports marketing than that. Consequently, it is useful, but not necessary, that readers of this book will have already studied principles of marketing offered in fine business schools everywhere. Third, this book is written from the perspective of those involved in marketing teams (or individual players) to a paying audience who consumes events, merchandise, and media that bring revenue to the organization. Other sports marketing books tend to mix the marketing of team sports and sport participation or fitness, which is quite a different thing. The motivation to participate in sport is much different than a fan's motivation to attend a sporting event. A glance at the typical fan guzzling a beer at the ballpark crystallizes that point.[1] So, if you're looking for guidance in running your own fitness center, you should read this book

---

[1]Although it is possible that the latter motivates the former, in that the beer-guzzling fan may be motivated to start working out to get in shape. But, we doubt it.

because it's entertaining, but it won't be of any help whatsoever in your work. Well, OK, it may provide some help, but not much. Those most likely to benefit from reading this book are those who (want to) work in professional and collegiate sports and plan to put the practices spelled out in these pages into action.

Much thanks and appreciation is given to those individuals and organizations who have allowed me to research their fans, accompany them in their game-day activities, pick their collective-brains, and to otherwise learn from them. While many have helped along the way, in particular I would like to thank the following individuals and their respective organizations for their sincere friendship and willingness to be involved in the learning process: Russ Bookbinder (Executive Vice President), Lawrence Payne (Senior Vice President of Broadcasting), and Joe Clark (Vice-President of Ticket Sales) with the **San Antonio Spurs**; Colin Faulkner (Vice President of Ticket Sales) and Geoff Moore (Executive Vice President of Sales & Marketing) with the **Dallas Stars**; David Peart (Executive Vice President of Sales & Marketing) with the **San Francisco 49ers**; Jamey Rootes (Senior Vice President of Sales & Marketing) and John Vidalin (Vice President of Corporate Sales) with the **Houston Texans**; Andy Silverman (Vice President of Tickets) and Jeff Cogen (Chief Operating Officer) with the **Texas Rangers**; Matt Fitzgerald (Vice President of Marketing), George Killebrew (Senior VP of Corporate Sponsorships), and George Prokos (Vice President of Ticket Sales) of the **Dallas Mavericks**; Chris McGowan (Senior Vice President of Sales & Marketing) with **AEG/LA Kings**; Robin Woith (Director of Marketing and Corporate Partnerships) with the **Dallas Cowboys**; John Dillon (Vice President of Marketing) and Tad Brown (Senior Vice President of Sales) with the **Houston Rockets**; Aaron Bryan (Director of Database Marketing) with the **National Basketball Association**; Steve Schanwald (Executive Vice President of Business Operations) with the **Chicago Bulls**; Kerry Sewell (Vice President of Marketing and Communications) with the **Memphis Redbirds**; Michael Hansen (Director of Licensing) with **Nike, Inc.**; Bill Glenn (Vice President of Analytics) with **The Marketing Arm**; Tena Griffith (Manager of Sports Marketing) with **Southwest Airlines**; Kelly Roddy (Director of Sales & Marketing) with **HEB Groceries**; and Ronnie Vandiver (Texas Zone Marketing Manager) with **State Farm**. I especially want to thank (a) Kerry Stover (Principal) with **www.ithinkinc.com** for his technical research support and services for some of the primary research reported in this book and for his continued friendship and support given to me and Baylor University, and (b) Eric Fernandez (Director of Sponsorships) with **AT&T** for providing excellent insights into how effective sponsorships are created, managed, and evaluated—and for basically being an all-around great guy. Finally, I would like to thank noted Pulitzer-Prize winner, author Dave Barry, for his inspiring words when I asked him to write the Foreword for this book, "I'm sorry, but I am <u>WAY</u> behind in a book deadline and I'm just not doing anything else right now. P.S. <u>WAY</u> BEHIND."

What Is Sports Marketing?

1

A Special Case of What?

Some might argue that sports marketing is a "special case" of marketing, meaning that there are theoretical and practical dimensions of marketing that are peculiar to sports marketing. For instance, courses are offered in services marketing, international marketing, internet marketing, business-to-business marketing, and the like because the applications of marketing to these particular contexts require some adaptation specific or special to each case. Following this logic, we should accordingly treat sports marketing as a special case to study because its processes do not function or generalize well for other goods and services. That is, special cases of marketing do not possess theoretically sound (or law-like) principles or axioms that guide practice across a variety of other business contexts.

If, however, sports marketing better explains and predicts effective marketing when compared to other product and services marketing, then one might argue that *marketing* is actually a special case of sports marketing. General theories of marketing should ultimately possess superior predictive and explanatory powers of marketing effectiveness. As we examine the differences between typical goods/services marketing and sports marketing, consider which characteristics better explain optimal buyer-seller relationships.

What's the Difference?

If a customer is a loyal Folgers coffee customer, we can predict that he or she will likely continue to buy Folgers coffee at the grocery store.

A loyal Folgers' customer may, however, switch to similar coffee (Maxwell House) or buy Folgers at another store if appropriately discounted. You won't see many Folgers' customers wearing shirts with its brand name emblazoned across the chest.[1] Nor are you aware of many people who, of their own free will, frequently visit www.folgers.com. If so, they must be the same people who are visiting www.tide.com, www.zest.com, or www.crest.com. The consumer's purchase of Folgers is primarily an economic decision based upon the perceived value of what one gets (coffee) for what one pays (e.g., $2.99 for a 13 ounce can). Some may also perceive that the best part of waking up is Folgers in the cup, but we know of no empirical evidence to support this.

If an individual is a fan of a professional or major college sports team, even a losing team,[2] we can predict that the fan will likely:

1. Identify with and follow the behavior of the team and individual players on that team, on and off the field (via www.espn.com, team Web sites, newspapers, television, radio, wireless, etc.).
2. Purchase licensed merchandise (jerseys, automobile paraphernalia, caps, mugs, etc.) promoting the team.
3. Donate or pay for permanent seat-licenses (PSLs) in order to buy season tickets.
4. Travel to see games of that team outside the local market.
5. Support tax-based initiatives to pay for a new arena or stadium for the team.
6. Be a supporter of the conference or league in which the team plays.
7. Devote significant social time attending, watching, and discussing the team with others devoted to the same or other teams.

The fundamental reason that fans are willing to exert effort and expend resources to support their team is due to consumer surplus. Consumer surplus is the difference between what the fan is prepared or willing to pay and the price that a team charges for a ticket. Specifically, teams sell tickets when the value (V) the fan places on the experience of being at the event equals or exceeds the price (P) that the team charges for admission to the event. In general, a transaction can take place (viz., tickets can be sold) as long as V exceeds the cost (C)

---

[1] Folgers has, however, sponsored NASCAR drivers with the Folgers' name prominently displayed on caps, shirts, and other merchandise that fans have worn.

[2] Fisher, Robert J., and Wakefield, Kirk L. 1998. Factors leading to group identification: A field study of winners and losers. *Psychology & Marketing* 15 (January): 23–40.

Components of Fan Value Analysis

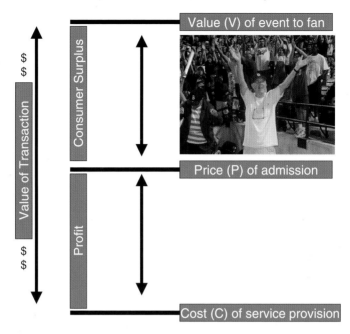

Source: Adapted from Roberts, John H. 2000. Developing new rules for new markets. *Journal of the Academy of Marketing Science*, 28 (Winter): 31–45.

to the team providing the event. Figure 1.1 illustrates the situation in which fans' perceived value exceeds the price of admission.

While consumers of most goods and services see value as primarily an economic evaluation (Which detergent is the best buy?), the value fans derive from attending sporting events is likely to be more than a mere economic decision. In fact, when teams make fans focus on the price they are paying, they are focusing on the wrong side of the equation. The whole point is to make them fans—not consumers in the traditional sense. This is the first fundamental difference between sports marketing and marketing of most goods and services.

Compared to typical goods and services marketing, sports marketing differs in at least ten respects (see Table 1.1). We begin by discussing the difference between customers and fans.

1. Fanatics

A central point of differentiation between sports marketing and traditional goods/services marketing (hereafter, GSM) is how we view individual purchasers. One typically refers to customers when the subject is goods and services. Sports teams and players have fans. Dictionary.com defines a customer as: "One that buys goods or

Table 1.1

Top 10 Differences between Goods/Services Marketing and Sports Marketing			
Top 10	**Dimension**	**Goods/services**	**Sports teams/events**
1	Purchasers	Customers	Fanatics
2	Adoption	Loyalty—repeat purchasers of the same brand (viz., lack of switching behavior)	Psychological identification with individuals and teams that goes beyond mere loyalty
3	Promotion and Media	Owner pays media for promotion	Fans, sponsors, and media pay to promote team/event
4	Distribution Channel	Static; more site-limited	Mobile; more flexible
5	Product	Adapted	Global
6	Price	Customer pays a given price for good/service	Two-part: Fans frequently pay for the *right* to pay for tickets
7	Facilities	Corporate owner buys/ builds own facilities	Government (taxpayer) typically pays for facilities
8	Competition	Individual branding in competitive markets	Cooperative contractual relationships → monopoly power and antitrust exemption
9	Exchange	Principally economic exchange	Principally social exchange
10	Employees	Contractual power favors owners	Contractual power favors employees (players)

services." A fan is "An ardent devotee; an enthusiast"; a fanatic is "A person marked or motivated by an extreme, unreasoning enthusiasm, as for a cause."

Current GSM focuses primarily upon creating customer satisfaction. Satisfaction occurs when expectations are met or exceeded. Satisfied customers mean three things to the company.[3] First, satisfied

---

[3]Gruca, Thomas S., and Rego, Lopo L. 2005. Customer satisfaction, cash flow, and shareholder value. *Journal of Marketing* 69 (July): 115–130.

customers increase the value of the firm to shareholders. Second, satisfied customers assure the firm of future cash flow. Third, satisfied customers reduce the variability in future cash flow.

As with GSM, sports teams seek to satisfy customers. We would expect, however, that fanatics of a team or brand are more than satisfied. Fans experience pleasure and satisfaction with successful teams; but, they also experience feelings of *delight* or excitement that deeply resonates within the identity of the individual fan, such that the effects are likely to be long-term.[4] Delight is a combination of pleasure and arousal with an element of surprise that is frequently experienced in the sports world. Further, fanatics are resilient in the face of service failure (viz., the team loses), and delight and excitement turn to distress and gloom. Sports teams develop a faithful fanatical following primarily due to high levels of identification, which is the second point of differentiation between GSM and sports marketing.

2. Identification

Consumers are loyal to goods and services while fans identify with teams and individuals. Loyalty is the repeat purchasing of a good or service by a consumer. A loyal customer is sensitive to differences in brands and prefers a brand or set of brands over others. Identification is when an individual reacts to events that occur to the team or player as if the events happened to him or her. A highly identified fan will describe one's self to others in terms of being a team fan, perhaps to the point that the fan feels like he or she is part of the team. Fans are certainly loyal to the team in terms of repeat purchases, but fan identification is a deeper psychological affiliation that is a basis for a fan determining his self-esteem and self-worth. Chapter 2 deals more specifically with how teams and players can build fan identification. Because of high fan identification, fans seek out ways to promote the team to others.

3. Promotion and Media

The manufacturer and/or retailer of goods and services pays for the development and placement of brand advertising and promotions. In contrast, sports teams and individuals (players and drivers) receive

---

[4]See Oliver, Richard J., Rust, Roland T., and Varki, Sajeev. 1997. Customer delight: Foundations, findings, and managerial insight. *Journal of Retailing* 73 (Fall): 311–336.

indirect and direct financial support to advertise and promote themselves. Fans indirectly promote the team by buying and wearing or displaying licensed team merchandise. Sponsors directly promote the team and pay for the advertising and media to do so. For instance, AT&T initially paid the Dallas Stars to host the team Web site (attwireless.dallasstars.com). Similarly, radio and TV broadcasts of sporting events are "brought to you by" the sponsors.

Much of the actual product, particularly in terms of revenue, is in the broadcast of the games or event. The fact that sports are broadcast, in and of itself, differentiates sports from other goods and services. Typical goods and services find it difficult to entertain using its product as the star of a broadcast, although more than a few have created infomercials featuring already fit models promoting either the Ab Doer Pro, Ab Dolly, Ab Energizer, Ab Flex, Ab Force, Ab Rocker, Ab Roller, Ab Slide or the Abtronic—guaranteeing that you will look just like the model without "any effort from you." Anyway, the point is that sports are different because others pay for the team's advertising, promotion and broadcast in a way that typical goods and services find difficult to achieve.

Goods and services marketers typically pay for media to broadcast or to print advertising and promotional information while the media pays sports teams for the right to broadcast or print team and event information. For example, beginning in 2007, the networks (Fox, ESPN/ABC and Turner Broadcasting) are paying $4.48 billion over eight years for all media rights to NASCAR events. In contrast, no network is bidding hundreds of millions of dollars to broadcast, "Inside the Making of Tide Detergent."

The revenue generated from TV contracts is the principal differentiating factor between the healthiest sports leagues (NFL, NBA, MLB, NASCAR) and the less healthy (NHL and WNBA). The proliferation of broadcast and other media outlets for sports also points to the fact that the distribution for sports is increasingly electronic and not limited to static locations.

4. Distribution Channel: Static vs. Mobile

Goods and services designate specific geographic outlets. Customers purchasing from Sears buy products at a local Sears store or order products to be shipped from a Sears distribution center. The distribution channel for Sears is relatively static, changing only when stores open or close. Sporting events and teams, on the other hand, are basically traveling road shows, moving from location to location, city to city, nationally and globally.

The experiential and transitory nature of sporting events (as well as other competitive broadcast events such as "Survivor") lends itself to electronic forms of distribution. The NFL, for example, is broadcast in 205 countries across 24 time zones for upwards of 4,500 hours of weekly programming (http://www.nfl.com/international/globalTV.html, 2001). Similarly, cable and internet broadcast systems have developed new distribution channels such as NBA.TV that blur the lines between traditional broadcasts and online services that make the product available anytime, anywhere.

5. Product: Adapted vs. Global

Due to the nature of the events and the distribution channels, sports such as soccer, basketball, baseball, tennis, golf, and motor sports are truly global products needing little translation or alteration of the marketing mix to gain acceptance across cultures. The marketing mix (product, place, promotion, pricing) for typical goods and services are frequently adapted to local markets.

Compared to most sports, frequently cited "global" products such as Coke and McDonald's are not actually standardized global products. Coke alters its packaging, name, and syrup *content* in foreign countries. McDonald's offers beer in German restaurants and cooks its hamburgers rare in France. In contrast, the *content* or product of the NFL, Formula 1 Racing, Olympics Downhill Racing, or the NHL remains the same throughout the world. In a sense, given its electronic broadcasts, the distribution is standardized around the world. Obviously, the promotion (e.g., language) and pricing (e.g., costs of cable or pay per view) aspects of the marketing mix may be adjusted by global markets.

6. Two-Part Pricing

Customers typically pay one price for a given product or service. When you go to a grocery store such as Kroger's, you select your favorite grocery items[5] and pay the prices marked on the items. You are not required to pay admission to the store so that you can shop. However, some exceptions do exist that resemble the fan loyalty—and even fanaticism—in customer products. For instance, people do pay an annual fee to shop at Sam's Clubs or Costco. Some people we know actually get very excited about being able to shop at these places. Such

---

[5]Namely Pop-Tarts, Cheese Whiz, Cool Whip, and frozen pizza.

organizations are the exception to the rule—and add evidence to the premise that the most successful marketers are those that emulate sports marketers.

Professional sports and major college sports fans frequently pay a two-part tariff (or price). While some services with relatively inelastic demand (electricity, utilities, etc.) use a two-part pricing system (basic fee + additional user fees) due to monopoly power, even sports organizations operating in competitive entertainment markets frequently charge two prices. In sports, an initial payment (donation to the university, payment for a seat license, membership fees) is frequently necessary to allocate a limited inventory of preferable seats. Fans paying the initial fee are then given the opportunity to purchase tickets.

Another aspect of two-part pricing in sports is the event itself. Fans pay for a ticket to enter the event (initial payment) and then purchase other products (food, drink, souvenirs) after entering. Thus price-setting in most sports settings must consider various forms of price bundling. Season tickets are offered at a bundled price for the entire season and are de-bundled in the form of smaller ticket packages or individual tickets. Offering tickets with a hot dog and soft drink for a single price is another example of price bundling in that it combines the prices of what would normally be two-part pricing. Price bundling is common among services (e.g., vacation package of flight, hotel, and ground transportation; cable TV packages), so this aspect doesn't by itself differentiate the marketing of goods/services versus sports. Yet, it is common practice in *all* sports marketing contexts, but is not common to all goods/services contexts. Interestingly, fans are typically paying for admission to a publicly owned facility, even though the bulk of the ticket sales proceeds go directly to the team owners.

7. Facilities: Taxpayer vs. Corporate Support

Although the subject of much public policy debate, sports team owners frequently do not pay for their own facilities. A new Nissan automobile plant may be able to acquire favorable tax status and property in Mississippi ($695 million in tax breaks and incentives over 20 years), but will still pay for building their own facilities ($930 million in Canton, MS). In contrast, the majority (18 of 29) of NBA owners' facilities are largely or entirely paid by taxpayers (see http://www.marquette.edu/law/sports/sfr/nba22.pdf, 2001). In addition, naming rights by sponsors add additional revenue to the team. Even when owners invest private dollars into the facility, it is not necessarily because public monies are unavailable, but is often due to revenue control issues that will favor the team owners if they also own the facility.

Why do city, county, and state officials want to attract sports organizations? Why are they, and their taxpayers, willing to pass referendums to pay for these facilities? The case can be made for a variety of motives (mainly political and economic) for this support. However, from a broader sociological perspective, sports teams provide a city (or state) with a social identity that can represent who they are to others. The successful state university sports team allows constituents to represent themselves to others as winners. The tough blue-collar character of the Steelers over the years symbolizes who Pittsburgh fans are to the rest of the country. The black uniforms, skull-and-crossbones, and intimidating players for the Oakland Raiders, for better or worse, mostly identify their fans. We are not sure what the men dressed up as hogs in dresses at Washington Redskins games means. In contrast, judging from media reports in places like Cleveland (OH), Memphis (TN), Louisville (KY), and Houston (TX) and some empirical evidence,[6] major cities who have lost or have been without major league sports teams spend considerable effort searching for an identity by way of alluring sports franchises.

Consider what is sold in airport gift shops. You will always find jerseys, mugs, and other merchandise that represent the city to others who pass through the area. The merchandise may feature the licensed logos of local golf courses or minor league teams in Charleston (SC), the Cowboys in Dallas (TX), or the Jazz and Olympic logos in Salt Lake City (UT). The point is that communities represent themselves to others through their identification with a sports organization. Interestingly, visitors buy the licensed merchandise from these cities to represent to others that they visited there. The identity of the sports organization offers social meaning and value both to those who live in the city and to those who visit the city. In any case, the social value of the professional sports team often goes beyond simply the directly relevant economic value of the team to the community.

8. Competition: Cooperative (monopoly) vs. Individual (monopolistic)

Branded goods and services marketers have traditionally not cooperated in their marketing efforts. At the wholesale level and in some highly competitive retail markets, goods and services may engage in cobranding or cooperative strategic alliances in order to offset or

---

[6]Wakefield, Kirk L. 1995. The pervasive effects of social influence on sporting event attendance. *Journal of Sport and Social Issues* 19 (4): 335–351.

balance competitive weaknesses and strengths. As a rule, however, goods and services marketers do not cooperate in cross-promotions and work in league with each other on a permanent basis as do sports. Admittedly, this is an area in which some sports organizations do better than others. In addition to the major professional leagues, excellent examples are also found in major college sports conferences (SEC, Big 10, etc.) that negotiate and promote for the benefit of the league and its members. Fans of the teams are also ardent supporters of the league and enjoy following other team members or players in addition to their favorites (e.g., NASCAR and NASCAR drivers).

The nature of sports leagues, particularly at the professional level, has evolved to the point where the leagues operate as monopolies, controlling entry and exit into the industry. For both practical and legal purposes, Major League Baseball is a monopoly. The league continues to be exempt from antitrust laws. While Microsoft is sued by the U.S. Justice Department for restraining trade, and other major industries vital to U.S. markets (telephone, transportation, airlines) have been broken up to allow free entry into markets, Major League Baseball is still allowed to control the granting and retraction of franchises, develop television contracts that preempt feasible entry into the market, and (depending upon the source you listen to) control the labor market.

Other pro sports leagues operate in a similar fashion, such that virtually any new league has no opportunity to compete. A clear example of this monopoly control of sports leagues is in the NFL, where the city of Los Angeles has no NFL team, despite the fact that it is the second most populated market in the United States. The NFL's revenue sharing plan has contributed to the fact that the barrier to entry in the form of an initial franchise fee into the Los Angeles market for a prospective team owner exceeds $700 million (the amount the Houston Texans paid for entry into the Houston market). Obviously, a free market would have a pro football team in Los Angeles. A monopoly, in this case, does not.

In summation, the point here is that every other goods and services marketer must abide by federal antitrust laws; professional sports, in large part, do not. The logic presented is that the leagues must maintain control for the integrity of the sport, as they seek to protect the social welfare of fans.

9. Exchange: Economic vs. Social

As inferred earlier, customers pay an economic price for the goods or services that they purchase while fans make a social investment in the transaction. Customers typically give up monetary value in exchange (what one gives up for what one gets) for the good or service, although time and search effort may also be expended. In most cases, however, only limited social exchange occurs. When you go out with friends to eat dinner on Friday night, you may be largely motivated by social reasons to go to a particular restaurant and consume certain food and beverages. In the same venue, however, individuals and groups of customers may at the same time purchase a meal where social exchange accounts for little or no part of the encounter. In either case, the exchange with the restaurant is still premised on the purchase of the meal. Clearly, the more that the restaurant can do to make the purchase based more on the experience (e.g., Rainforest Café, ESPN Zone, etc.), the more they are practicing what is common to sports marketers.

In sports, attendance is nearly always (98–99 percent of the time) with at least one other person. The sports fan pays a price for the right to enjoy an emotional experience with others. The fan goes to the game to be with others, to share the experience in this social exchange. More broadly speaking, unlike most other retail settings, large crowds have positive psychological effects. No line at the grocery checkout will make most shoppers happy, but no line to see a ballgame is a definite cue to a fan that either this is a lousy sporting event or that the fan has arrived at the stadium on the wrong date. The excitement of the competition and the aura of the star power of the players on the team are such that the experience is best enjoyed in the presence of others.

10. Contractual Power: Owners vs. Employees

Finally, the size and power of the manufacturer or retailer of goods and services affords the owner contractual leverage over its employees in most goods/services contexts. Salaries, benefits, and tenure are largely controlled by the owners. Employees have mobility, but are rarely able to single-handedly affect the outcome of the firm by making contractual demands.

Employees (viz., players) of sports teams, however, are more likely to possess contractual power over employers. Contract concessions, renegotiations, and arbitrations generally favor players. At the same time that union membership has declined in manufacturing over the past four decades, union membership in professional sports leagues has grown relatively strong due to the leverage held by the players. Consequently, work stoppages in major sports leagues have become commonplace in the past decade. In 2004–2005, the NHL shut down due to the players' unwillingness to abide by owners' demands in its new labor contract. Similarly, MLB players forced the cancellation of most of the season and the World Series in 1994.

Although the first nine differences are positive aspects of sports marketing, the leverage or power of individual players in major college and professional sports has clear negative implications. The average fan has difficulty in identifying with 21-year-old multimillionaires who often appear ungrateful for what they have. Players and coaches willingly trade team allegiances for more money. Teams uproot overnight and move to another city. Motor sports drivers trade sponsors for more money. While most fans may not blame the teams or players for maximizing their financial positions, the ultimate fact is that such fluctuations erode loyalty and identification. Just as brands lose customers when they change advertising agencies and campaigns from year to year, teams lose identified fans as they shift player personnel and team names in search of making more money.

So, What Is Sports Marketing?

As with any taxonomy, exceptions exist. Some entertainment services, such as the movie industry, share some characteristics with sports teams and players. In the same way, we can think of some sports marketing contexts in which the owners do not share some of these characteristics. Yet, as can be seen from these ten dyadic illustrations, the norm in sports marketing is different from the norm in other forms of marketing.

In summary, then, what is sports marketing? Sports marketing is building a highly identified fan base such that fans, sponsors, media, and government pay to promote and support the organization for the benefits of social exchange and personal, group, and community identity within a cooperative competitive environment. The following chapters will offer the necessary components for effective sports marketing strategies that result in maximizing fan identification.

Conclusion

Does conventional goods and services marketing best explain and predict effective marketing? Or does sports marketing?

Effective sports marketing is primarily premised upon building fan identification. Customers can identify with a branded good or service, as when customers wear FUBU, Harley Davidson, or other name brands prominently displayed on their clothing. As such, it can be argued that identification is merely a deeper level of loyalty. However, the best examples of fanatical followings are within the realm of sports marketing.

Branded goods and services that emulate sports marketing practices can build highly identified customers. Services such as eBay can generate fanatical support such that users form and meet in clubs for social benefits associated with being with fellow eBayers. Branded products such as Sony Playstation can generate enough unreasoning enthusiasm among its fans that they will pay a premium in order to purchase the product before others. Food service operators such as Taco Bell, KFC, Pizza Hut and A&W can join forces to cooperate to build customer patronage. These, however, are the exceptions to the rule.

Nonsports organizations can benefit from understanding and practicing sports marketing principles. Brands that seek to build levels of identification like that found in the wide world of sports can generate fans that are willing to proudly wear their brand names (e.g., Nike) and otherwise display unyielding devotion. So, whether your career is in sports marketing or grocery shopping, this text should provide guidance for excellence in marketing.

Sell an Identity

2

If you were asked to identify yourself to others, what would you say? Most of us would give our name, where we are from, and identify our university or organization. In so doing, you would be telling us something about the family, the community, and social group to which you belong. And since you are a sports fan, you might also add something about the fact that you are a [put your team here] fan or are otherwise associated with a successful team or individual.

Since no one knows where Oxford, Mississippi, is, for instance, people from Ole Miss might say that they are from Oxford, home of the Ole Miss Rebels and John Grisham (except that he moved, primarily because he kept waking up with tour groups on his front porch or someone having a wedding in his yard without his permission). Similarly, Baylor students might identify themselves as being students at Baylor (Jerusalem on the Brazos) in Waco, which is close to President Bush's ranch, but is not really that close to David Koresh's compound. The point is that we identify ourselves to others by successful groups or individuals with which we are associated. We feel better about ourselves when we think that others think that we are winners in one way or another.

So, in general, individuals have an intense need to express who they are to others by means of group membership. One prominent way that individuals do this is through identification with sports teams and individual athletes.

Within the realm of sports, identification is when an individual reacts to events that occur to the team or player as if the events happened to him or her.[1] A highly identified fan will internalize or adopt the team's or player's attitudes and behaviors as their own. If you are highly identified with a team, you feel good when the team wins and bad when the team loses. You believe that the team is a representation of who you are to yourself and to others. You feel as though you are practically part of the team.

Since how the team performs affects our egos, we react psychologically, physiologically, and behaviorally in ways to protect our egos. If we win, we attribute the team's success as our success and to our being winners. If the team loses, we may justify the loss, make excuses, be overly optimistic about future performance, or simply blast the opposing team or players in a way that will make us feel better. In any case, winning or losing, our body physically reacts to the situation, as our heart rate increases and our bodies are otherwise stimulated (more on this later).

Not every fan is highly identified with a team or player. However, the more the sports marketer can build identification with the team, the more fans will support the team. The bottom line is that sports organizations must sell an identity that benefits and builds fans' self-esteem.

A Model of Identification

So, how do organizations build an identity and identification among fans? Figure 2.1 summarizes research findings, illustrating five factors that lead to fan identification:

1. Attractiveness of players
2. Social acceptance
3. Variety seeking (negative influence)
4. Involvement with the sport
5. Performance (team/player)

Similarly, identification leads to five consequences that generally benefit the sports organization:

1. BIRGing (Basking In Reflected Glory)
2. Attributions

---

[1]See Hirt, Edward, et al. 1992. Costs and benefits of allegiance: Changes in fans' self-ascribed competencies after team victory versus defeat. *Journal of Personality & Social Psychology* 63 (November): 724–738.

Figure 2.1

Model of Identification

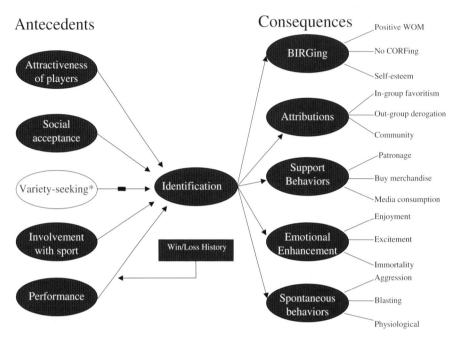

*Variety-seeking has a negative effect on identification.

3. Support behaviors
4. Emotional enhancement
5. Spontaneous behaviors

The astute reader will note the acronym. Namely, if sports organizations treat their fans ASVIPs then they will have covered all of the BASES when it comes to fan identification.

Attractiveness of Players

Fans may find players to be attractive due to the player's success and similarity.

Success. Fans will generally find successful athletes and teams as attractive. When the team performs poorly, attractive members of the team offer fans a basis by which they can identify with the team and still protect their self-esteem. A fan of the Chicago Cubs, for instance, may identify with the team because of a particular star player: "Hey, I don't care if the Cubs win. I just love to watch Derek Lee knock the ball out of the park."

Emerging stars. Teams that do not have established star players have a more difficult time in building identification. In such cases, a team's marketing campaign may be able to grow its own by featuring an individual rising star in their advertising and promotional efforts. For instance, when the NBA's Grizzlies moved from Vancouver to Memphis, the team featured Jason Williams (who, despite his undisputed commitment, is still a distant #2 in the league at the guard position—behind Allen Iverson—in tattoo percentage) as well as rookies Pau Gasol and Shane Battier as star players in 2001–2002. The Memphis newspaper carried an ongoing series on the life of a rookie in the NBA, featuring interviews with Shane Battier during this same year. So, even when the team performs poorly, the fans can identify with the rising stars, perhaps also identifying with the struggles of Battier as he adapted to the style and level of NBA play.

Personal contact. If you've ever met a professional player in person, odds are that you have continued to follow that player and his team. The more familiar that you become with the player, the higher is the likelihood that you will want to watch the player on TV or attend a game.

The more that the team can facilitate indirect (e.g., interviews) and direct (e.g., autograph signings, public social service events, etc.) contact with the players, the more fans will be able to identify with the players. Players that make themselves available through these indirect and direct means are valuable assets beyond what they do at game time. The reverse is also true. You can probably think of some players who have been successful in competition but were unattractive in some other way (e.g., Albert Belle, Mike Tyson, or Rasheed Wallace). These individuals dilute identification among the majority of fans who value positive traits such as fair play and integrity.

Similarity. We find those who are similar to us attractive.[2] For those of us with healthy self-esteem, we psychologically react to others by thinking: "If you are similar to me, then you must be attractive—because I am attractive" or "If you are attractive, then you are similar to me—because I am attractive." The blue-collar fans of the Pittsburgh Steelers are likely to identify with the team more easily when the players exemplify blue-collar football: run the football and play tough defense. Pittsburgh fans love Jerome Bettis (The Bus), because they feel as though they have similar characteristics. The "Steel Curtain"

[2]Byrne, D., and Nelson, D. 1965. Attraction as a linear function of proportion of positive reinforcements. *Journal of Personality and Social Psychology* 36 (June): 659–663.

defense of the 1970s is a good example of a team's players representing characteristics similar to its fans.

The team doesn't have to win for fans to feel as though the players are similar and attractive. The old Brooklyn "Bums," as the Dodgers were locally called before they moved to Los Angeles, had a strong fan following among individuals who could identify with the struggles and mishaps of the team. This could be some of what goes on with the Cubs and other teams with long-standing absences from playoffs and championships.

Curse of the Billy Goat: *Why the Cubs Will Never Win It All?*

As the story goes, William "Billy Goat" Sianis, a Greek immigrant who owned a nearby tavern (the now-famous Billy Goat Tavern), had two $7.20 box seat tickets to Game 4 of the 1945 World Series between the Chicago Cubs and the Detroit Tigers, and decided to bring his pet goat, Murphy, with him. Sianis and the goat were allowed into Wrigley Field before the game and even paraded about on the playing field before ushers intervened and led them off the field. After a heated argument, both Sianis and the goat were permitted to stay in the stadium occupying the box seat for which he had tickets. However, before the game was over, Sianis and the goat were ejected from the stadium at the command of Cubs owner Philip Knight Wrigley because of the animal's objectionable odor. Sianis was outraged at the ejection and allegedly placed a curse upon the Cubs that they would never win another pennant or play in a World Series at Wrigley Field again (Sianis died in 1970).

Fast forward to the 2003 NLCS. The Cubs were five outs from the World Series. Cubs' Moises Alou, thinking he could nab a foul ball for the second out in the eighth inning, headed toward the stands with his glove held high and was just about to fit his glove around the ball when Cubs fan Steve Bartman interrupted Alou's poise and the ball deflected off his hand and into the stands. Even though the Cubs tried to get a fan interference call, the field umpire labeled it foul, declaring it "up for grabs." The Cubs went on to lose the NLCS after being ahead three games to two.

In one of the odder baseball media events, the actual ball was eventually bought by a local restaurateur, Grant DePorter, who had it exploded into shreds by Academy Award-winning special effects expert Michael Lantieri in a nationally televised event. The remnants of the ball, infused in vodka and beer, were used to flavor a special "Foul Ball Spaghetti." While no part of the ball itself was in the sauce, the ball was boiled and the steam captured, distilled, and added to the final concoction, which was then sold to some 4,000 diners, Cubs fans all.

Source: Adapted from "Curse of the Billy Goat." *Wikipedia.* Wikipedia, 2005. Answers.com 16 Jan. 2006. www.answers.com/topic/curse-of-the-billy-goat

The issue of similarity and attractiveness has important implications for the two primary marketing management issues of positioning and personnel. Sports organizations must consider how they will position the players they acquire and retain (within a team concept) with their target markets. If the team's fans are primarily blue-collar (Pittsburgh Steelers), white-collar (Los Angeles Lakers) or no-collar/frequently collared (Oakland Raiders), then promotional efforts and personnel decisions should follow suit.

In summation, teams can build identification by acquiring, retaining, and featuring attractive players through indirect and direct contact with fans within a well-designed promotional campaign.

Social Acceptance

Have you noticed that when people move from one city to another they become more of a fan of that city's teams? The extent to which you identify with some team or player is likely to have something to do with time you have spent in the hometown or state of the team or player.

From a broad perspective, Americans will identify with the U.S. athletes in the Olympics because it would simply not be American to root against the United States. Intense social pressure exists that influences us to support the American athletes. Because of our culture, we have difficulty thinking of anything but supporting the Americans. To illustrate more vividly the role of social influence, imagine the social pressure one might feel at a local sports bar while watching the university's team play on TV against an archrival. The likelihood that anyone will stand up and yell for the opposing team is directly proportional to the number of beers consumed. I, for one, am glad that you have better sense than to put yourself in that situation. The point is that the extent to which the team or player enjoys social acceptance is directly related to the degree to which fans will be willing to identify with the team or player.

Social acceptance typically originates from at least three sources: family, peers, and community (including the city, state, and national level). Interestingly, we tend to get our information about what the community thinks by inferring from the views of our families and peers.[3] So, the way to improve community acceptance is by targeting actions that will make families and small groups accept the team and sporting event. Minor league sports often do this by focusing on the entertainment value for the family, which in turn influences acceptance of the team in the community.

Two primary ways to increase social acceptance are to improve the place and to give fans ownership of the team.

The place. Perceptions of social acceptance of a sporting event are directly tied to the place the sporting event is held. In Table 2.1, which sporting events do you think people are likely to perceive as more popular?

Table 2.1

Dimension	Sporting Event "A"	Sporting Event "B"
Location	Dangerous part of town with few access roads	Near other entertainment and restaurants off major roads
Facility	Old and deteriorating	New equipment and modern amenities
Food	Popcorn, hot dogs (boiled), peanuts, soft serve ice cream in a little helmet	Southwest chicken salad, BBQ, pizza, chicken, Häagen-Dazs ice cream
Parking	Entry and exit are bottlenecked	Entry and exit facilitated by layout and shuttles
Maintenance	Dirty restrooms, food service, and seating areas	Clean restrooms, food service, and seating areas
Service Personnel	Facial hair, unkempt uniforms, long hair	Clean shaven, clean uniforms, short hair
Comfort	Cramped seating and aisles	Ample knee, arm, and seat space

---

[3]Wakefield, Kirk L. 1995. The pervasive effects of social influence on sporting event attendance. *Journal of Sport & Social Issues* 19 (8): 335–351.

If you selected sporting event "B," then you are like most other Americans who attend sporting events. If you selected sporting event "A," then you were once an Expos or Phillies fan. Or, if you live in England, the confines of sporting event "A" may look pretty good compared to some place like Gillingham's Priestfield Stadium. For Americans, it's hard to imagine visiting a stadium built in '92— that's 1892.

Worst Grounds in England
1. Priestfield, Gillingham
2. Kenilworth Road, Luton
3. Millmoor, Rotherham
4. Withdean Stadium, Brighton
5. Fratton Park, Portsmouth
6. Selhurst Park, Crystal Palace
7. Blundell Park, Grimsby
8. Ninian Park, Cardiff
9. National Hockey Stadium, Milton Keynes Dons
10. Stamford Bridge, Chelsea

Source: Clarke, Gemma (2004), "Simply the Worst," *The Observer*. For a truly engrossing account of just how bad some stadiums are in Britain, read: http://observer.guardian.co.uk/sport/story/0,6903,1323809,00.html

---

A chief reason that progressive sports organizations invest so much capital in facilities is for the obvious reason: people like nice places and they don't like bad places. It's that simple. If a facility becomes known nationwide as unfriendly to fans and even the players (see "Worst Grounds in England"), then it is probably time to get a new stadium or do major renovations.

Ownership. Perceptions of social acceptance are connected to the extent to which individuals in the community feel as though they have ownership of the team. Fans of the Green Bay Packers literally do own a piece of the team, but fans can feel as though they own the team in other ways. The Memphis Redbirds (AAA) baseball team's not-for-profit status helps the community feel as though they are supporting the city when they support the Redbirds. Providing fans the opportunity to have input and communication with team ownership and management also breeds ownership feelings.

Teams that move to new communities are especially vulnerable because they may be perceived as not being "our team." Consequently, teams relocating, as well as established teams, may consider doing as much as possible to have their social acceptance PREPAID:

- Proactively involving fans to give input to management and the team (e.g., publicizing the fact that you can email the team owner at mark.cuban@dallasmavs.com or can visit him at his day job at Dairy Queen).
- Researching fans to determine fan satisfaction and what aspects of the event they would change.
- Encouraging or requiring key players to move residences to community.
- Publicizing efforts to reach diversified customer base (e.g., Utah Jazz's $5 Value Tickets).
- Acquiring or attracting players with local connections.
- Initiating and maintaining public service activities involving players and management.
- Developing marketing campaigns, announcements, and other communications that emphasize that this is "your team" or "your event."

An excellent case study of how not to gain social acceptance can be found in the Canadian Football League's attempt to bring the CFL to the southern U.S. cities of Memphis, Birmingham, San Antonio, and Shreveport in the mid 1990s. Players were brought in from other CFL teams that were largely unknown in the United States. The CFL positioned itself as uniquely Canadian and as direct competition with the hugely popular NFL. Comparing itself to the NFL, the CFL promoted itself in the United States with the slogan, "Our balls are bigger." Needless to say, things deflated from there.

Variety Seeking

While the first two factors of attractiveness and social acceptance increase fan identification, individuals who are variety seekers are unlikely to be highly identified with the team. Variety seekers attend a game simply for a change of pace. These weakly identified fans may come to the game because of a sales promotion (fireworks or concert), for a bit of excitement, or to experience something new. These "entertainment hoppers" may go to the game one weekend and then not return for the rest of the season.

The importance of understanding variety seekers is that a good deal of the sales promotions that are offered at sporting events are likely to attract variety-seekers (e.g., the Dynamite Lady[4] or price discounts) and may do little to convert the fan into a more loyal or identified fan. Although the objective of such sales promotions may be to reach secondary or less loyal fans to fill unoccupied seats, without coordinated marketing efforts the sports organization may be wasting sponsorship and promotional dollars on individuals who will be unlikely to return until the next promotion. Borrowing from Wakefield and Barnes (1996),[5]

> Sales promotions objectives are typically positioned as either maintaining customer loyalty or boosting short-term sales, although the latter typically comes at the expense of the former. . . . Properly designed sales promotions may, however, boost short-term sales while also building customer loyalty. If sales promotions of [sporting events] tend to attract variety-seekers, then the sales promotions could be designed not only to stimulate, but also to reinforce positive aspects of the [sports] experience that are likely to increase loyalty or perceived value of the [event]. . . . For instance, sporting events are often sponsored by restaurants, which in turn offer coupons, contests, or drawings for free dinners. Instead of simply using the giveaways as the sales promotion, the promotion could be reinforcing and developing involvement and loyalty by giving away a limited number of free meals with members of the team.

In short, sports marketers must evaluate what the objective and effect of sales promotions are on fans. While some infrequent spectators might attend due to a promotion and decide that the event is enjoyable enough to return more frequently, sports-irrelevant sales promotions and discounts are likely to send the signal to spectators that the event is not valuable enough to attend in its own right. In any case, the marketing manager can build identification in weakly identified fans by offering promotions that are somehow related to the team, the event, and its players.

---

[4]The Dynamite Lady was known for her ability to place herself in a large box at sporting events and then blow herself up with the aid of actual sticks of dynamite. She was last seen by the author in the mid 1990s at a minor league baseball game. In a personal interview, she confessed to having broken most of the bones in her body doing this stunt.

[5]Wakefield, Kirk L., and Barnes, James H. 1996. Retailing hedonic consumption: A model of sales promotion of a leisure service. *Journal of Retailing* 72 (Winter): 409–427.

Involvement with the Sport

Within the sports setting, fans may have an enduring involvement with the sport and situational involvement with the event. Enduring involvement is an ongoing interest or concern with the sport on a day-to-day basis.[6] An individual who has an enduring involvement with motor sports is likely to closely follow NASCAR or NHRA results throughout the season and read or watch whatever media is available regarding motor sports. On the other hand, situational involvement with the sport or sporting event occurs due to the circumstances of the event itself. An individual does not have to have enduring involvement to experience situational involvement. A university alumnus may return for the Homecoming football game and become involved with the game at that time, but not be involved in any way with football or the team for the rest of the year. An individual who has enduring involvement can also experience situational involvement that heightens the emotional experience, as when archrivals meet or playoff games ensue.

Unless individuals understand the nature of the game and something about the participants in the game, they can't identify with the team. For those of us who grew up in the south, where it was difficult to get involved with ice hockey due to the lack of ice (see article in January 18, 1968 Bryan-College Station Eagle, "Hockey Sticks Wash Ashore Lake Bryan: Dozen A&M Students Presumed Drowned"[7]), we find people less identified with hockey teams.

Sports marketers can increase fans' enduring involvement with the sport and thereby increase fan identification. Table 2.2 illustrates methods to increase enduring involvement. Increased situational involvement is likely to result in more strongly felt emotional and social exchanges and reinforce team identification. Situational involvement can be increased by promoting key match-ups and pivotal games and including in-depth information about the opposing team and players.

Performance

Countless studies confirm the fact that winning increases team identification and attendance. It is important to point out, however, that the team's history plays a role in this relationship. For teams with

---

[6]Richins, Marsha L., and Bloch, Peter H. 1986. After the new wears off: The temporal context of product involvement. *Journal of Consumer Research* 13 (2): 280–285.

[7]This headline is not entirely accurate. A&M refers to Texas A&M University. Reader should insert name of local lake and school's archrival in headline.

Table 2.2

Increasing Enduring Fan Investment	
Method	**Example**
Increase opportunities for sports **participation**	• Sponsor local sports teams and leagues • Offer sports clinics staffed by coaches and players
Provide **information** on **rules** of the game	• Feature something like the ESPN/NHL's "NHL Rules" on Web sites • On broadcast and live games, show "You make the call!" programming that illustrates rules • Announce the availability of printed rules of the game at stadium information centers or from section attendants
Provide complete game and **player** information	• Handout halftime stats in the stands • Install scoreboards that post real time game stats • Introduce players with personal information • Feature in-depth player information in freely accessible formats (read: not only in expensive programs)
Facilitate **media** exchange	• Give reporters ready access to players and management • Arrange player/coach appearances in non-sports settings

strong winning traditions, fans do use team performance as a source of identification. However, for teams without winning traditions, fans overlook objective performance records and focus on either relative performance or the other positive sources of identification.[8]

Fans may perceive their team as performing relatively well even if the team is below .500 with justifications such as:

• We're better than last year!
• At least we beat the #1 team.
• We've got the talent; we just haven't put it together yet.
• Given how small our budget is, we do pretty well compared to the big guys in the conference.

[8]Fisher, Robert J., and Wakefield, Kirk L. Factors leading to group identification: A field study of winners and losers. *Psychology & Marketing* 15 (December): 23–40.

- We've got some of the best players in the league, we just need one more (pitcher, lineman, point guard, etc.).
- Wait till next year.

Although improved performance in the standings will nearly always lead to increased attendance, it is the fans' perception of performance that influences attendance. Marketing managers can influence this perception by focusing on the achievements and performance of individual players, progress from previous years, isolated successes (e.g., Top 10 Finish in a Nextel Cup race or PGA event), or changing the point of reference from winning to some other trait on which the team or organization performs well. For example, a hockey team can be characterized as scrappy, tenacious, hard-nosed, or even "guys who like to fight" whenever they hit the ice. Fans can identify with the style of play and justify focusing less on the won/loss record. Of course, winning usually helps.[9]

Since objective performance is a fickle marketing element from season to season and even game to game, even for the best of teams, sports marketers are better off promising something besides a winning effort. Fans are satisfied when expectations are met and dissatisfied when expectations are not met. Promotional campaigns are frequently prepared in advance of the season. Campaigns that essentially promise or refer to a winning team during what turns out to be a downturn will not resonate well among fans. Promotional campaigns should focus on benefits of identifying with the team that the organization can be certain of delivering.

Consequences of Identification

BIRGing

Highly identified fans are likely to Bask In Reflected Glory by doing such things as wearing team-identifying apparel after a team win, describing team wins in terms of what "we" did, and, in general, seeking to enhance their public image by connecting with positive

---

[9]Winning does not always help. The Pittsburgh Pirates won division and league titles with Barry Bonds as the NL MVP in the early 1990s, yet were near the bottom of the league in attendance. The Boston Celtics won 9 straight NBA titles but suffered through poor attendance. The New Jersey Nets were first in their division in 2002 and were next to last in the league in attendance.

aspects of the team.[10] BIRGing is also recursive, in that it also serves to reinforce one's identification with the team. BIRGing has three related consequences.

Self-esteem. As you have likely observed, highly identified fans will BIRG in other ways. If you attended a sporting event featuring your favorite team on Saturday night and they win, why do you watch the sports report of the event on TV after you get home? Why do you eagerly read the newspaper account of the event the next day? Why do you recount the game over and over with your friends? You are BIRGing because it reinforces your self-image and public image. The result of BIRGing is enhanced self-esteem in the highly identified fan.

CORFing. Fans may engage in CORFing (Cutting Off Reflected Failure) following a loss, seeking to distance themselves from the team in a way that will protect their self-esteem. While some evidence exists that CORFing occurs for those who are identified with a group,[11] research related to those identified with a sports team or player suggests that the highly identified fan will do less CORFing than the less identified fan.[12]

Highly identified fans are likely to BIRG and not to CORF. That is, they will refer to wins and losses in the same way: "We won" and "We lost." Less identified fans are likely to BIRG ("We won.") and to CORF ("They Lost.").

Positive word-of-mouth. Highly identified fans expend considerable amounts of time expressing positive sentiment regarding the object of their identification. This positive word-of-mouth may take the form of oral or written communications with family and peers, as they encourage others to join them in attending the sporting event or otherwise supporting the team or player. This positive word-of-mouth is also likely to influence social acceptance among families and peers, which, in turn, builds fan identification.

Like any other services marketing, generating positive word-of-mouth is critical in determining the success of the organization. Building highly identified fans may serve as a form of a temporary firewall

---

[10]Cialdini, Robert B., et al. 1976. Basking in reflected glory: Three (football) studies. *Journal of Personality and Social Psychology* 34 (36): 366–375.

[11]Snyder, C. R., Lassegard, M., and Ford, C. E. 1986. Distancing after group success and failure: Basking in reflected glory and cutting off reflected failure. *Journal of Personality and Social Psychology* 51: 382–388.

[12]Wann, D. L., and Branscombe, N. R. 1990. Die-hard and fair-weather fans: Effects of identification on BIRGing and CORFing tendencies. *Journal of Sport and Social Issues* 14: 103–117.

against negative word-of-mouth when some aspects of the sports experience may deteriorate. For self-esteem reasons, highly identified fans are less likely to denigrate the team and organization with which they have identified. To do so causes internal psychological tension ("If this team is so bad, then why am I associated with it?"). Obviously, at some point, fans will recognize poor performance, weak social acceptance, or unattractive players and reduce their identification in order to protect their self-esteem ("I used to be a _____ fan, but I just couldn't take it any more.")

Attributions

People make inferences about themselves and others based on behaviors and situations they observe.[13] If you see someone going to church, you might attribute religious convictions to that person. If you are attending the same church, you might attribute religious convictions to yourself. If you frequently see that person in church, you might consider that person as a member of your group who has affiliated with that church and make positive inferences about that person. Conversely, while passing by the church on your way to Sunday brunch, you might attribute hypocritical actions to those entering the church and consider them to be a group with which you do not want to associate. This is a good thing, because you gave up being hypocritical some time ago.

The point is that people make inferences about themselves, groups, group memberships, and group characteristics. If you are in a group, you will tend to make self-serving attributions, assume responsibility for group decisions greater than is deserved, and will be biased in favor of the in-group and be biased against an out-group.[14] We're sorry, but that's just the way it is.

Within the sports setting, highly identified fans do these same things. We sometimes make self-serving attributions regarding how smart we were to support (or wager on) a particular winning team, almost as much as we are to attribute the winning to the team—as if we actually had something to do with the outcome. Highly identified fans will actually take credit for successful team strategies, such as

---

[13]Kelley, Harold H. 1967. *Attribution theory in social psychology.* Nebraska Symposium on Motivation. Lincoln: University of Nebraska Press.

[14]Folks, Valerie S., and Kiesler, Tina. 1991. "Social cognition: Consumers inferences about the self and others," in *Handbook of Consumer Behavior*, eds. Thomas S. Robertson and Harold H. Kassarjian, New Jersey: Prentice-Hall.

completing a long touchdown pass: "I've been saying that we should just throw the ball deep. Haven't I been saying that?" It's a good thing the coach was listening.

While self-serving attributions are more internal in nature, in-group favoritism, out-group derogation, and perceived community acceptance are more externally focused.

In-group favoritism. Highly identified fans are likely to attribute positive characteristics to other fans of the same team or player: "He's pretty cool. He's a Spurs fan." Deeper than that, however, highly identified fans spend a good deal of time with other fans and are likely to know them better than they do fans of other teams. The relatively rich social experiences and relationships developed by fans, combined with selective memory, lead highly identified fans to attribute positive traits to other fans, as well to the team or players.

One favorable consequence of in-group bias is that fans tend to accommodate and cooperate with other fans. Highly identified fans see each other as part of a group, facilitating positive fan behavior. Another favorable consequence of in-group bias is that fans attribute positive characteristics to the players. You can probably think of some role players on your favorite team that you think are pretty good, but when it comes down to it, might not even make another team in the same conference or league.

While it may seem obvious that highly identified fans will think and say positive things about the team, it is interesting to observe the effects of in-group versus out-group bias with respect to player trades. Identified fans have an amazing ability to change their minds about a player once they arrive on their team. Similarly, when a player is traded away, fans highly identified with the team (as opposed to the player) will likely make disparaging remarks about his ability ("He wasn't that good anyway.") However, if fans highly identify with the player, trading the player may decrease the fans' identification with the team.

Out-group derogation. It probably comes as a surprise to you that highly identified fans think and say bad things about the opposing team and its players. Although fan behavior at events can be problematic, the positive effect of out-group derogation is primarily in building a home-field advantage. Highly identified fans tend to make opposing teams and fans feel unwelcome, making some venues extremely difficult for visiting teams to succeed.

Community. A consequence of in-group/out-group bias is that it serves to build community and solidarity among fans. Again, you can see how identification has a circular effect. High identification leads to greater feelings of community, which, in turn, is likely to influence fans' perceptions of community acceptance. One can observe, for instance, highly identified fans congregating for tailgating with other fans prior to sporting events. Entire communities of campers, RVs, and tents can develop overnight on many college campuses on football game days and at NASCAR events.

Support Behaviors: 3Ms

Spectators reinforce their identification with the team by engaging in support behaviors. The more identified fans are, the more they will engage in:

- Meeting (games, events, fan clubs, etc.)
- Merchandise buying (souvenirs, licensed logo items, etc.)
- Media consumption related to the team (online, newspaper, TV, radio, etc.)

These support behaviors are the primary sources of revenue for sports organizations.

Meeting. Fans will seek opportunities to meet or join other fans to support their favorite team or player. An obvious effect of identification is that highly identified fans will attend games (home and away) and other related events. Highly identified fans will join fan clubs and other support groups, such as university booster clubs.

A critical outcome related to this willingness to meet and join with others is the willingness to spend money in support of the team. Highly identified fans are likely to see their expenditures as an avenue of supporting the team, as opposed to simply paying money in exchange for a good or service. Further, highly identified fans who expend significant amounts to obtain luxury box seats or other signs of team-related prestige are able to represent themselves to others as important team fans. While there may be other motivations, identification and self-representation to others is likely to explain why anyone would be willing to donate $36,488 to Duke University's sports program in order to be a "Cameron Wade Donor." Although not well researched, identification and self-representation may also be the principal motivation for corporate sponsors who spend upwards of $250,000 to meet with other executives and clients in skyboxes, plus the cost of a dozen or more tickets for each event.

Source: Courtesy of Dallas Mavericks.

Source: Courtesy of Dallas Mavericks.

Sports marketing managers can facilitate meeting opportunities by:

1. Offering promotions geared toward bringing highly identified fan groups together, such as the Dallas Mavericks "Self-Expression" contest (sponsored by Cingular Wireless) that invites fans to paint or otherwise dress themselves to compete for free prime seats (see pictures above).

Source: Courtesy of ATP Masters Series.

2. Including fans in public service efforts or other community events, such as the Masters Series ATP tournament's Lady's Day (see above) that includes a fashion show moderated by players and an autograph session at the end.
3. Building and supporting booster fan clubs which allow more access to players and athletic facilities. In addition to traditional booster club efforts, some minor league hockey clubs arrange for families to adopt players during the season—inviting them into their homes for meals or other activities. During this time, families can offer helpful advice concerning dental care, personal hygiene, and social skills.[15]

Merchandise. Fans buy team or player-related merchandise to reinforce their identification and to represent themselves to others as fans of the team or player. This has important implications for promotions and for licensed product sales.

Identified fans will desire promotional items that are somehow related to the team or event to enhance and reflect their self-concepts. Team jerseys, t-shirts, equipment, and other items (e.g., bobble-heads on office desks) that are frequently on display to others are likely to be highly desired by fans. Items that are unrelated to the team and not frequently on public display are likely to have less appeal to identified fans (e.g., Sears' sponsorship of ice scrapers to Chicago Bulls fans).

Licensed logo apparel sales are an important source of revenue for many sports organizations. Since identified fans are seeking to bolster their self-esteem by associating themselves with the team or player through how they appear, it is critical that the quality and styling of the apparel is obvious to those wearing and observing the apparel. Although price sensitive segments exist among sports fans, the majority of sports fans who are willing to spend money on season tickets are likely willing to spend proportionate amounts on team or player merchandise.

Media. In order to feed their feelings of identification with the team, highly identified fans will spend more time following their favorite team or player in the various media. A highly identified fan of NASCAR and a given driver will get online at www.nascar.com and its related sites, watch NASCAR races on ABC and Fox's Speedvision Network

---

[15]This sentence is meant to be funny. Unfortunately, it is not. At least not to those hockey players who have few remaining teeth, shave on a weekly basis, and settle most disagreements with a swift blow to the head.

on cable, read motor sports newspaper articles and NASCAR magazine, listen to NASCAR radio broadcasts, and pay attention to virtually every other communication regarding NASCAR.

Since merchandise and media are so important to the success of sports organizations, they are the primary subjects of chapters in this text. However, by now, you should understand that identification is the driver that leads to sports success.

Emotional Enhancement

Individuals react to events and places along a circumflex of affective responses (see Figure 2.2). The highly identified fan is likely to experience more positive affective responses to the sports organization, team, and players than will less identified individuals in terms of excitement, pleasure/enjoyment, and relaxation. Less identified fans may find sporting events to be sleepy, boring, displeasing, and perhaps distressing due to lack of identifying with the team or players. Even as a hard-core sports fan, you may have experienced this when flipping through the TV channels, as you pass by games or events that do not include teams or players that you cared about. This, of course, doesn't mean that you won't watch Australian rugby matches if that's the only sports programming available.

In addition to enhanced feelings of excitement and enjoyment, evidence suggests that one's identification and involvement with a sports team in some ways makes the highly identified fan feel immortal. While sports fans pass on like everyone else, identification with a sports team seems to shield against the potential consequences of death.[16] For instance, highly identified sports fans are likely to be more optimistic when reminded of death concerns, as their interest in the sports team acts as a form of buffer against death. Highly identified sports fans are in search of the "perfect moment" in sports, that when experienced (e.g., Christian Laettner's turnaround jumper that allowed Duke to beat Kentucky with time expiring in the 1992 Final Four), gives them feelings of salvation and victory that last a lifetime.[17,18]

---

[16]Dechesne, M., Greenberg, J., Arndt, J., and Schimel, J. 2000. Terror management and the vicissitudes of sports fan affiliation: The effects of mortality salience on optimism and fan identification. *European Journal of Social Psychology* 30: 813–835.

[17]Grimshaw, Michael. 2000. I can't believe my eyes: The religious aesthetics of sport as postmodern salvific moments. *Implicit Religion* 3 (November): 87–99.

[18]Yes, this does all seem a bit out there. But that's the point. Building highly identified sports fans transcends normal goods and services marketing.

Figure 2.2

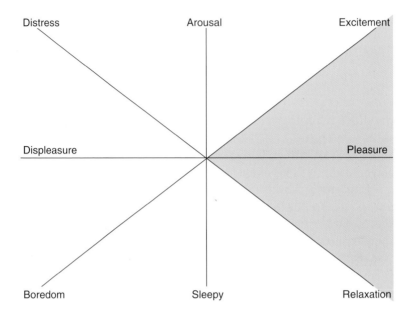

Circumflex of Emotions. *Source:* Adapted from Russell and Pratt (1980).

Sports organizations can enhance fan excitement and enjoyment in a variety of ways:

- Pregame music and video that fits the demographics of the fans.
- Innovative player introductions that build excitement and chances to BIRG even before the game starts.
- Event-specific music and sound effects that ignite fan excitement at key points in game.
- Post-game rallies on the field or court (helps if team comes back out) after big wins.

Spontaneous Behaviors

Just as affective responses are involuntary, highly identified sports fans learn behaviors which become spontaneous or automatic. Highly identified sports fans can't make themselves not feel excited when they go to see their favorite team play. Highly identified fans also can't help but respond physiologically to the sports environment, actually experiencing higher blood pressure, endocrine levels, and, among males, actually producing greater levels of testosterone when winning.[19] Similarly, many highly identified fans have learned through conditioning processes to respond to game stimuli (people, events, and circumstances) in some relatively negative ways.

If you are a highly identified fan at your favorite team's game, what have you learned to do when the referee makes a call against your team? If you are like most other fans, you will affirm the referee on the good job he is doing. You will tell your friends that it sure must be difficult making those tough calls within a split second and with thousands of people watching. You will think to yourself or mention to others, "That's the way it goes. Maybe we'll get the next call."

Maybe that's not quite it. Actually, if you are like most other highly identified fans, you have likely learned that the appropriate reaction is to begin blasting the referees, the opposing players, their fans, their coach, and their bus driver, if available. It doesn't matter if they can hear you or not. You can be sitting on the top row near the rafters and you will still want to offer your words of encouragement to the referee. You might even be watching the game on TV and still attempt to communicate your disagreement with the call to the referees, perhaps by pounding on the TV set.

The point is that highly identified fans are more likely to be aggressive and to engage in blasting at sporting events. This can be a serious problem for event management. Sports organizations that desire to curb overly aggressive behavior can alleviate the problem by:

- Developing announcements and presentations by the head coach and players to encourage fans to follow specific rules of behavior while at the game. For example, Duke's Coach Mike Krzyzewski (pronounced "K") spends time talking to students before games to encourage them to be model fans.

- Training and placing event attendees in each section to actively look for potential dysfunctional fans. This often includes evaluating sobriety, which leads to the next issue.

- Having no-drinking sections in the venue and eliminating the sale of alcohol late in the game (e.g., after seventh inning, etc.).

---

[19]Bernhardt, Paul C., Dabbs, James M., Jr., and Fielden, Julie A. 1998. Testosterone changes during vicarious experiences of winning and losing among fans at sporting events. *Physiology & Behavior* 65 (August): 59–62.

Conclusion

Sports organizations must build fan identification through attractive players, building social acceptance in the community, converting variety seekers into more identified fans, building local involvement with the sport, and fielding competitive teams in a way that fans can have some source of feeling like a winner. The sports organization that increases its numbers of highly identified fans will reap the consequences of increased support—namely, more fans in the seats, giving more money to support the team, watching more broadcasts, and buying more team merchandise.

Precision Marketing

3

Marketers have traditionally segmented markets on the basis of demographic, geographic, psychographic, and behavioral variables. Individual customers with similar attributes and needs are grouped into segments. The firm targets those segments that best match the firm's objectives and resources given the competitive environment, typically investing resources in mass media such as newspapers, magazines, radio, or television.

While sports marketers work under these same basic principles, the process has shifted from relatively static marketing planning models (year-to-year plans) to include more dynamic customer relationship management (CRM) models that quickly adapt to changing customer states and behaviors that can result in day-to-day or even second-by-second adjustments. As teams understand that they can precisely tailor their marketing mix to meet the needs of the different target markets through interactive network programs, they can produce creative and profitable results. Precision marketing offers customized benefits targeted to specific individuals based upon personal characteristics collected through the organization's customer database.

For example, the Dallas Stars recognized that all of their staff's email contacts were potential customers. Prior to the beginning of the 2003–2004 season, every business employee working for the Stars selected individuals from their personal email contact list and emailed what amounted to a trial offer to come to a Stars game (see Box below). The immediate results were that over 52,000 people responded to the email to attend a preseason or early season game. Many more than originally received the email responded, as the email was forwarded from the initial recipients to their friends.

The Stars campaign illustrates the nature of effective viral marketing. Venture capitalist Steve Jurvetson first referred to viral marketing as "network-enhanced word-of-mouth." If individuals receive electronic communications with obvious personal benefits, they will spontaneously pass the information on to others. The benefits might be economic, emotional, or social in nature. Combining all three provides excellent motivation to pass the message on to others. The Stars offer provides a price deal (economic) to enjoy a sporting event (emotional) with another person (social). Subsequent email offers were made to the individuals that responded to the first offer, thus building an ongoing relationship resulting in increased attendance and exposure to the Stars.

Dallas Stars Email Campaign to Infrequent Attendees

I am sending you this great offer because I work for the Dallas Stars and we are looking for new fans to sample our games. Knowing you, I thought you would be interested in getting 2 free tickets to a Dallas Stars game.

The Dallas Stars want you to:

1. Click here for 2 complimentary tickets to an available game and
2. Forward this offer to anyone you know that likes the Stars, hockey in general, or just wants to go see something exciting at American Airlines Center! When you register, don't forget to put in my reference number RAN2776D to be eligible for this offer.

Unlike many Internet email offers that have come before (you remember the Bill Gates Microsoft/AOL hoax), this one is real! It won't last very long. This offer is only valid until September 30th. Seats are limited and offered on a first-come, first-served basis so click here now for your free tickets.

If the above links do not work, simply copy this URL into a browser and hit enter: http://dallasstars.rqst4.info/dspSurvey. cfm?N=163&SID=2&SEQ=1

Get your free tickets to a Dallas Stars game now!

These are other results associated with the Stars viral marketing campaign:

- Extensive publicity (articles in the Dallas Morning News and Sports Business Journal)
- Verbal word-of-mouth about the campaign and the game experience from the fans that attended
- The majority of those responding also subscribed to receive future offers from the DallasStars.com Insider
- The team's database doubled throughout the campaign
- Their story gets to be in this chapter on precision marketing

Goals of Precision Marketing through CRM

For the purpose of sports organizations and sporting events, CRM seeks to achieve three goals through precision marketing:

1. Generate new fans
2. Enlarge attendance and purchases of current fans
3. Motivate and maintain current fan loyalty and identification

The Stars viral marketing campaign generated approximately 20,000 new fans who attended a Stars game. Subsequent emails sought to get these fans to come back to other games via 2-for-1 specials on upgraded seats (see Box below) and then a 3-game micro-plan designed to increase loyalty and identification through increased exposure and involvement at the Stars games. Hence, the Stars generated new fans with a free offer, enlarged attendance and purchases by offering the 2-for-1 deal, and then finally motivated greater loyalty and identification with the team by those who subscribed to the 3-game micro-plans. For those that bought into all three deals, the Stars brought fans from attending zero games to six games throughout the season.

It is important to note that the Stars found a sponsor (a local sports radio station) for these campaigns—with little added effort or cost to the team, given the difficulty of typing "SportsRadio 1310" into an email (see Box below). Clearly, the target market for the sponsor and the team heavily overlap, making the sponsorship deal of benefit to the radio station. Adding the radio station as a sponsor helps the Stars, as the radio station will also promote the Stars and the special deal on air.

Dallas Stars: *"The Ticket" 2-for-1 Special*

SportsRadio 1310 "The Ticket" and the Dallas Stars would like to offer you the perfect ticket package for holiday gift giving (or you can just treat yourself!).

Buy a StarsClub Luxury ticket to see the Stars take on Ken Hitchcock, Jeremy Roenick, and the Philadelphia Flyers at American Airlines Center on December 29th and get a StarsClub Luxury ticket to the Friday, January 30th game vs. the San Jose Sharks for FREE!

Great for stocking stuffers and last minute holiday gifts!

These lower level tickets are limited and only available by calling 214-GO-STARS and asking for "The Ticket 2-for-1" ticket special.

Brought to you by the Dallas Stars & SportsRadio 1310 "The Ticket."

Thank you for your interest in the Dallas Stars!

The Key to Successful Precision Marketing

The key to all network-enhanced precision marketing efforts is the quality of the customer information in the database. As sports fans seek to affiliate themselves in some way with the team or players, the organization has ample opportunity to gather customer-specific data. Every time a ticket to a sporting event is purchased, vital customer information can be obtained. As fans buy individual tickets, mini-paks, or season tickets online, over the phone, or at the ticket office, the organization can gather information that will allow the organization to implement incentive plans that seek to convert these fans into even more frequent attendees. As fans attend games, fan surveys can gather customer information, so that specific fan segments can be identified, rewarded, and encouraged to motivate and maintain their commitment to the organization, its team, and its players.

Through any means of customer contact, the organization must evaluate and search for ways to be market oriented. Market oriented organizations do three things effectively:[1]

---

[1]Jaworski, Bernard J., and Kohli, Ajay K. 1993. "Market Orientation: Antecedents and Consequences." *Journal of Marketing* 57 (July): 53–70.

1. Generate customer information
2. Disseminate customer information
3. Respond to customer information in a way that meets customer needs and fulfills organizational goals.

This chapter provides specific guidance for sports organizations regarding the types of customer information that can be collected and disseminated to guide sports marketers in segmentation, precision marketing, and marketing planning decisions. Since it is typically not the sports marketing manager's responsibility to actually design the database information system, one should develop close, personal friendships with the organization's information technology (IT) employees.[2] However, everyone in the organization should be familiar with the capabilities and possibilities available through CRM software packages (see Appendix 3B).

Without customer information, the organization is merely working from management's intuition and experience. This can lead to ineffective management, inasmuch as professional sports organizations have traditionally been managed by individuals whose backgrounds have been:

- A player (professional, collegiate, or otherwise) who retires and aspires to work in sports management,
- Media or team employees without technical or business training, or
- An individual whose father or other relative owns the team.

In any case, no matter the background or training, management requires knowledge of their customers that exceeds their own abilities to observe and analyze. Even relying upon open access to fans (such as team owners Mark Cuban of the Mavericks or Ted Leonsis of the Capitals—see Appendix 3A) does not mean that management will make effective marketing decisions.

In this chapter, we examine traditional segmentation variables that sports organizations use to segment markets. Sports marketers are not likely to gather all of the information discussed in the following section at one time. Rather, given their needs, the organization will gather selected spectator information that facilitates generating new fans, more fans per game, and more long-term fans for their organization.

---

[2]Most IT employees are appreciative of gifts containing caffeine or nicotine. You might also provide team logo apparel to replace the shirt he or she has worn for the past three days.

Segmenting in the Sports Marketing World

Table 3.1 depicts three major types of segmentation variables (geographics are merged into demographics) and appropriate measures for gathering this information. Once gathered, this information can become part of aggregate customer profiles that can be used to attract sponsors and to plan targeted marketing efforts. On an individual basis, customers can be selected for precision marketing efforts via phone, mail, or email. We look at each set of segmentation variables,

Table 3.1

Sports Segmentation Variables	
Personal characteristics	**Measure**
Demographic	
Gender	Male/Female
Age	Year of birth: 19____
Marital status	Married/Single
Homeowner	Rent/Own home
Children	Number of kids under 18 living at home?____
Heritage	African American, Caucasian, Hispanic, Asian, Native American, Other
Education	High school or less, some college, 2-year degree, BA/BS, Master's, Dr/MD
Household income	<$25,000, $25–49,999, $50–74,999, $75–99,999, $100,000+
Vicinity	Miles you live from venue?
Zip code (address)	Zip code:
Email	Email:
Psychographic	*How accurately do these statements describe you? (inaccurate—accurate)*
Price sensitivity (*tickets, food/ drink, parking, team merchandise, etc.)	I am willing to make an extra effort to find low prices for *. I will change what I had planned in order to take advantage of a lower price for *. I am sensitive to differences in prices of *.
Social motives (can substitute friends for family)	I go to the game to spend time with family as much or more than for the game itself. I go to the game only if (some of) my family goes. My family is the main reason I go to games.

Table 3.1 *Continued*

Personal characteristics	Measure
Promotion-proneness	Promotions influence when I attend games. Promotions play a big part in my choice to attend games. If there's a promotion I like, I just go to that game instead of another one.
Variety seeking	I enjoy going to different entertainment spots for the sake of comparison. If I have a choice when I go out, I'd rather try someplace new than go to places I already know. I tend to go to a lot of different entertainment spots, just for the sake of a change of pace.
Behavioral	*How frequently do you use the following media to find information about the team? (not at all—very frequently)*
Information-gathering	Newspaper (list names or editions as needed) Radio (list stations) Television (list stations) Internet (team Web site or emails) Signage at/near stadium Magnet or pocket schedules
Consumption/Usage	Including this game, how many games have you attended this season? (____/N) How many games will you have attended at the end of this season? (____/N) When the team's games are on TV, how frequently do you watch? (never—all the time) When the team's games are on the radio, how frequently do you listen? (never—all the time) What seats do you prefer to buy? (list seat type; do not prefer—strongly prefer) How much did you spend on food and drink for yourself (not others) at this (last) game? How much did you pay for parking at this (last) game? How many team licensed logo items do you personally own? (1–5+) • Apparel: Jerseys, shirts, sweaters, shorts, jackets, caps, jewelry, etc. • Home use: pennants, posters, signs, mugs, clocks, etc. • Vehicle: license plate frames, license plate inserts, windshield signs, etc.

discussing segmentation issues relative to the sponsor, the team (or sports organization), and CRM.

Demographics

Demographics are the staple of the sports marketer's information system. Demographic profiles are used in selling sponsorships to corporations and organizations wishing to target markets overlapping with those of the sports organization. Table 3.2 contains sample data from customers at a professional baseball game.

Table 3.2

Sample Customer Demographics		
Variable	**Majority**	**Additional information**
Gender	58.1% Male	41.9% Female
Marital status	71.1% Married	29.9% Single
Age	42 (mean)	17.4% <30 years old; 27% >50 years old
Home	77.8% Own	22.2% Rent
Miles fans live from park	50% within 18 miles	85% within 30 miles
Kids at home	56% have no kids under 18	21.1% have 6–12-year-olds; 18.5% have 13–18-year-olds
Heritage	87.2% are Caucasian	6.1% are African American, 3% Native American
Household income	69.5% earn over $50k (30.8% earn over $100k)	Only 17.7% earn less than $35k
Tickets bought per party	90.6% of tickets were purchased for parties of 5 or less	Two (39.6%) and four (24.6%) tickets were most common.
Seats purchased	13.2% Club 17.1% Lower Dugout 17.9% Upper Dugout 27.3% Field Box 16.3% Outfield/Pavilion 8.2% Bleachers	73% of these are individual ticket (not season) purchasers.
Reported expenditures	$15.00 on food & drink (median)	Parking: 23.2% paid less than $2 or nothing; 51.8% paid $5
Games planned to attend this season	50.2%—10 games or less 66.3%—20 games or less	Median games = 10 Average games = 19.8

Sponsor target markets. What kinds of sponsors might be interested in reaching customers with the demographics provided in Table 3.2? Given the high income levels, marital status, and mean age, marketers of professional services (e.g., airlines, e-commerce, consulting and accounting firms), leisure services (e.g., resorts, cruise lines, casinos, etc.), and automobile dealers are organizations likely to have relatively high customer overlap with attending fans.

Team target markets. Sponsors are interested in targeting advertising to the majority of sports fans attending. While the sports organization also seeks to understand their own primary target markets, the organization is often interested in understanding the segments they are *not* attracting. In other words, what are the opportunities? Reviewing Table 3.2, which segments could this team seek to grow or develop? What kinds of people aren't attending? Before going to the next page, write your answers here: _____

_____

_____

Stop. Go back and do what you were told.

So, what did you come up with? Or, did you just keep reading? Well, either way, here's one thing you might have figured out: Efforts could be mounted to increase visits to the ballpark by younger, single, lower-income females living in apartment buildings within a given radius of the stadium (e.g., ten miles). For instance, the team could stage an exhibition between the home team and the New Jersey Nemesis, a traveling women's baseball team, or have a scrapbook-sharing night. You may be able to think of better ideas.

CRM. Demographic data can be easily collected whenever individuals purchase any form of ticket package. If properly coordinated, this data can be collected or augmented via onsite surveys as fans attend a game or event and compiled within the organization's customer information systems. Online registrations, either on the organization's Web site or other points of ticket purchase, routinely gather this demographic information.

How can the organization build and maintain relationships with customers based on the demographic data in their database? Look at Table 3.2 again. The baseball team knows the names and emails of single or married individuals living or working within five miles of the stadium, who make over $50,000, are not season ticket holders, and who paid $5 or more for parking at the last game they attended. The team could email parking passes (sponsored, of course) to the married individuals ("good with four or more in your car") or a price-bundled offer that includes dinner at the ballpark on weekday games for the singles.

Psychographics

In addition to identifying with the team, individuals may be motivated to attend or not attend games due to individual psychological differences. In particular, sports organizations may wish to identify those game attendees who, within the sporting event context, are more or less:

1. Price sensitive: willing to respond to changes or differences in prices
2. Socially motivated: desire to spend time with friends and family
3. Promotion prone: willing to shift consumption behavior based on promotional incentive
4. Variety seekers: desire to seek variety in leisure and entertainment activities

In general, individuals who are more price sensitive, socially motivated, promotion prone, and variety seeking are less likely to be frequent attendees in a given season or a particular sporting event. The more highly identified the fan is with the team, the less the likelihood that behavior (attendance, purchases, media habits, etc.) will be determined by changes in prices, social context, promotions, or need for variety. Identification with the team tends to supersede these tendencies. Less identified and involved fans may, however, be motivated to attend or make purchases for other reasons besides a great love for the sport and identification with the team.

Sponsor target markets. Fans that are particularly price sensitive, socially motivated, promotion prone, and/or variety seekers may be targeted by sponsors of events or promotions that are otherwise unrelated to the sporting event. HEB grocery stores may sponsor a Fourth of July post-game concert or fireworks that reach a broad spectrum of their own customers and the team's fans. HEB may also offer in-store special ticket packages (with bonuses or discounts) for these events for those buying four or more tickets to take advantage of social motivations and price sensitivity for those willing to make the effort of advance purchases.

Team target markets. From the sports organization's perspective, the objective of promotional efforts aimed at price sensitive, socially motivated, promotion prone or variety-seeking segments is to increase patronage of infrequent fans, who hopefully will enjoy the experience, gain exposure to the sport and the team, and subsequently intend to return more frequently. Care must be taken that these promotional efforts maintain or enhance the perceived value of the ticket price. Although sponsors may be paying or trading value for the right to distribute discounted or free tickets, frequent availability of cheap or complimentary tickets will reduce the value of the ticket to those who otherwise are willing to purchase regularly priced tickets.

Sports marketing managers are always interested in finding out what fans think of prices for tickets, merchandise, and the like. By collecting information on these psychographic measures, management may find that they have been overestimating the price-sensitive or promotion-prone segments. It is important to correlate what people say they do (i.e., shop for low prices) and what they actually do. For example, the fans may report via survey that ticket prices are too high, but these same fans may also be frequent attendees who spend $15 a game on concessions at current prices. Although sizeable segments may report high price sensitivity, the actual segment size of those who actually do want to buy the cheapest seat and bring their own food to the game may be considerably smaller.

Ticket.Com/Ticketmaster.com: *Great for the League, Bad for the Team?*

In order to facilitate ticket purchases on the Internet or by phone from any location on the globe, Major League Baseball, the National Basketball Association, and the National Hockey League have signed league-wide contracts with organizations such as Ticketmaster.com and Tickets.com. The average fan purchasing tickets is likely to encounter familiar Web site interfaces and familiar ticket surcharges. While consumers may have become accustomed to the ubiquitous Ticketmaster and its fees, individual sports teams are not always able to market efficiently under these contracts. The ticketing vendor controls the customer information that is generated due to fans' interest in the team. The team would often like to customize the information they receive from fans to be able to more effectively market to the fans' needs. Unfortunately, the ticket vendors have difficulty customizing a program that the vendors essentially mass market. Fans lose out because teams would be able to efficiently target specific products and promotions to fans based on their interests and backgrounds. Teams lose out because they miss the opportunity to build strong relationships with fans through effective precision targeted marketing. Obviously, teams can turn to other vendors and other sources of fan information to build their databases, but they do so at additional costs beyond what the league has already obligated them to pay to the league-wide ticket vendor.

CRM. Clearly, the best opportunities to target individuals who really are price sensitive, promotion prone, or variety seekers are through precision direct marketing efforts. Sophisticated customer information systems can track those customers who respond to specific deals. Importantly, the availability of discounted ticket prices are not broadcast in mass media in a way that is likely to change the perceived value of the ticket for the entire market.

Sports organizations are beginning to adopt the marketing practices of grocery stores and casinos with respect to customer information systems and club/store memberships. You have probably signed up for membership cards to receive special discounts and promotions geared toward your shopping patterns and characteristics. Interestingly, when customers of grocery stores (e.g., Sam's or Kroger's) and casinos (e.g., Harrah's) offer these membership cards, customers willingly provide these marketers with massive amounts of information that is then used to effectively target each individual. The point is that collecting the customer data is relatively easy.

Sports organizations at the top of their marketing game, such as the San Antonio Spurs with their AT&T Rewards program, use software that enables them to track customers when they swipe their tickets or cards at the gate or otherwise interact with the organization. Individual customers (fans) who infrequently attend Spurs games can receive targeted emails and mailings to increase patronage. The more those fans attend games and swipe their Rewards card at kiosks around the AT&T Center at each successive game, the value of the rewards increases (see AT&T Point-Level Rewards box). The rewards range from items that reinforce involvement and identification with the team (schedules, posters, basketballs, etc.) to those geared more to the price-sensitive or promotion-prone segments (buy-one-get-one-free tickets) to the socially motivated and variety-seeking segments (restaurant meals, Six Flags tickets, etc.). Again, note that the Spurs have sponsors (Sprite, Pizza Hut, IHOP) for this program that are targeting some of these same segments.

While it is obvious that season ticket holders are likely to be treated as "members," sports organizations can also develop other levels of memberships that facilitate information collection and marketing targeted at individuals who are price sensitive, promotion prone, socially motivated, or are variety seekers.

Behavioral

Sports marketers are particularly interested in behavioral differences in fans with respect to (a) how they search for information and (b) their consumption/usage. This information can guide media buys, as well as to help teams understand differences between infrequent and frequent fans. Returning to Table 3.1, you can see the methods used to gather this information from fans as they complete various surveys or enroll in programs either online or at the sporting event.

Information Search

Fans purposefully seek information that may be of enduring value (news stories about a favorite player or last night's game) or temporary value ("When is tip-off?") to the fan. However, different fan segments may gather this information from different sources (TV, Internet, newspaper, etc.), at different times (weeks in advance of the game vs. game day), and for different purposes (e.g., curiosity, BIRGing, etc.).

Sponsors/teams. Sports organizations and their sponsors are interested in determining how fans get information about the game or event, such as game times, dates, opponents, and promotions. For instance, infrequent fans that attend a weekend game as part of a weekend in the big city may access game information three to four weeks in advance in order to make ticket purchases. Alternately, frequent fans may look on their pocket schedules or team-sponsored calendars. The team and sponsors may use this information to guide media purchases (e.g., Weekend Entertainment Guide in newspaper vs. TV ads on evening news) supporting games or events they sponsor.

CRM. In a general sense, much of this information may be obtained from syndicated services such as Arbitron (radio) and Nielson (television) ratings. However, sports organization that can obtain information search tendencies associated with specific customers in their relational database can more effectively target communications to them. If a large group of individuals in the database may be queried (selected) based on their tendency to access email or the Internet, then marketing information can be communicated through those media to those fans. If another group is identified that does not have Internet access, then direct mail or phone may be used to communicate. The efficiency (versus bulk mailing or calling all customers) from such an approach is obvious.

AT&T Point-Level Rewards

AT&T Center Rewards members earn 100 points for every Spurs, Silver Stars, or Rampage game* they attend at the AT&T Center and swipe their card. Rewards listed are cumulative. You can receive every reward up to the level of points you have earned for the season!

100 points
FREE 16 ounce Sprite and Rampage Buy-One-Get-One Free Ticket Offer

200 points
Free Beef or Chicken Taco from Taco Cabana and Silver Stars Buy-One-Get-One Free Ticket Offer

300 points
Spurs and Rampage Schedule Poster

400 points
Spurs or Rampage Window Cling and Rampage Buy-One-Get-One Free Ticket Offer

600 points
Invitation to an exclusive Rampage Practice (must be earned by March 19)

800 points
Spurs or Rampage Stress Ball/Puck

1,000 points
Rampage Buy-One-Get-One Free Ticket Offer

*Reward levels are based on pre-season and regular season games only.

1,200 points
Rooty Tooty Fresh and Fruity Breakfast from International House of Pancakes

1,400 points
Spurs Yearbook and Rampage Buy-One-Get-One Free Ticket Offer

1,800 points
Spurs or Rampage Poster

2,000 points
Spurs Buy-One-Get-One Free Ticket Offer

2,200 points
Spurs or Rampage Lapel Pin

2,600 points
Rampage Buy-One-Get-One Free Ticket Offer

3,000 points
$10 Gift Card from Taco Cabana

3,500 points
Six Flags Fiesta Texas One-Day Complimentary Admission Ticket

4,100 points
Spurs or Rampage Sunshade

4,500 points
Spurs Championship DVD

Special Super Fan Reward

5,000 points
Hard Cover Spurs Championship Book

Random Rewards Given Away Every Game

At each and every Silver Stars, Spurs, and Rampage home game, AT&T Center Rewards members will automatically have a chance to win one of the instant Random Rewards listed below:

- One (1) Limited Edition 2.4 GHz Cordless Speakerphone (Digital Spread Spectrum Technology)
- One (1) SBC Center Family 4 Pack to a select SBC Center Family Show
- Twenty (20) IHOP Full Stack Breakfast with coffee
- Fifteen (15) Pizza Hut Personal Pan Pizza with Drink Purchase
- Seventy-Five (75) Pizza Hut Lunch/Dinner Buffet with Drink Purchase
- Five (5) Frost Bank Saddles and Spurs Club Access Passes
- One (1) Conn's $25 Gift Card (by mail)
- Ten (10) Best Buy Free DVDs
- Five (5) Ripley's Believe It or Not and Plaza Wax Museum passes
- Five (5) San Antonio Children's Museum passes

Consumption/Usage

Return to Table 3.2 regarding the data collected from fans attending a professional baseball game. How do you think sponsors and the team might use the consumption data?

Sponsor target markets. Sponsors are particularly interested in the reach and frequency of their sponsorship activities. Reach can be determined by estimating the number of unique individuals attending and watching games. For an individual game or event, this is relatively easy to determine by attendance figures and television ratings. Frequency, on the other hand, can be determined if one knows how often a typical fan is exposed to the sponsorship.

For example, if the average baseball fan attends 20 of the 70 (Minor League) or 81 (MLB) home games, one would expect that this frequency of exposure would have a substantive effect on awareness and recall of the sponsor's brand. Teams armed with this data can present proposals to sponsors indicating the benefits of in-stadium sponsorship in reaching a typical baseball fan:

- attends 20 games,
- earns in excess of $50,000 annually,
- is married, owns home, and lives within the city.

We will spend more time in a later chapter on sponsorship recall. However, you should be able to see that frequency is an important factor in determining why corporations spend what seem to be excessive amounts of money for sponsoring sporting events. The company is able to reach these fans in an environment where the individual is having a good time and is likely to make the association between the brand and the property—particularly if the fan is looking at the scoreboard signage following most plays.

Team target market. Like any other organization, the sports organization is interested in designing marketing efforts at those identified as infrequent, frequent, and very frequent attendees. The goal is to increase consumption by infrequent and frequent fans and to maintain consumption by very frequent or hardcore fans. Methods discussed in Chapter 2 are employed to build and enhance the level of identification in each segment.

Listening to and understanding the needs of loyal season ticket holders are critical to any sports organization's success. Organizations need to spend as much or more effort in maintaining and keeping their current loyal fans due to the lifetime value (LTV) of a customer. To understand this concept, consider how much money you spend at your favorite restaurant, hair salon, dry cleaner, or other retail/service outlet while you are in college. (Or, if you smoke, calculate how much money you spend killing yourself over a four-year period.) Pick one of these and write your calculations here:

- $_____ spent per week
- × 50 weeks (you're gone for at least two weeks) = $_____
- × 4 (or 5 or more) years = $_____

For the four or more years that you are in school, you may find that you will have spent tens of thousands of dollars at a given restaurant or store. Wouldn't those places treat you a lot better if they saw you as a $10,000 customer when you walked through the door, rather than as a person who rarely leaves a decent tip?

The LTV of a sports fan can range from relatively small amounts to hundreds of thousands of dollars, to millions of dollars for corporate accounts. For example, consider the lifetime value of yourself as a season ticket holder at your university after you get out of school.

As you may be aware, it is far cheaper to keep current customers than to acquire new ones. So, if your university administrators were very smart, they would be doing everything they could to be good to you while you're in school so that you'll want to continue buying tickets to games after you leave school.

In general, then, what can sports organizations do to maintain current fans and build value?

1. Provide open communication between the fans and the organization. Open communication doesn't mean that you act like Capitals' owner Ted Leonsis (see Appendix 3A). Fan forums, online surveys, and community relations departments can solicit and channel fan information without burdening executives who may have better ways to spend their time.
2. Ask for fan input on decisions from fan groups via announcements, Internet, surveys, and other means.
3. After #2, explain fully any changes in pricing, seating arrangements, changes in uniforms, or anything else that might mess with fans' expectations.
4. Following #3, only offer good surprises.[3] Keep in touch by way of unsolicited bonuses and benefits that build value in the relationship. If you only communicate when you want more money out of their pockets they will eventually notice the pattern.

CRM. Sports organizations that track actual consumption behavior of ticket purchasers can increase revenues for the organization and satisfy customers at the same time. Many season ticket and other ticket purchasers do not use the tickets that they hold. Although the ticket revenue is already obtained upon purchase, the fan does not derive full satisfaction from the purchase and the sports organization misses important additional revenue that is gained when the ticket is used.

Season ticket holders who are identified as infrequently using their tickets can be approached in a variety of positive ways:

1. Automated and personal emails elicited following patterns of unused tickets.
2. Personal phone calls to see if the organization can help them make better use of their tickets, such as:
    a. using the tickets as donations to disadvantaged individuals,
    b. using the tickets as promotional items on sports talk shows, or
    c. helping or encouraging them to distribute the tickets to clients or others who will use the tickets.

---

[3]This is also not bad advice for maintaining marriages or keeping one's job.

Given the problem that unused tickets are in many successful organizations, hiring one or more individuals to monitor the relevant customer information system data and creatively dealing with unused tickets is likely to be worth far more than the salary of the employee(s) responsible for this duty. Teams today are also turning to technology solutions, such as the online ticket exchanges facilitated by Ticketmaster (go to http://teamexchange.ticketmaster.com).

Implementing Creative CRM Solutions

Now that we have outlined the types of data that are useful to collect for marketing purposes, we turn to an overview of implementation issues pro teams will face as they incorporate CRM into their marketing planning and execution. CRM is still in its infancy in the world of sports, and major league franchises are only now beginning to harness the power of marketing on a one-to-one basis with its customers.

The Goal: Real-Time Connectivity

Anxious to reconnect with fans following the NHL lock-out, the Chicago Blackhawks have turned to CRM solutions offered by GoldMine[4] (see http://www.frontrange.com/). When fans go to the tickets section of the team's Web site to make a ticket request (http://www.chicagoblackhawks.com/tickets/), the fan's contact information is downloaded into a CRM database and each fan is automatically assigned to a sales representative. The sales rep, in turn, can actually contact the fan in real time while the fan is still browsing the team's Web site. Of course, even better would be an online chat with a sales rep. However, the point is that through CRM you can achieve real-time results in a 1-to-1 relationship with a qualified prospect.

The Issues

There are seven keys that will determine whether or not your sports organization will be successful implementing CRM.[5]

---

[4]See Beasty, Colin. 2005. The Blackhawks' revitalized game. *Customer Relationship Management* 9 (October): 19.

[5]Adapted from Krell, Eric. 2005. CRM's 7 Deadly Warning Bells. *Customer Relationship Management* 9 (September): 28–32.

1. *Commitment:* The senior executives of the organization must have buy-in for the CRM initiative or else it will falter when the process hits snags. And it will hit snags, as individuals from marketing, sales, information systems, and operations must work together to make the CRM program work effectively and efficiently. Without the backing of senior management, the project can get sidetracked or delayed as different units seek disparate goals. If you're at the lower end of the organizational totem pole, be careful in volunteering to lead up the CRM initiative unless you know for a fact that the top management is in support of the effort.

2. *Hardware match:* The temptations presented to those given the responsibility for buying equipment, software, and hardware for the CRM implementation may be too much for some to handle. First, the team may have an existing relationship with a key sponsor (e.g., IBM), but the IT people like Dells or Apples. Second, the needs and preferences of the IT people may not match the needs and skills of those on the CRM project team who will have to use the systems. So, if left up to the technology gurus, you could come up with a great system that others have difficulty actually using.

3. *Healthy data:* An early threat to the life of the CRM project is unclean data. Data may be collected in a variety of ways from a variety of sources. Dependent upon how the data is collected, the same customer could be identified as multiple customers based upon multiple transactions. For instance, a customer could buy a ticket at the box office, purchase a jersey on the team's Web site, and complete a contest form at the game. All of these should collect vital data in the same format and identify customers in the same manner.

4. *Measurement expectations:* The allure of fantastic increases in productivity through CRM possesses some to set performance goals that are unrealistic. When finance wants to know what the return on investment (ROI) is on the CRM investment, be cautious of promising staggering returns. It is often difficult on the front end to determine where the biggest paybacks will occur. Instead of offering over-the-top results, you are better off with conservative estimates.[6] Then, when things do go well, expectations have been exceeded and everyone is happy.

5. *Change management:* Assuming you have paid attention to the first four keys, you know that you have to have top management's

---

[6]Otherwise known as "sandbagging."

support to make the CRM initiative successful. However, just because they're on board doesn't mean that everyone else in the organization gets it. In fact, unless the mid-level managers and other employees who will actually be handling and managing the data understand the importance of the CRM effort, the system will not reach its goals. For instance, you will probably need to hold meetings with different department heads and relevant employees to sell the importance of the CRM program.[7]

6. *Right people on the CRM bus:*[8] Effective management of the CRM implementation requires the proper mix of talent from technical, marketing, database management, and analytics personnel. Difficulties arise if the project implementation team is imbalanced, with too strong a presence from one of these functional areas. Similarly, even though the team might equitably represent each of these areas, the skill levels of the team members should be adequate and comparable for the tasks. If you are unable to get the people who can best perform the implementation tasks, you may as well not do the project at all. That may mean paying salaries above and beyond normal market levels to make sure the right people are on the bus—and are sitting in the right seats. You can't go anywhere until the bus is ready to roll.

7. *Sell and sell again.* Once the CRM project takes off and people see its value, the tendency is to let the fervor cool down. Instead, CRM leadership must continue to sell the program, tooting its own horn, and documenting the successes. This means that you should plan out each year's calendar with key events to get yourself in front of company decision makers and opinion leaders to update them on the progress of the CRM program. Once you get started, you have to keep the momentum of the CRM program going in order to stay on the cutting edge.

Conclusion

In order to effectively target precision marketing campaigns, teams must collect precise, reliable, and valid customer data. The more

---

[7]We suggest threatening to release their individual personal data to everyone on the Internet unless they comply with your demands. On the other hand, this may also create what some would call a "negative workplace environment." Consequently, you may do better with veiled threats of reading their personal emails through the new CRM system.

[8]See Jim Collins. 2001. *Good to Great.* New York, NY: HarperCollins.

precise the database, the more precise is the targeting. The result is less wasted effort by the organization and achievement of the CRM objectives of generating more fans, enlarging purchases, and maintaining loyal, identified fans. For the fans, they receive information and offers from the team that are beneficial not only to themselves, but to others with whom they share the information and offers. Without precise customer information, fans experience confusion ("Why did they send me this?") and waste effort viewing (and deleting) irrelevant emails or ignoring other poorly targeted media. Gathering customer data related to demographics, geographics, psychographics, and behavioral variables allows the sports organization to make effective pitches to those organizations seeking to sponsor or advertise with the team due to similar target markets. In sum, everyone wins with network-enhanced precision marketing.

Capitals' Owner Clashes With Fan at Game

3A

By Jason La Canfora
Washington Post Staff Writer
Tuesday, January 27, 2004;
Page A01

In this space, we intended to share a story about Washington Capitals owner Ted Leonsis and his experience with Jason Hammer, a Capitals fan. According to this story, Mr. Leonsis got a little too close to his fan base, resulting in a physical altercation with Mr. Hammer at a game. Mr. Leonsis was subsequently suspended by the NHL for fighting with a fan and the team fined $100,000.

Unfortunately, we were unable to relate this entire story from the Washington Post verbatim, due to the untimely request on the author's part and the excellent customer service provided by the Post.

To obtain permission for the use of the Post's articles, one must apply online at http://postwritersgroup.com/reprintsform.htm. This form has this header:

"NOTE TO USERS: Please provide as much information as possible so that we can expedite the handling of your request."

AFTER completing the form and submitting the request online, applicants THEN receive a notice that the Post's typical response time is 15 days. Apparently the author's submission referring to an imminent publishing deadline did not sit well with the Permissions Editor:

Dear Mr. Wakefield,

Thank you for your interest in the *Washington Post*. I cannot meet your immediate deadline. I don't like to jump people ahead of others. It's not fair to those who have waited patiently. Request for reprinting is denied.

Sincerely,

Name Omitted, Permissions Editor, The Washington Post Writers Group

Interestingly, this response from the Post was received precisely four hours after the request. Admittedly, the author was duly punished for allowing insufficient lead time for the Post to respond in a positive manner. On the other hand, we wonder: If there was enough time in the day to read and deny the application, would it be possible in the same amount of time to either approve the permission or to politely reiterate the 15-day waiting period? We might have felt somewhat better if the application page would have also had something similar to this warning:

NOTE TO USER: If you so much as hint that you want us to help you in some way other than the way that we prescribe in the subsequent page that you have not yet read, we will have no other recourse than to deny your request immediately so that we don't do any more work than we have to. Thank you very much for your patience.

Top CRM Software Packages (2003)

Top 15 CRM suppliers as rated by ISM (ISMguide.com) in accordance with 171 selection criteria, including 105 business functions, 48 technical and 18 user friendliness/support features:

- Amdocs ClarifyCRM v. 11.5—by Amdocs Limited
- C2 CRM v. 5.4—by Clear Technologies, Inc.
- Client Management Software 6.0—by Oncontact Software Corporation
- E.piphany E.6—by E.piphany, Inc.
- ExSellence v. 4.5—by Optima Technologies, Inc.
- iCRM (Applix iEnterprise v. 8.3.1)—by iET Acquisition, LLC
- mySAP CRM 3.1—by SAP AG
- Onyx Enterprise CRM 4.0—by Onyx Software
- PeopleSoft CRM 8.8—by PeopleSoft, Inc.
- Pivotal CRM—by Pivotal Corporation
- S1 CRM Solutions—by S1 Corporation
- SalesPage open.space 4.0—by SalesPage Technologies, Inc.
- Siebel 7.5—by Siebel Systems, Inc.
- Staffware Process RM v. 9.0—by Staffware plc
- Worldtrak v. 5.6—by Axonom, Inc.

The next 18, in alphabetical order:

- ACCPAC eCRM™ 5.5—by ACCPAC International
- Ardexus MODE 4.0—by Ardexus, Inc.
- Connect-Care v. 7.1—by Connect-Care, Inc.
- Firstwave eCRM v. 8.1—by Firstwave Technologies, Inc.
- Goldmine FrontOffice 2002 (HEAT® and Goldmine® Sales & Marketing™)—by FrontRange Solutions
- growBusiness Solutions—by Software Innovation
- iAvenue v. 6.1.3—by Saratoga Systems, Inc.
- iBaan for CRM—by Baan
- J.D. Edwards CRM 2.0—by J.D. Edwards & Company
- marketing.manager-Generation V—by update software AG
- Maximizer Enterprise 7—by Maximizer Software, Inc.
- Maximizer Enterprise for Notes-2002.7—by CGI Group, Inc.
- Net CRM v. 8.5 and NetSuite v. 8.5—by NetLedger, Inc.
- Oracle CRM Suite 11i—by Oracle Corporation
- Salesforce.com—by Salesforce.com
- SalesLogix v. 6—by Best Software
- UpShot—by UpShot Corporation
- Visual Elk 9.0—by StayinFront, Inc.

Research Your Fans

4

Without customer information an organization cannot be customer oriented. A market-oriented organization, you will recall, generates, disseminates, and responds to customer information. If you have no information, you cannot disseminate or respond to it.

Although the best sports organizations regularly conduct market research to determine fans' characteristics, needs, preferences, and wants, many have no systematic approach for conducting fan research. Decisions are often made on the basis of intuition, experience, or observation rather than quantifiable, definitive information.

The Value of Market Research

Sports marketers are faced with a myriad of marketing mix decisions that could benefit from fan input (see Table 4.1). Gathering information requires time and money and must be balanced against the relative benefit of gaining that information. A baseball team may have 20,000 season ticket holders who, on average, use their tickets to only half of the team's 82 home games. Although the team already has the revenue from these ticket sales, they could conceivably gain the opportunity to resell 10,000 prime seats for each game. The problem is that management does not know what will motivate season ticket holders to either use their seats (and thereby contribute to concession revenues) or to make their seats available to others. Obviously, this is worth a substantial investment in research.

In addition to understanding target markets (see Chapter 3), sports organizations can gauge fan reactions to other facets of the marketing mix, such as new pricing schemes, changes in facilities, quality of employee service, and the like. An increasingly important aspect of

Table 4.1

Marketing Mix Decisions	
Marketing mix decision	**Related research questions**
Product Assortment	What are fans' perceptions of our licensed apparel and merchandise? What are fans' perceptions of our team's logo?
Ticket Prices	How willing are season ticket holders to participate in a program to exchange unused tickets? What will motivate them to exchange unused tickets?
Facility Management	How do fans perceive the • information provided on the scoreboards? • wayfinding signage? • comfort and physical condition of seats?
Promotions	How do fans value our promotions? Which do they prefer? Which influence them to attend (early)?

sports marketing research has to do with the effectiveness of the sponsorships provided to the sports organization (see Chapter 9).

Presuming that the reader has some background in marketing research, we first provide a brief overview of the basis for market research and then discuss issues and measures of importance to sports marketing researchers.

Marketing Research: What Do You Mean?

Marketing research involves collecting data directly from individual fans or members of organizations. We are particularly interested in how sports marketers conduct market research for specific marketing problems, as opposed to ongoing information system needs (such as ticket sales). The objective is to expose you to the many types of market research needs of sports organizations and to give you a means to measure important attitudes and perceptions that sports marketers use in developing and adjusting marketing plans.

The research process boils down to the five steps of the scientific method that you learned in your high school science class:

1. Define the problem.
2. Develop hypotheses.
3. Collect data.
4. Analyze data.
5. Derive conclusions.

Sports marketers can think of a thousand questions they would like to slap down on a questionnaire. You, however, being the rigorously trained research methodologist that you are, must maintain focus on what problem is being solved. You must center on what management needs to know so that they can make a better decision. Sometimes the problem can be solved by searching through relevant background information (e.g., search the Web, library, or syndicated sources of information) for the answer. Failing that, you proceed to develop hypotheses, collect data, analyze the data, and solve the problem.

Types of Sports Marketing Research

Marketing researchers design exploratory, descriptive, and causal research projects. Exploratory research, as the name implies, explores the marketing problem further through primarily informal, qualitative (rather than quantitative) means, such as personal interviews, observation, or focus groups. For example, the Memphis Grizzlies selected a panel of fans to visit other NBA arenas (via observation) to provide input (via interviews and focus groups) as to what they would like to see in the Grizzlies' new arena prior to its construction.

Descriptive research, surprisingly, is most often used to describe a particular state of affairs in quantitative terms. Every sporting event or organization conducts (or purchases) research that describes their typical customer in demographic terms. Other descriptive research might include describing the average fan's opinion about service quality or some other facet of the sporting event.

Source: Courtesy of Rovion, Inc.

Causal research seeks to understand factors (cognitive, affective, or behavioral) that cause, explain, or predict other perceptions, feelings, or behaviors. In a strict sense, researchers design experiments to isolate causal factors. For instance, the NBA might want to determine if using Rovion's Bluestream technology (see http://www.rovion.com/Showcase/DRJ_demo.htm) is more effective in driving business to team Web sites for ticket purchases than traditional Web site video technology. Subjects could be exposed to both Web sites (identical Web sites, except one employs the Bluestream technology and one does not) and differences measured. Interestingly, we conducted this experiment and found that the Rovion technology does make a significant difference in fans' feelings about the Web site experience and subsequent intentions to purchase from the Web site—as long as the subject liked the celebrity used in the "video-over" technology. The presence of the celebrity adds a social cue (similar to attractive sales people in a bricks-and-mortar store) that enhances the online shopping experience.

On a practical basis, researchers build predictive models to help understand factors that theoretically and pragmatically influence variables of concern. Sports marketers are often interested in determining what factors related to fans and the event lead to attendance. Our model of identification presented in Chapter 2 is an example of a causal model. In general, the form of a causal model is patterned after attitudinal structure:

$$\text{Perceptions} \rightarrow \text{Affect} \rightarrow \text{Behavior}$$
$$\text{Think} \rightarrow \text{Feel} \rightarrow \text{Do}$$

What an individual thinks about the Dallas Cowboys (winners or losers) influences what he or she feels (excited or bored), which, in turn, influences what he or she does (attends or avoids Cowboys' games).

Researchers are sometimes interested in just one or two aspects of attitude. For example, you might be interested in finding out how individual perceptions of event quality (food and beverage quality, employee service quality, facility quality) influence fans' overall perceptions of event quality. Alternately, you might be interested in finding out how fans' feelings regarding one aspect of the event (e.g., satisfaction with team performance) influence their behaviors (e.g., attendance). The methods described in this chapter are geared particularly toward descriptive and causal research projects.

Sports Marketing Research: Current Issues and Measurement

Sports marketers face a variety of different sports marketing problems. Most research problems in sports can be classified in terms of marketing mix variables that need to be evaluated from the fans' point of view. That is, sports marketers are often interested in finding out what fans think or feel about the product and service provided, ticket prices, promotion schedules, and facility quality in order to adjust plans to increase attendance for the upcoming year. What fans think about service quality and the like are virtually all post-purchase evaluations. We examine five prevalent market research issues, providing survey measures and managerial implications for conducting each type of research. We begin our discussion with brand equity, followed by perceptions of service quality, perceived value of tickets and entertainment, perceived value of promotions, and fans' identification or recall of sponsors.

Perceived Brand Equity

A sports organization's brand equity is related to the organization's perceived quality, brand loyalty, brand associations, and brand awareness (cf., Aaker 1991[1]). For example, the New England Patriots have high brand equity due to:

- Fans' perceptions of its high quality team, coaching staff, front office, and stadium
- High fan loyalty
- Strong associations with the Patriots name (such as Tom Brady and his calm demeanor as the leader that places the success of the team above personal accolades)
- High brand awareness across the United States, where even people who don't care about football are aware of the Patriots, their players, and their achievements

Why is brand equity so important? Research confirms at least six reasons that sports organizations should be concerned about brand equity.

1. *Profits.* Brand equity predicts earnings and financial market value.[2]

---

[1]Aaker, David. 1991. Managing Brand Equity: Capitalizing on the Value of a Brand Name. New York: The Free Press.

[2]Aaker, David A., and Jacobson, Robert. 2001. The value relevance of brand attitude in high technology markets. *Journal of Marketing Research* 38 (November): 485–493.

2. *Product.* Since no tangible product exists for a team or sporting event, the image of the team or sports venue is the driving force behind market success.[3] The brand is represented by the licensed logo (e.g., Patriots) that sells merchandise.

3. *Promotion.* Brand equity is diluted by price promotions and strengthened by deeper image advertising and promotions.[4]

4. *Planning.* Brand equity considerations drive strategic planning processes to build and leverage brand equity over the long run.[5] Decisions are made with the long-term effects on brand equity in view.

5. *Perceived performance.* Particularly on the amateur level (NCAA and lower), teams with high brand equity are perceived to perform at high levels even when they are not (viz., inflated national rankings[6]). Sponsors of teams with high brand equity can afford to stick with the team during cyclical downturns (e.g., San Francisco 49ers, who have won 5 Super Bowls but have not been competitive from 2002–2005), as fans expect the team to return to its previous form.

6. *Participation of sponsors.* More and better sponsors want to associate with teams with high brand equity to leverage and build their own company's brand equity.[7] Poor brand equity means the sales staff is scrambling for sponsors, *any* sponsors. High brand equity means that the sales staff can focus on obtaining sponsors that best fit the desired image of the organization.

Sports marketers should monitor shifts in its perceived brand equity from year to year and across key segments and groups (e.g., season ticket holders). Table 4.2 contains measures for the constructs related

---

[3]Berry, Leonard L. 2000. Cultivating service brand equity. *Journal of the Academy of Marketing Science* 28 (Winter): 128–137.

[4]Jedidi, Kamel, Mela, Carl F., and Gupta, Sunil. 1999. Managing advertising and promotion for long-run profitability. *Marketing Science* 18 (1): 122–143; Yoo, Boonghee, Donthu, Naveen, and Lee, Sungho. 2000. An examination of selected marketing mix elements and brand equity. *Journal of the Academy of Marketing Science* 28 (2): 195–211.

[5]Varadarajan, P. Rajan, and Jayachandran, Satish. 1999. Marketing strategy: An assessment of the state of the field and outlook. *Journal of the Academy of Marketing Science* 27 (Spring): 120–143.

[6]See Seggar, John F., McBride, Darl, and Cannon, Lucile D. 1985. Pareto, powerhouse football and AP Polls. *Sociology of Sport Journal* 2 (December): 334–344.

[7]Cornwell, T. Bettina, Roy, Donald P., and Stenard, Edward A. 2001. Exploring managers' perceptions of the impact of sponsorship on brand equity. *Journal of Advertising* 30 (Summer): 41–51.

Table 4.2

Measuring Brand Equity	
Brand Equity	**Loyalty** I am loyal to the *team*. The *team* is my favorite team. I would rather see this *team* play than any other team in the league.
	Perceived Quality The likely quality of play for this *team* is extremely high. The likelihood that this *team* will play well is very high.
	Brand Awareness and Associations Some positive characteristics of this *team* come quickly to mind. I can quickly recall what the *team* logo looks like. I have difficulty imagining the *team* logo in my mind (reverse scored)
	Overall Brand Equity of Licensed Logo Apparel and Merchandise It makes sense to buy *team* logo merchandise instead of any other teams, even if all else about the merchandise is the same. Even if other apparel has the same features, I would prefer to buy apparel with the *team* logo on it. Even if there is another team as good or better than this *team*, I still prefer to buy this team's apparel.

Source: Adapted from Yoo, Boonghee, and Donthu, Naveen. 2001. Developing and validating a multidimensional consumer-based brand equity scale. *Journal of Business Research* 52 (April): 1–14.

to brand equity. In particular, these measures may give management a good indication of the factors that determine merchandise sales. A team with relatively low merchandise revenue may find that fans do not see the team's brand marks as distinctive from other teams, indicating a need to revise the logos or merchandise. Furthermore, if these measures are tracked over time, the team can determine if the brand and its reputation remain consistent or if certain incidents (e.g., trading key players, winning championship, etc.) are associated with changes in brand equity.

Perceived Service Quality

Service quality is one of the most researched subjects in services, in general, and sporting events, in particular. The service provided on the field in the form of the sporting event is the core service provided fans. The service in the stands is a secondary service provided fans, but is vital to keeping fans once they come to see the game.

Why is service quality so important? For those fans who attend the game for reasons apart from the sporting event itself (e.g., social reasons, business reasons, family obligations, etc.), the service in the stands may be the most important aspect in determining their satisfaction with the event. For those highly identified fans who attend for their love of the team and the game, the service provided in the stands will determine

- How long they will spend at the stadium, arriving late and leaving early if dissatisfied,
- How much they will spend while at the stadium, given how long they are there, and
- How many games they attend throughout the season.

Most service quality surveys are variations of an instrument known as SERVQUAL[8] (see Table 4.3). This instrument measures four key intangible characteristics of employee service (empathy, reliability, responsiveness, and assurance) and less reliably measures tangible aspects of the service (viz., the facility or stadium quality). The tangible elements of the service delivery will be addressed in a moment.

Intangibles

To date, service quality research related to intangibles can be seen as unreliable (viz., identical studies produce different results) due to two reasons.

First, SERVQUAL was developed primarily for relatively pure services (e.g., home telephone service) and does not account for the multiple sequences of service scenarios within more complex service deliveries such as sporting events. Consider the different groups of employees you encounter as you attend a sporting event:

Parking/Security personnel → Ticket office → Ticket takers →
Ushers → Vendors → Concessions

The delivery of service at sporting events is like the unfolding of a drama or theatrical play, where each scene depends upon the preceding

---

[8]Parasuraman, A., Berry, Leonard, and Zeithaml, Valerie. 1988. SERVQUAL: A multiple-item scale for measuring customer perceptions of service quality. *Journal of Retailing* 64 (Spring): 12–40.

Table 4.3

SERVQUAL Employee Service Dimensions
EMPATHY Show a sincere interest in solving your problems when you have one. Give you individual attention. Have your best interests at heart. Understand your specific needs. Care about their customers.
RELIABILITY Perform the service right the first time. Start everything on time. Make sure that everything in the place is ready before customers arrive. Insist on having everything in the place in perfect working order. Have office [operating] hours convenient to all its customers.
RESPONSIVENESS Give you prompt service. Are always willing to help you. Are never too busy to respond to your requests. Tell you exactly when services will be performed. Are always concerned with giving fast service. Do everything they can to make sure waiting lines go smoothly.
ASSURANCE Are consistently courteous with you. Have the knowledge to answer your questions. Make you feel safe in your transactions with XYZ. Instill confidence in customers. Make you feel comfortable when you talk with them.
Source: Parasuraman, A., Leonard Berry, and Valerie Zeithaml. 1991. "Refinement and reassessement of the SERVQUAL scale." *Journal of Retailing* 67 (Winter): 420–450.

scene. Importantly, the fans are involved in the production of the play, as they take part in the service encounter at each stage. The situational context of the service delivery varies by person and the setting—so that a fan could have a negative experience with an overzealous security guard and a pleasant experience with an usher. Hence, it is important to know what aspect of the service drama a given fan is evaluating when measuring service quality.

For reliable research that allows management to pinpoint any deficiencies, one would need to specify the employee group when administering SERVQUAL surveys. Otherwise, management does not know whether fans are thinking of the good (bad) service they received from the ushers, the concessions employees, or maybe the marketing intern that just started today. Consequently, if the survey indicates that the employees are not very responsive, management needs to know which employee group is causing the negative perceptions among fans so that they can remedy the situation.

Second, the four employee dimensions most often used in SERVQUAL surveys are actually derived from a larger set of dimensions that may be more applicable in some settings than in others. Using only these variables may exclude other important service aspects within sports settings. Table 4.4 offers a complete set of attributes that can be used in service quality surveys. Further research would likely be needed to develop items for the specific constructs such as "availability" or "courtesy," but could be derived from the definitions.

Table 4.4

Service Quality Attributes	
Access	The physical approach to the food service area, including finding your way to the food you want and the clarity of in/out lines.
Aesthetics	The appearance and ambience of the food service area, including the appearance of the facilities, food and drink, and service staff.
Attentiveness-helpfulness	How well service employees help, including the impression you get of their wanting or willingness to help you.
Availability	The availability of service employees and the availability (stock) of food and drinks; includes the employee/customer ratio and the amount of time each employee has to spend with each customer.
Care	The concern, consideration, sympathy, and patience shown the customer, including how well the employees make you feel at ease and emotionally (rather than physically) comfortable.
Cleanliness/tidiness	The cleanliness and neatness of the food service area, including the service environment, facilities, equipment, serving areas, and employees.

Table 4.4 *Continued*

Commitment	Employees' apparent commitment to their work, including the pride and satisfaction they apparently take in their job; their diligence and thoroughness.
Communication	How well employees communicate in a way that you understand, including the clarity, completeness, and accuracy of information communicated AND the ability of employees to listen and understand you.
Competence	The skill, expertise, and professionalism with which the service is performed, including the carrying out of correct procedures, correct execution of customer instructions, degree of product/service knowledge shown by employees, AND the general ability to do a good job.
Courtesy	Politeness, respect and propriety shown by employees, including the ability of employees to be unobtrusive and not interfering when appropriate.
Flexibility	The willingness and ability of employees to amend or alter the nature of the service or product to meet the needs of customers.
Friendliness	The warmth and personal approachability of employees, including cheerful attitude and ability to make you feel welcome.
Integrity	The honesty, justice, fairness, and trust in the way employees treat you.
Product quality	The taste, freshness, and quality of the food and drink, including the appropriateness of the food and drink temperature (hot/cold).
Reliability	The reliability and consistency of service, including punctual service delivery and keeping agreements made with you (doing what they said they will do).
Responsiveness	The speed and timeliness of service delivery, including the speed and ability to respond promptly to requests with minimal waiting and queuing time.
Security/safety	The personal and financial safety you have in completing transactions with employees; includes the way you feel about the employees when you exchange money for food and drinks.

Source: Driver, Carole, and Johnston, Robert. 2001. Understanding service customers: The value of hard and soft attributes. *Journal of Services Research* 4 (November): 130–139.

Tangibles

As you have already learned, the quality of the physical environment in terms of the stadium, arena, or facility can make or break sports organizations. Organizations that have brand new facilities will need to monitor fans' perceptions of the facility as it ages. Those with older facilities must know how fans perceive the current facilities in order to know what and when to renovate or to build new facilities.

Table 4.5 provides selected items to measure the interior decor, wayfinding signage, scoreboards, entertainment areas for children, seat comfort, space allocation, and cleanliness of the facility. For example, in addition to the incarceration and prolonged group therapy for international football fans, proper research—regarding fans' perceptions of facility space allocation that might have indicated the need to renovate European football facilities—could have prevented accidents causing the loss of hundreds of lives over the past few decades.[9]

The perceived value of the ticket or the entertainment received at a sporting event is based upon what fans think they get for what they give. Sports marketers are not so much interested in what fans think about prices. If you ask fans about prices, they inevitably will report that they would like them to be lower or that they are too high. Fans' perception of the value of the ticket or the event, however, gives you a better understanding of what they are willing to give up to attend the game or event.

Why is perceived value so important? If fans perceive a ticket to have high value, they will pay more money for it and be willing to give up additional time and effort to obtain that ticket. What is the perceived value of a Super Bowl Ticket? Is it the face value? Generally not.[10] What would you be willing to do to get tickets to the Super Bowl if your favorite team was playing and your favorite singing group was performing at half-time? Clearly, the perceived value of a ticket may exceed, meet, or fall short of the face value of the ticket depending upon the bundle of benefits one receives in exchange for purchasing the ticket.

Sports organizations may wish to measure other aspects of the sporting event that are likely to contribute to fans' perceptions of

---

[9]For a history of such disasters caused primarily due to poor space allocation and facility quality, see http://news.bbc.co.uk/sport1/hi/football/1273347.stm.

[10]Tickets are normally sold at prices above face value, with the exception of the 2002 Super Bowl in New Orleans, where scalpers were reportedly unable to sell all of their tickets even at face value—seriously.

Table 4.5

Facility Quality					
Rate this stadium in terms of its	**F**	**D**	**C**	**B**	**A**
Attractiveness of interior color schemes					
Attractiveness of wall/facade decorations					
Attractiveness of playing field					
Clarity of signs in helping me know where I am going					
Clarity of signs showing where things are located					
Entertainment provided on video scoreboard					
Completeness of information provided on scoreboards					
Scoreboards' provision of interesting statistics					
Attractiveness of entertainment areas for children					
Quality of entertainment areas for children					
Amount of knee room in the seats					
Amount of elbow room in the seats					
Comfort of seats in the facility					
Availability of concession areas to handle the crowds					
Availability of restrooms to handle the crowds					
Walkways/aisles wide enough to handle the crowds					
This facility makes me feel crowded. (Reverse scored.)					
Restroom cleanliness					
Food service areas cleanliness					
Seating area cleanliness					
Overall Inside Quality of the Stadium					
Perceived Value of Tickets and Entertainment					

Source: For these and additional items, see Wakefield, Kirk L., and Blodgett, Jeff G. 1994. The importance of servicescapes in leisure service settings. *Journal of Services Marketing* 8 (3): 66–76; Wakefield, Kirk L., and Blodgett, Jeff G. 1996. The effect of the servicescape on customer's behavioral intentions in leisure service settings. *The Journal of Services Marketing* 10 (6): 45–61; Wakefield, Kirk L., and Blodgett, Jeff G. 1999. Customer response to intangible and tangible service factors. *Psychology & Marketing* 16 (January): 51–68.

value. The perceived value of a sporting event is a function of all that one receives when attending a sporting event. Perceived value, in turn, influences fans' willingness to attend future games. A causal model of perceived value is depicted in Figure 4.1. We have already discussed measurement of perceived quality related to stadium quality and

Figure 4.1

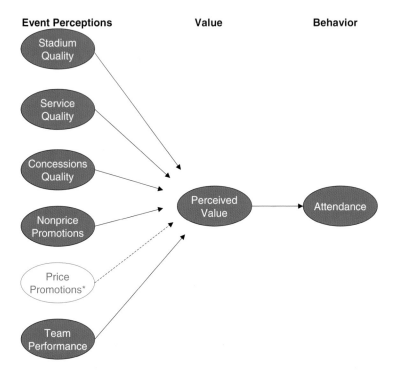

Causal Model of Perceived Value

*Negative effect. All others increase perceived value.

service quality. The following section discusses promotion (price and nonprice) value.

The perceived value of a ticket, entertainment, or virtually any other aspect of sporting events can be measured by adapting the following three items.

Perceived Value[11]
Generally speaking, the regular prices [to games here] are:
A bad buy—A good buy
Not worth the money—Worth the money
Too high for what I get—Not too high for what I get

Perceived value of promotions. In some people's minds, sports marketing is all about developing clever sales promotions to manipulate fans'

---

[11]Wakefield, Kirk, and Barnes, James. 1996. Retailing hedonic consumption: A model of sales promotion of a leisure service. *Journal of Retailing* 74 (4): 409–427.

behavior to attend games. Sales promotions are a single component in the organization's promotion mix, along with public relations, advertising, and publicity. Notwithstanding, the nature of sports marketing over the past two decades has led to an undue interest in sales promotions as a way to counter negative publicity generated by poor performance or other weak aspects of the team's marketing mix (i.e., product, price, and place).

Source: www.eBay.com.

Sports organizations have also been driven to offer a wide variety of promotions due to the growth in sponsorships. Sponsors who want to get the most out of their sponsorship investment are likely to seek a complete sponsorship package that produces multiple exposures to fans and involves them on an interactive level. Sponsored sales promotions provide that means. The fan who receives a Chris Pronger bobblehead sponsored by Pepsi (eBay price = $51.00) and displays it on his or her desk will be reminded of Pepsi each time he or she sits at the desk and looks at Chris Pronger's feet.

Why is promotion value so important? The primary goal of most sports promotion giveaways is to induce immediate response in the form of ticket purchases and early arrival at the event. Secondary or alternate goals may include enhancing team loyalty. As illustrated by the Buffalo Bills' experience in using boring bobble-heads (e.g., Coach Marv Levy) to promote game attendance, research is important to ensure that the team *and* the sponsor are effectively spending their time and effort in a way that will result in meeting promotional objectives. If the promotional item is discarded or otherwise disregarded, the team will not draw more fans and the sponsor will not benefit from repeated exposure.

Exploratory research in the form of focus groups is useful in screening the value of promotions. Descriptive research that seeks to determine the relative value of individual promotions can be measured with one or more of the items below.

> *Promotion Value* [This promotion]:
>   Has no value to me—Has high value for me
>   Adds no value to the ticket price—Adds great value to the ticket price
>   Isn't worth arriving early at the game—Is definitely worth arriving early at the game

As can be seen in Table 4.6, promotions that are related to the event tend to be more popular with fans. Research shows that price promotions have value for infrequent, low-income, price-conscious customers who are not loyal fans. Nonprice promotions have value for frequent fans who are highly involved with the sport and the team.[12]

Sponsorship Identification

Despite the fact that corporations annually spend billions of dollars on sports sponsorships, how fans process and recall sports sponsorship information is not well understood. Research conducted by Joyce Julius (see www.joycejulius.com) assumes that mere exposure is important. Certainly the amount of exposure a sponsor receives in view of fans is important. Exposure to a sponsor's logo blazing around an oval at 200 mph, however, does not necessarily translate into fan recall and identification of the sponsor.

---

[12]Wakefield, Kirk L., and Bush, Victoria D. 1998. Promoting leisure services: Economic and emotional aspects of consumer response. *The Journal of Services Marketing* 12 (3): 209–222.

Table 4.6

Price and Nonprice Sales Promotions at a Minor League Baseball Stadium	
Sales promotion	Customers with positive attitude toward deal
Fireworks	77%
Bat night	77%
Proof of Purchase[a]	74%
Cap day	71%
Coupon Books[b]	70%
Seat cushion	69%
Baseball night	69%
Pennant night	68%
Helmet night	67%
Monday All-Faiths[c]	66%
Fill 'er up Cup	65%
Team t-shirt	64%
2-for-Tuesday[d]	64%
Ladies Night[e]	64%
Mapco/Pepsi Discounts[f]	64%
Squeeze bottles	62%
Concert in the park	62%
Silver Bullets	62%
Field of Dreams charity night	61%
Lunch bags	58%
Baseball Collector's Cups	57%
Chamber of Commerce night	53%
Wild & Crazy Nickelodean Kids	53%
Power Ranger show tickets	51%
Seniors Night[e]	51%

Bold-faced print denotes organization-related nonprice promotions.
[a]Discounts based upon collecting cereal box tops.
[b]Discount coupons bought as part of entertainment coupon book.
[c]Discounts received when customer brings church bulletin.
[d]Discounts (2-for-1) received when customer brings Nestle wrappers.
[e]Discounts (½ off) received on Wednesday (seniors) or Thursday (ladies) nights.
[f]Discounts received by patronizing Mapco gas stations.

Fans' identification of sponsors is important because the association of the sponsor with the event (team, driver, etc.) allows the sponsor to leverage the positive association with the event to build its brand equity.[13] The sponsor frequently develops a complete advertising and sponsorship campaign that is designed to enhance the image of the brand. In order for the "lever" to be pushed, fans must make the association between the sponsor and the event.

Fans tend to recall those sponsors that are prominent (well-known, familiar) and related in some way to the event or participants in the event.[14] The prominence of a company like McDonald's or Coca-Cola aids fans' recall of the sponsorship because the brand names are instantly recognizable and easy to retrieve from memory. Nestle's Crunch is memorable as a sponsor of NBA Crunch Time because of its relatedness. Similarly, Dutch Boys Points in the Paint NBA promotion fits due to the relatedness between Dutch Boy products (paint) and paint.

Because of the prominence and relatedness phenomenon, measuring fans' sponsor identification is more difficult than most other market research projects discussed thus far. Prominent and related sponsors will be recalled more so than those less prominent and unrelated to the event. Of course, this also implies that smaller firms sponsoring events unrelated to its brand in some way are very likely wasting their money.

One way to measure sponsorship identification is to ask fans to identify sponsors from a list of companies, some of which are not sponsors. In this list, one can develop a list containing an equal number of *nonsponsoring* companies who are:

a. prominent and related
b. nonprominent and related
c. prominent and unrelated
d. nonprominent and unrelated

Randomly mixing these company names with the event's actual sponsors helps control some of the guessing that fans will do, compared to

---

[13]Cornwell, T. Bettina, Roy, Donald P., and Stenard, Edward A. 2001. Exploring managers' perceptions of the impact of sponsorship on brand equity. *Journal of Advertising* 30 (Summer): 41–51.

[14]Johar, Gita V., and Pham, Michel Tuan. 1999. Relatedness, prominence, and constructive sponsor identification. *Journal of Marketing Research* 36 (August): 299–312.

if you just asked them to recall sponsors from a list consisting only of actual sponsors.

The recall data generated from this research, when favorable, can be used to report to sponsors. When recall data suggests that fans are not effectively recalling sponsors, this should suggest the need to improve the quality of the sponsorship package. While little can be done to make a less prominent sponsor more prominent in the short run, sports marketers can develop sponsorship packages that better integrate the sponsor into the event. For instance, NASCAR or NASCAR driving teams could assist the United States Navy by integrating the Navy's "Accelerate Your Life" ad campaign into an effective sponsorship opportunity.

A critical issue in sponsorship research is determining the return on investment of sponsorships. What is the value of American Airlines sponsorship of the American Airlines Center in Dallas and Miami? To what extent does fan affinity for a given team (viz., the Stars and Mavericks in Dallas) transfer to the companies that sponsor the venue or the team? We trust that you can survive without knowing the answer to these questions until you read an entire chapter devoted to sponsorship valuation later in this text.

Conclusion

Let's conclude this chapter by returning to its beginning. Sports teams are faced with marketing problems. Management meets, discusses, and dissects what is believed to be the causes of a specific marketing problem. The next step is to collect data and analyze the results to form conclusions that lead to action steps to remedy the problem. This chapter provides a ready source of methods of data collection that address some of the most common sports marketing problems pertaining to marketing mix issues, as seen below.

Sports marketing research issue	Marketing mix variable
Brand equity	Product
Perceived service quality (intangibles & tangibles)	Distribution
Perceived ticket/entertainment value	Pricing
Perceived promotion value	Promotion
Identification/recall of sponsors	Promotion

You are clever enough to realize that other problems may require different measures and approaches in your job. If so, we advise that you simply refocus whatever your boss is saying back to one of these five problems, because at least you know how to research these.

Build the Season Ticket Base

5

Season ticket sales are the financial foundation of any sports team. Gate receipts account for roughly one-third of total revenue for Major League Baseball (33.9%, 2004) and National Basketball Association (34.3%, 2003–2004) teams, with media revenue and venue revenue making up the remainder. The UK's Premier League (29%, 2003) and the NFL (23.4%, 2003) rely less on ticket sales due to its media revenue—and the fact that these teams routinely sell out contributes to the high demand for media coverage. Average attendance in the NFL in 2004 was 67,462, with only the Arizona Cardinals (37,533) managing to attract less than 50,000 fans a game. A team or league without a loyal fan base does not have the clout to generate attractive media contracts. Basically, the relationship is the higher the average attendance, the higher the revenue that can be generated from media and sponsorship sources. That brings us back to the point that season ticket sales are the financial foundation of any sports team.

The process of selling tickets has changed dramatically in the past decade, as the vast majority of tickets (up to 70%) are now sold online via the teams' Web sites (or associated vendors such as TicketMaster). For those of you too young to remember, fans would either visit the box office or use their rotary phones to call the ticket office located at the stadium to buy tickets, where they would be put on hold until Blanche got back from her cigarette (or cigar, in NYC) break. Today, phone sales are still a critical element in selling tickets, but more so for outbound (team to customer) than inbound (customer to team).

Entry into sales and marketing positions in most sports organizations begins as part of the inside sales team, making outbound phone calls to prospective buyers of mini-plans and other ticket packages. Inside sales people generate leads from recent single-game purchases, as well as other names in the team's database. The goal of inside sales teams is to convert single-game ticket buyers into multiple-game ticket buyers. While some organizations allow full-menu selling to inside sales people, most limit these entry-level positions to selling only partial-season game plans. These entry level positions are essentially trial positions to see who can actually sell tickets. Those who do are then moved into full-time, salaried positions to sell a full menu of individual tickets, mini-plans, season tickets, groups, game day packages (parties/events/picnics), and suites. Others may also sell admissions to fantasy camps, children's camps, and clinics.

In this chapter, we will discuss methods and issues specific to those responsible for managing and selling a full menu, paying particular attention to building and maintaining season ticket sales. Successful season ticket sales are based upon understanding and implementing three fundamental concepts related to

1. Segmentation of season ticket holders,
2. Reducing churn of season ticket holders, and
3. Building and monitoring relationships with season ticket holders.

Segmentation of Season Ticket Holders

Season ticket holders are typically classified according to whether they are individual/family, corporate, and whether or not they include suites. For most professional teams, season tickets will consist of 60 percent corporate buyers and 40 percent individual buyers. In pursuing corporate season tickets and suites buyers, the clientele base is relatively obvious. Teams typically target executives in the top 1,000 corporations in major cities. The benefits sought by corporate buyers may be different from that of individual buyers; however, their individual characteristics and attitudes toward the property are likely to be similar to other season ticket holders. Consequently, to delineate the differentiating characteristics of season ticket holders, we treat corporate and individual buyers alike. The primary difference is that when considering prices and payment, it is a question of corporate versus household budget that restricts the decision making of the buyer. Household income is still a factor, however, since attending a game is not cost-free even when the ticket is paid for (e.g., see Team Marketing Report's Fan Cost Index at http://www.teammarketing.com/fci.cfm). Further, recent changes in tax laws have reduced the amounts that corporations and their executives, particularly for pharmaceutical firms, can deduct for entertainment/selling expenses.

Season ticket holders and buyers of other multiple-game packages can be segmented along four dimensions: Demographics, Media-Related Behaviors, Barriers to Attendance, and Incentives to Attend. Table 5.1 presents the variables in each of the four dimensions and how buyers of full-season tickets, half-season tickets, mini-paks, single-game tickets, and nonattenders differ on each variable in each dimension. Each dimension and its associated variables are discussed in turn in relationship to how an individual salesperson for the team would evaluate potential ticket buyers. Each section closes with power questions that can be used to qualify prospects for season ticket packages. Power questions provide you with the information that you need to effectively match customer needs with the appropriate inventory at your disposal as a salesperson.

Demographics

Whether you are selling season tickets for major league sports, NCAA Division I athletics, or even for most minor league teams, your primary group of season ticket buyers will have similar characteristics. Since the cost to frequently attend professional and major college sporting events exceeds the ability to pay for most young employed individuals, season ticket holders are likely to be middle-aged (mid-40s) or older, compared to the average single-game and mini-pack buyers (mid–upper 30s). Accordingly, season ticket holders are almost by necessity going to be in the upper-income brackets. However, those that are not in the highest income brackets ($75–99,999 and over $100,000) may be good candidates for half-season or mini-paks. The more critical element related to income has more to do with how often the individual goes out each month for entertainment (spending at least $25 each time out). Some people have money, but they just don't like to go out for entertainment. They would rather sit at home, read a book, drink some tea, spend quality time with family members, or engage in some form of service to others in the community. Obviously, these are not the kind of people that you want at a ballgame.

If you find that a prospect already goes out at least once every week for entertainment, it's just a matter of shifting his or her selection of entertainment. If the individual is more of a homebody, your task is more difficult because that person must drastically change routine to frequently attend sporting events.

Note from Table 5.1 that full-season ticket buyers are almost evenly split between male and female, are likely to be married (64%), and most have no children living at home (64%). This suggests that many

Table 5.1

Ticket Buying Segments

Surveys were conducted with over 5,000 fans regarding three different NBA teams. Fans were asked about their attitudes and behaviors related to the local NBA team. The table below illustrates the results.

Demographics

Ticket Purchase	Age	Distance (miles)	Male (%)	Go out (monthly)	Household income $100k+	Married (%)	No kids at home (%)
Full-season	44	22	51	4.9	46%	64	64
Half-season	40	23	55	4.8	33%	56	68
Mini-paks	39	24	60	4.5	25%	49	62
Single-game ticket	36	30	48	4.2	14%	52	55
Nonattender	40	37	40	3.4	9%	56	58

Statistically significant differences exist between at least two groups of ticket purchasers for each variable (e.g., nonattenders are significantly different from season ticket holders in all cases).

Media Consumption

Ticket Purchase	TV	Radio	Newspaper	Game-talk
Full-season	●●●●	●●●	●●●●	●●●●
Half-season	●●●●	●●●	●●●●	●●●●
Mini-paks	●●●●	●●●	●●●●	●●●
Single-game ticket	●●●	●	●●●	●●●
Nonattender	●	—	●	●

Barriers

Ticket Purchase	Psychic costs	Venue convenience	Popularity	Perceived ticket availability	Perceived ticket value	Hometown acclimation
Full-season	●	●●●	●●●	●●●	●●●	●●●●
Half-season	●	●●●	●●●	●●●	●●●●	●●●●
Mini-paks	●	●●●	●●●	●●	●●●	●●●
Single-game	●●	●●	●●●	●●	●●	●●●
Nonattender	●●●	●	●	●	●	●●

Incentives

Ticket Purchase	Involvement	Loyalty	Identification	Similarity
Full-season	●●●●	●●●●	●●●	●●
Half-season	●●●●	●●●●	●●●	●●
Mini-paks	●●●●	●●●●	●●●	●●
Single-game ticket	●●●	●●●	●●	●●
Nonattender	●	●	●	●

The number of ● indicates the level for each variable. Differences in the number of ● between ticket purchase groups indicates that statistically significant differences exist between the groups.

of these are couples who do not have someone nagging them about how they are always leaving home to go the ballgame. Rather, they are attending the game together, as a true example of wedded bliss. Seriously, this data represents an important point in team marketing and sales: Decisions to spend relatively large sums of money in a household are most likely to be joint decisions with another household member. If the other primary decision maker in the household is not supportive of spending time and money on season tickets, you're either going to have no sale or no marriage. OK, that may be a bit strong, but you get the picture. (Note: As a point of ethics, you should prefer that the marriage remains intact, no matter the commission level.)

Most season ticket holders will live close enough to the venue so that the commute from home to the venue is no longer than the commute they typically take to work. Frequently, the sports venue is located in close proximity to the central business district so that it actually is the same distance for many. In a major metropolitan area, this may range from 20 to 25 miles. For sports with relatively more games (basketball, hockey, baseball) compared to others (football), individuals who live 30 or more miles away will be unlikely to travel that far that often to warrant getting season tickets.

Power questions. You may be able to acquire the income and age data from your customer database. For corporate customers, you can inquire about the budget available for hospitality. Hopefully you can observe the gender. With respect to demographics, the following questions (in order) will help you qualify them as prospects for full-season, half-season, mini-paks, or individual game tickets.

1. How many times each month do you go out for entertainment (spending at least $25)?
2. Tell me about your family living at home with you. (Listen for marital status and kids.)
3. Where do you live? How far is that from the stadium/arena?

Media-Related Behaviors

After finding out whether or not an individual has the ability to pay for tickets, one of the best indicators of future attendance (besides past attendance) is the fan's media habits. Full-season ticket purchasers will tell you that they watch the team on TV whenever they can (viz., away games), that they frequently listen to the games on the radio when they're in the car, that they always read whatever is in the paper about the team, and that they were just talking with some of their friends about the latest trade, last night's game, or some other team-related issue.

One of the ways to differentiate between the multiple-game ticket prospect and the single-game purchaser is how frequently they listen to the team on the radio. Individuals who listen to games on the radio must be able to visualize the game in their minds, and likely have favorite players that matter to them enough to want to follow their performance in real time—not just read about it in the paper or see it on SportsCenter.

You know that you are wasting your time with a prospect if they tell you that they don't watch the team's games when they (the team) are on TV. Most prospects will be polite with you, expressing some interest in the team, just because you work for the local team. You can purposely probe into their real interest level by asking them if they saw one of the recent games on TV or read about the team's most recent trade in the paper. To them, you are making conversation. The real purpose is to understand how much the individual follows the team in order to qualify them as a prospect.

People talk about what is important to them. For some people, that means they talk about themselves all the time. These are the kind of people that you'd like to spend less time with, even if it is your boss. Back to the point at hand, people who are interested in sports—and your team in particular—will spend a good deal of time talking about it with others, not just occasionally. Consequently, if the prospect enjoys talking about the sport and the team with you, you have a pretty good clue that the prospect would be interested in attending games. This seems obvious, but you would be amazed how many salespeople waste time trying to sell tickets to someone who is providing clear evidence that he or she really isn't all that involved with the team. Your objective in selling is to be efficient, making the most use of your selling time that will result in actual sales—not just to be able to fill out another call report.

Power questions. Media-related behaviors are some of the easiest to determine through probing questions. However, a problem is that TV viewing is high among virtually all attenders, so knowing that they watch games on TV mainly only separates non-goers versus goers. Even then, research provided to NBA teams reveals that as many as 80 percent of the local market may watch the team on TV, but only 20 percent will actually attend a game. Our research shows that a key differentiating factor is listening to the game on the radio. If you find someone who listens to games on the radio, he or she is a good prospect to increase current attendance.

With respect to media-related habits, variations of the following questions will yield appropriate information to qualify prospects (in order):

1. How often do you listen to our games on the radio?
2. Do you find yourself talking with others about the team/game?
3. Did you see any of the games on TV last week?
4. Did you read the article in the paper about _____ this week?

Barriers to Attendance

Over time, individuals frequently fall into entertainment inertia, where they continue seeking the same forms of entertainment in the same places at the same times. Individuals may reach and remain in this inert state for at least two reasons. First, they have become satisfied with their current choices and have come to the point where changing habits would require a great deal of time and effort to acquire new information, evaluate alternatives, and then to choose a different course of action. In short, time is valuable and they don't want to waste time and cognitive effort on an unknown alternative when they are happy now. Second, and related to the first reason, is the risk associated with making a wrong choice. Individuals may be willing to just continue going to the same place and doing the same thing every weekend because of the financial, social, and intellectual risk associated with deciding to do something new *and* expensive. Asking someone who attends two to three games a season to purchase season tickets poses substantial risk and requires the individual to spend time determining whether or not the tickets are worth it to them. Too often it is far easier (no effort and no risk) for them to just tell you that they'll think about it—which, translated, means they're not going to think about it.

To overcome entertainment inertia, you must recognize the barriers that people have that keep them from shifting from their current state of attendance (zero or low) to purchasing multiple-game ticket packages. The barriers to attendance include psychic costs, venue convenience, popularity with friends and family, acclimation to hometown, perceived ticket value, and perceived ticket availability. We address each of these and the power questions that will aid in the determination of these factors.

Psychic Costs

Psychic costs refer to the nonmonetary mental, physical, and emotional expenditures incurred in the selection and execution of an alternative. Individuals learn to follow scripts for events that require an expected sequence of steps to complete (e.g., your morning breakfast ritual). Once that script is learned, additional psychic costs are incurred to learn a new script or to alter an established one.

Consider the script that fans follow to attend a sporting event. A fan who has not previously attended a particular sporting event at a given venue will put out significantly more psychic effort to attend than someone who has previously attended. Individuals who are not natives of the area will be unfamiliar with many of the aspects of going to the game, particularly compared to those who have grown up or lived in the area for a long time. Given the high level of mobility in major cities, if sports organizations want to maintain and grow their fan base, they must always be acculturating new fans to adapt and adopt the home team as their team—and to learn new scripts that lead them to the ballpark. Once scripts are learned, it is much easier to repeat.

Suppose that a Boston Bruins fan moves to the Dallas area due to job relocation. If this person does not feel like Dallas is his new hometown, he is more likely to have high psychic costs associated with going to a Dallas Stars game, primarily because he does not know "how to go to the game" in Dallas. Of course, if he was a season ticket holder or regular attender in Boston, he will have a better clue than someone who was an infrequent attender.

The problem many sales and marketing people have is that they have forgotten what it was like the first time they went to a sporting event. They assume that everyone knows the best way to go about getting tickets (i.e., best seats, best value, where to buy them, when to buy them, how to pick them up at will-call, etc.), the best places to park (including where NOT to park), the easiest way to get into and around the venue and the like. For instance, literally thousands of fans will wait in long lines at the main entrance of an arena when there are no lines at the other end of the arena, just because they don't know the best way to get into the game. Similarly, these same fans will wait for an hour in traffic leaving the venue because they don't know alternate routes. Just getting in and out of the place can result in high psychic costs that can make such a trip not worth a return visit for these fans.

The solution to reducing psychic costs is to identify those fans who are otherwise interested in attending the sporting event (e.g., they watch games on TV, etc.) and to offer ways that reduce the mental, physical, and emotional expenditure—as well as reducing the monetary risk that may allow for a tradeoff in risks. In other words, if an interested, but non-attending, fan receives an opportunity to attend a game at little or no financial risk, he or she is more willing to invest the psychic costs to attend. For instance, reduced tickets, free parking, or a coupon for dinner in the club restaurant could be offered. The key here is that you must first identify those who fit the profile (nonattender, interested in team, new to city) so that you do not offer an incentive to those who have already attended and have decided to infrequently return.

Another way to reduce the psychic costs is to help them learn the script vicariously. This can be achieved through advertising media (direct mail, email, pamphlets, etc.) that illustrate important steps in the script. One creative approach would be to have a tab on the homepage of your Web site for new fans, perhaps entitled "New fans: Score tickets for your first Dallas Stars game." Fans would be directed to a sub-web that provides in-depth information about each sequence in going to the event. Streaming video or pictures could show fans where to park, where the will-call window is, to know to yell the word "Stars" at the top of their lungs during the United States national anthem (viz., "... O say, does that STARS-spangled banner ..."), what food choices are available at the venue, and what routes are available to exit. If properly designed, fans could enter drawings online to win tickets or other incentives—which could be used to identify new prospects for sales calls.

Script for Attending Game

Step	Psychic Effort Required Fan:
Buy ticket ▼	Knows the best way to go about buying tickets for events.
Drive ▼	Is familiar with the traffic routes around the venue.
Park ▼	Is familiar with the parking options around the venue.
Find seat ▼	Knows way in and around the venue.
Watch game ▼	Knows what you're supposed to do at an event at the venue.
Drive home	Knows the best traffic routes out of the venue.
Overall Comfort Going to the Game	**Feels very comfortable about going to a game at the venue.**

Power questions. The questions you need to ask to determine the likelihood that psychic costs are holding prospects back from committing to ticket purchases are straightforward. Most venues have multiple events (e.g., concerts), so the prospect may be familiar with the place from other events. You basically want to find out if they have been to an event at the venue before and if they have any questions about attending events at the venue. The difficulty is in asking questions in a way that won't get socially desirable responses. If you ask someone, "You know how to get around down here, don't you?" the tendency will be to agree so as not to reveal ignorance. Try questions like these:

1. How many events have you attended here before? (dependent upon response, follow up with questions 2–5)
   If you were to come to an event:
2. . . . how would you get here?
3. . . . where would you probably park?
4. . . . which side of the [venue] would you be likely to enter?
5. . . . do you know where to pick up tickets at will-call?

The key in asking questions similar to 2–5 is to not ask questions that can be answered "Yes/No" so that you can determine what they really do know. You should listen for responses that indicate uncertainty and then provide directions—preferably in a printable format so that they can visualize what they need to do.

Venue Convenience

Fans perceive venue convenience as a function of (1) distance traveled from home to the venue, (2) psychic costs, and (3) venue location and functionality. These interrelationships are important because if psychic costs are reduced, perceptions of convenience will increase. One of the reasons that fans have favored Wrigley Field over U.S. Cellular Field in Chicago is a matter of venue convenience. Wrigley is located in a relatively safe part of town, easily accessible by public transportation. The White Sox play in a new stadium and have significantly improved the facility since U.S. Cellular became title sponsor. However, the perception of many Chicago fans is influenced by the stadium surroundings and their experiences with the park when it was first built in 1989. To improve perceptions (and reality), the White Sox installed new "Scout Seats" directly behind home plate that offer personal wait service and convenient parking just outside the gate for those buying these seats. Other upgrades have been made to improve accessibility around the park. The amenities accompanying the Scout Seats are likely to appeal to those fans that cite venue inconvenience as a barrier to attending.

From the individual salesperson's point of view, if you are dealing with a customer that indicates that it just isn't very convenient to get to the game, you should realize two things: First, if the person actually does live over 30 miles away, you are not likely to sell this person season tickets. However, if the individual is otherwise very interested in season tickets, but just can't see driving to every game, you can suggest that the season tickets be shared with friends or business associates who wouldn't each mind traveling a few times a season to the game. Second, if the person lives within a relatively short distance, then your task is to probe to find out exactly what is perceived as inconvenient. Due to health or other reasons, going to the game may truly be inconvenient. It may be that offering a bundled parking pass with tickets or some other solution (parking and then taking the stadium shuttle) may resolve the conflict. If the individual really can't name anything concrete that makes it inconvenient, then you are likely dealing with psychic costs (so, go back and reread that section).

Power questions. You may have already determined from the demographic data where the prospect lives relative to the venue. What you want to know now is the prospect's perceptions of how convenient it is to attend an event. You could ask this directly or indirectly:

Direct: Is there anything about going to the game itself that makes it inconvenient for you?

Indirect: If someone gave you tickets to the game, would there be any chance that you might stay home to watch the game on TV instead?

Using the indirect approach, you could probe responses to determine what aspects of attending the game make it seem easier to just stay home. In either case, you may be able to overcome objections with the benefits of attendance (excitement, social interaction with friends/family, etc.) or offers to increase convenience (e.g., parking pass, etc.).

Popularity with Friends and Family

Social acceptance can be an incentive or a barrier to attendance. We address it primarily as a barrier because an individual may have an interest in attending a given sporting event, but because few others in his or her immediate circle of friends or family have any interest in attending he or she may choose not to attend. Since sporting events are rarely attended alone (<2%), you will have difficulty selling season ticket packages to prospects if they do not have friends or family that will also attend.

As you might suspect, popularity with friends and family is inversely correlated with psychic costs. If friends and/or family follow the team, enjoy watching the games on TV, and would like to go to games, the difficulties and risks associated with deciding and attending the game are substantially reduced. Notice from Table 5.1 that popularity with friends and/or family is high for every segment that actually attends a game, but is low for nonattenders. This indicates that social acceptance is a necessity for any kind of attendance, not just for season ticket sales. Without it, there's almost no chance of selling the prospect multi-game packages or season tickets.

Power questions. You really just want to find out if any friends or family would like to attend the game with the prospect. So, simply ask: "Who else of your family or friends would like to go to the game with you?"

This is also a useful time to consider the possibility that the prospect might not be able or willing to buy season tickets alone, but might be willing to share season tickets with others. In that case, ask these two questions:

1. Is there someone you know that might like to share season tickets with you?
    If there is someone, follow up with:
2. Would you mind if I contacted them to see if they are interested?

If at all possible, do not rely upon them to contact the referral. It is too easy for the prospect to put it off. Then, when you call back, it makes it too easy for the prospect to object. You would rather manage the relationship. If the referral does want to share tickets, then you can easily close the deal because it is unlikely that the original prospect will back out. If the referral isn't interested, you may be able to generate additional referrals, or even add a third or fourth party in the season ticket purchase. In any case, you do not want to take a passive role in the relationship.

Acclimation to Hometown

According to the U.S. Census Bureau (2002–2003), over 14 percent of Americans move each year, with about 6 percent moving outside of their current county. More dramatic is the high mobility of 20–29-year-olds (28–30% move residences each year) and 30–44-year-olds (14–20% move residences each year). While many of these are movements within the same county, a sizeable portion (4.5–6%) of 20–34-year-olds move into a county from outside the state each year. This would suggest that nearly three-quarters of the 20–34-year-olds in your market probably did not grow up in the area and most likely recently moved there. Three percent of 35–44-year-olds move from one state (or county) to another each year. Hence, approximately 30 percent of this market is likely to be a recent transplant. Once people reach 45, mobility is less pronounced; only about 2 percent of 45–54-year-olds move from outside a given state each year. Again, however, this would represent 20 percent of this market over a decade's time.

The effects of geographic mobility on fan (non)identification with the local team is relatively easy to observe. Large market teams, such as New York, Los Angeles, or Chicago in the United States, often have sizeable contingents of fan support when these teams play away games in smaller market cities. We should point out at this time that it is extremely bad form for a St. Louis resident to wear a Yankees jersey to a Yankees-Cardinals game in St. Louis. It is even worse form to yell against the hometown team, even though you did just move from New York. We also hope that the Cardinals fans treat you with the same respect and caring that Red Sox fans do when Yankee fans show up at Fenway Park.

The critical issue here is that the fan's identification and willingness to attend local games is influenced by the extent that the fan has acclimated to the community. Hometown acclimation refers to the degree to which a fan thinks of the current city (state) as home. If someone asks you where you are from, where do you say? If you say that you are from the city where you currently live, you are likely to have acclimated fairly well. On the other hand, all of us have met individuals who have not adjusted properly and keep reminding us that they are from somewhere else.[1] Sometimes these people will continue reminding us, even though it has been over 20 years since they moved. Hence, although the amount of time one lives in an area is usually a good indication of the degree of hometown acclimation, it is important to emphasize that one's feelings regarding home is based upon personal perceptions and emotions.

Geographic mobility of the population has important implications for marketing campaigns and strategies for building audiences for local sporting events. Transplants to the city will require information

---

[1]We don't understand why they just don't move back there, if it was such a great place and all. We would be happy to help them move, if the opportunity arose. Unfortunately, a key reason that these people no longer live where they used to live is because they were so annoying that their native state made them relocate to your state.

and education regarding the team and the venue and its history. Efforts must be made to identify recent transfers to the city to provide specific incentives to get them to "try" going to the game. Some teams take advantage of out-of-market loyalties to attract local fans to see their favorite team from their prior hometown. These are excellent prospects for future sales as they identify themselves as having high involvement with the sport. The key is to find methods to collect individual information on these customers (sign-ups, contests, etc.) to follow up with sales calls.

Power questions. Information about a prospect's hometown is not difficult to acquire. Ask questions such as:

1. How long have you lived here?
2. Where do you call home?

The first question provides objective data. The second offers subjective information that allows for an estimation of how acclimated the individual is to the community.

Perceived Ticket Value

Recall our discussion of consumer surplus in the first chapter. Consumer surplus is the difference between what the fan is prepared or willing to pay and the price that a team charges for a ticket. Teams sell tickets when the value (V) the fan places on the experience of being at the event equals or exceeds the price (P) that the team charges for admission to the event. Relatedly, perceived ticket value is the fan's perception of what he or she gets from the experience of being at the event for what they pay. In short, it's what I get for what I pay.

Perceptions of ticket value in most professional and major college sports have some similarities to prestige goods. That is, as prices increase, perceived value also increases, up to a point. Low-priced goods within the category have low perceived value. For instance, when it comes to men's cologne, most people perceive a low value for Stetson ($9.99, 64 oz. jug, by Cody) versus high perceived value for Black Code ($90, 2.5 oz., by Armani). However, perceived value also depends upon the usage segment targeted. Individuals who infrequently use the product see little value in any of the product offerings, although even this segment would perceive more value from the higher priced alternatives. Frequent users—or attenders, in the case of sports—are much more likely to have a high perceived value for the most expensive alternatives.

Figure 5.1 illustrates that individuals who never or rarely attend any games during a given season have relatively negative perceptions of ticket prices. Nonetheless, this segment still perceives that the more expensive ticket is a better value than the cheap seat. Probably everyone reading this book, with the exception of George Steinbrenner, has been in the nosebleed section at some sporting event—and realized that even if it was a cheap seat, you would still rather pay more to sit closer to the action. As individuals gain more experience at an event, they tend to desire better seats. The bottom line is that as ticket price increases commensurate with the quality of the seat relative to the game, so does perceived value—and particularly so for frequent attenders.

The battle many teams fight is finding ways to make the upper-level seats still seem valuable to season ticket holders or other multiple-game ticket buyers. For successful franchises, the lower bowl at most arenas and stadiums are sold out. To increase season ticket sales means that the organization must find ways to increase the perceived value of the upper bowl seats. Some of the methods used to increase the value of season tickets (whether upper or lower levels) are shown following the *Power questions.*

Perceived ticket value is typically seen as a barrier, because a common objection of prospects is to the price of the tickets or ticket package. The reality is that prospects are not objecting to the absolute price as

Figure 5.1

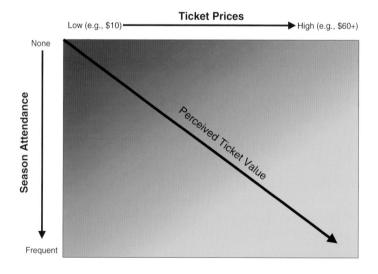

Perceived Ticket Value

much as the fact that they do not see that the benefits outweigh the costs. When it comes to going to sporting events, movies, dining out, and the like, only about one-third of the market is actually likely to make decisions primarily on price, and these are likely to be low-income individuals.[2] Consequently, if you've already qualified the prospect in terms of ability to buy (i.e., household income), the objection is almost certainly an issue of perceived value. Your job is to determine what benefits appeal to the prospect that would increase value to equal or exceed the price charged for the tickets.

Power questions. The objective is to find the price threshold of the prospect. One of the best ways car salespeople find out about a customer's needs is to ask what kind of car he or she is currently driving—and what the buyer does and doesn't like about that model. Similarly, ask:

1. Have you ever bought season tickets for any sport?
   - Follow-up if yes: Tell me about it. For what you paid for the tickets, was it a good value? What did you like or dislike in the package?
   - Follow-up if no: When was the last time you bought tickets to a game? For what you paid for the tickets, was it a good value? What did you like or dislike?
2. If you were to buy (season) tickets here, in what price range per game are you interested?

Ways to Increase the Perceived Value of Ticket Packages

- Options to renew same seat or upgrade to other seats as they become available
- Guaranteed playoff seats
- Invitation to special team sponsored events and other private functions
- Team store discounts
- Personal account executive assistance
- First right to purchase tickets for all other arena events
- Improved seating comfort (wider, softer, etc.)
- Guaranteed promotional items

---

[2]Wakefield, Kirk L., and Inman, J. Jeffrey. 2003. Situational price sensitivity: The role of consumption, occasion, social context, and income. *Journal of Retailing* 79 (4): 199–212.

- Parking passes
- Access to private club lounge and other "Goldmember" privileges
- In-seat wait service
- Access to private club-level restrooms
- Coupons for free/discounted events with team partners (ice skating, golf, movies, etc.)
- Ticket Exchange Programs (unused tickets transferred or sold to others)
- Assistance buying road game tickets
- Exclusive email offers for various ticket or merchandise discounts
- Subscriptions to team magazine or newsletters

From the first set of questions, you should note what represents value to the prospect. For example, you might learn that it is important to be able to get to the club level restaurants and restrooms or to be able to attend special functions held by the team. These become your selling points when presenting the various ticket packages available. For the upscale buyer who may be dissatisfied with upper bowl seats, an important selling point for these seats is that lower bowl seats are first offered to current season ticket holders as they become available.

Perceived Ticket Availability

As sports organizations become more successful, fans increasingly perceive that most of the good seats are unavailable. As a result, fans may not attempt to buy tickets even when they are available. As can be seen in Table 5.1, nonattenders have particularly poor perceptions regarding ticket availability. Hence, a barrier to getting infrequent or nonattenders to increase their attendance is both perceived and actual ticket availability.

For facilities that operate near capacity, quality seats are scarce. However, a sizeable gap often exists between fans' perceptions and reality. Quality seats may be made available through ticket exchanges. Some organizations hold back a portion of tickets to be sold on a game-by-game basis or for group sales that could otherwise be sold as season tickets. In other cases, not all of the lower bowl seats have actually been sold.

In markets where tickets are in high demand, fans may perceive that the only way to get a lower bowl seat is to go through a ticket broker.

Ironically, this may not be the case, as teams may withhold some lower bowl tickets or have access to ticket exchange programs.

Power question. What you want to know is whether or not the prospect has attempted to purchase tickets and was unable to acquire the tickets he or she wanted. If you find out that the prospect has gone online to buy a ticket, but did not purchase, at least you know that you have an interested prospect. Ask: "Have you ever attempted to buy a ticket to the game and couldn't find what you wanted?" You can follow up with information about ticket options that fit the prospect's interests (i.e., see questions on ticket value).

Incentives to Attend

Fans are motivated to attend sporting events due to three inter-related factors: involvement with the sport, loyalty to the team, and identification with the team. These three factors represent levels of commitment that allow you to classify the likelihood of a prospect becoming a season ticket holder (see Figure 5.2). Additionally, a key differentiating characteristic between attending and nonattending fans is the degree to which they feel some level of similarity with the players on the team. We deal with each of these four factors in turn and conclude with related power questions.

Figure 5.2

Levels of Fan Commitment

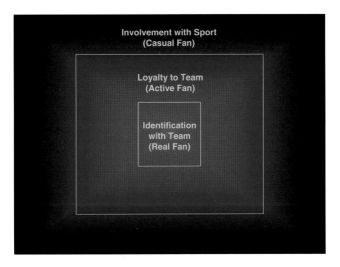

Involvement with the Sport

Involvement with the sport means that the individual has an ongoing interest or concern with the sport on a day-to-day basis. If a prospect has no interest in the sport, the only likely reason for them to want to buy season ticket packages would be to please others—either family members or corporate clients. Even then, it is highly unlikely that you are dealing with a hot prospect. Nearly 99 percent of NBA fans that attend more than five games indicate that they are avid basketball fans. It's hard to imagine differently.

Power question. Finding out if someone is a fan of the sport is probably one of the first things you will want to find out about a prospect. If he or she is not involved with the sport, you can hang up the phone and call your next prospect. Rather than asking generic questions (Do you like hockey?), you can get a better handle on how strong a prospect is by asking something like: "On a scale of 1 to 10, how much of a hockey fan are you?" If necessary, you can explain the scale in terms of 10 being equal to a fanatic and 1 meaning not a fan at all. Most people will grasp what you're asking. In some cases, it may be necessary to specify the level of the sport. For instance, some people are avid NCAA basketball or football fans, but not particularly avid NBA or NFL fans.

Loyalty to the Team

People must first have some interest in the sport before they can possibly be loyal fans. If they are very involved at all, they will have selected a favorite team. So, another way to determine if someone is very involved is to ask who his or her favorite team is. If prospects can't name a favorite team, it is fairly certain that they are not involved with the sport or their name is Bud Selig.[3]

In the first chapter, loyalty is referred to as the repeat purchasing of a good or service by a consumer. A loyal customer is sensitive to differences in brands and prefers a brand or set of brands over others. Loyal fans have made a decision to follow a particular team (or teams) over other teams, preferring that team based on personal preferences. Given that loyalty to a team is a choice, a loyal fan can choose to be disloyal at some point.

During the NHL strike season in 2004–2005, a Canadian Press[4] poll revealed that one-third of Canadians who claimed to be NHL followers

---

[3]Yes, I know that "they" is plural and "Bud Selig" is singular.
[4]"Poll: Hard-core NHL fans don't miss the game." Canadian Press, Wednesday, February 09, 2005.

did not miss the NHL games. About the same number of NHL followers did not look forward to the return of the NHL. Ken Dryden, Hall of Fame goaltender and Canadian parliamentarian, delineated the difference between just being repeat customers versus being highly identified fans when he said, "I think that there are a number of fans in this country who have sensed over the last number of months that actually, maybe, it was more habit than it was passion."[5] One-third of Canadians *were* loyal NHL fans, but did not actually miss their favorite teams when they were gone. And, they pretty much didn't care if they came back. If you were talking about your significant other, and found that that's how your significant other feels about you, you're probably not feeling very significant. The point is that loyal fans will attend as long as they are loyal, but loyalty can be a fleeting thing.

On the positive side, Table 5.1 demonstrates that anyone who buys multiple-game packages will identify themselves as loyal team fans. This is easy to find out, as our next questions of power show.

Power questions. Salespeople can determine fan loyalty by asking:

1. Across all sports, what is your favorite sport?
2. Within this sport, who is your favorite team?
3. On a scale of 1 to 10, how loyal would you say that you are to our team?

The reason to ask the first question across all sports is that it gives you an idea of where your team stands in the loyalties of the prospect. Due to expense in terms of time, effort, and money, most people will limit the number of season tickets that they will purchase. A prospect with no season tickets to any sporting event will most likely buy season tickets (if any) only for his or her favorite team across all sports.

Identification with the Team

When a fan develops a deep psychological attachment to the team that goes beyond mere loyalty, identification has occurred. As you recall, highly identified fans react to events that occur to the team or player as if the events happened to him or her. A highly identified fan will internalize or adopt the team or players' attitudes and behaviors as his or her own. If someone is highly identified with a team, he or she will feel good when the team wins and bad when the team loses. Highly identified fans believe that the team is a representation of who

---

[5]"Loving hockey is a habit: Dryden." Monday, Feb. 7, 2005, www.cbc.ca

they are, both to themselves and to others. Highly identified fans practically feel as though they are part of the team. Once fans move to a high level of identification, they are extremely likely to purchase multiple-game ticket packages.

If you find a highly identified fan that does not have some form of season tickets, it is likely that one of the other factors is acting as a barrier to attendance. Discretionary income is a frequent issue. If income is a determining factor in not buying season tickets, the prospect is still likely to be an excellent candidate for sharing a season ticket plan with others. The only thing that limits the purchase of a season ticket package in this case is how many interested friends or relatives the prospect has. The addition of others in sharing the ticket package reduces the perceived risk of the purchase to the individual, while also generating social support in favor of the purchase. Sharing tickets may also be a good solution for the highly identified, high income fan that is too busy to be able to use the entire package alone.

Power questions. A fan's level of identification is actually best captured by behaviors associated with highly identified fans. In particular, you can ascertain if a prospect is highly identified by gauging media consumption (TV, radio, newspaper, etc.) related to the sporting event. You can also estimate identification level by observing whether or not individuals refer to the team as "they" versus "we," with the latter indicating that they think of themselves as part of the team. Since most people wouldn't understand what you are asking in direct questions ("Are you highly identified with the team?"), you can indirectly query:

1. Who are some of the players on the team that you are familiar with?
2. What players on the team do you follow?

The more specific and complete the answers (i.e., they can name every player; quickly recall players' names), the greater is the likelihood that they are highly identified with the players on the team. In fact, you are measuring knowledge of the team, but it is a good reflection or evidence of identification.

Similarity with Players

Fans may believe that they are similar to players with respect to attitudes, personal characteristics, and behaviors. The more fans feel that they share attitudes, personal characteristics, and behaviors with the players, the more identified they become with the team. In this sense, similarity can be seen as a positive influence or incentive to attend games. In professional sports, the greater risk may be that fans feel as though they have little in common with the players. From that perspective, dissimilarity would be a barrier to increasing fan attendance.

In general, fans do not believe that they are all that similar to professional players. Table 5.1 demonstrates that even season ticket holders only hold moderately high feelings of similarity with the players. Similarity is not a frequent deal breaker, but can be in three cases. First, teams may trade star players that have a strong fan following. Fans that have grown to follow the team primarily on the basis of their identification with one particular player may reduce media consumption and attendance when that player is traded. Second, sometimes teams may make drastic roster or coaching changes altering the makeup of the team chemistry or style of play. Fans who appreciate an aggressive, fast-breaking style of play may not care much for a slow-down, defensive-minded approach dictated by the player personnel or the coach. Third, teams may acquire one or more players with antisocial or otherwise unattractive personal characteristics. It is useful to note here that Antoine Walker, who is probably on a different NBA team now than when writing this (viz., 2005 teams: Dallas Mavericks → Boston Celtics → Miami Heat), is a very talented, but annoying player whose shot selection forces most fans to pound their collective heads against the seats in front of them as soon as he (Walker) receives the ball. In addition to the damage to the facility equipment and the fans' foreheads, such players are generally not good for enhancing fan identification.

In those cases where the team makes notable player personnel changes (or happens to hold on to undesirable players), salespeople may encounter fans unwilling to purchase tickets primarily due to the underlying lack of similarity between the player(s) and the fan's preferences. A good way to overcome this objection is to point out to this person that you also pound your head on your desk whenever you see this player's name on press releases. Okay, that probably won't help much. You may just have to wait until this player is traded or retires. In the case of Antoine Walker, you shouldn't have to wait long.

Power question. Information relative to felt similarity with players is likely to be offered voluntarily by the prospect. These opinions are based on deeply held feelings that have built up over time and are not easily contained by sports fans. Prospects uninvolved with the sport or the team will not care or know enough to have strong feelings about particular players. However, if you believe the prospect may somehow have fallen into some form of psychological denial or compartmentalization, or for some other reason hasn't yet verbalized feelings about the players, you may ask: "How do you feel about the players on this year's team?"

Scorecard

Based upon the responses you receive regarding demographics, media consumption, barriers to attendance, and incentives to attend, you can qualify a prospect's likelihood of purchasing a ticket package. Table 5.2 represents a scorecard with each of the factors and the associated power questions. Dependent upon the nature of the prospect inquiry, you may not be able to go through the entire scorecard.

Table 5.2

Prospect Scorecard		
DEMOGRAPHICS	**Score**	**Power Question**
Age*		[check customer data or estimate]
Miles from venue		Where do you live? How far is that from the stadium/arena?
Male		[observe]
Go out*		How many times each month do you go out for entertainment (spending at least $25)?
Income*		Tell me about your job. What do you do for a living? [or check customer data]
Married*		Tell me about your family living at home with you. (Listen for marital status and kids.)
No kids		Tell me about your family living at home with you.
MEDIA		
Radio*		How often do you listen to our games on the radio?
Game-talk*		Do you find yourself talking with others about the team/game?
TV		Did you see any of the games on TV last week?

Table 5.2 *Continued*

MEDIA	Score	Power Question
Newspaper		Did you read the article in the paper about ____ this week?
BARRIERS		
Psychic costs*		How many events have you attended here before? (follow up with questions below) If you were to come to an event: . . . how would you get here? . . . where would you probably park? . . . which side of the [venue] would you be likely to enter? . . . do you know where to pick up tickets at will-call?
Convenience		Direct: Is there anything about going to the game itself that makes it inconvenient for you? Indirect: If someone gave you tickets to the game, would there be any chance that you might stay home to watch the game on TV instead?
Popularity*		Who else of your family or friends would like to go to the game with you? Is there someone you know that might like to share season tickets with you? Would you mind if I contacted them to see if they are interested?
Hometown*		How long have you lived here? Where do you call home?
Perceived value*		Have you ever bought season tickets for any sport? Follow up if yes: Tell me about it. For what you paid for the tickets, was it a good value? What did you like or dislike in the package? Follow up if no: When was the last time you bought tickets to a game? For what you paid for the tickets, was it a good value? What did you like or dislike? If you were to buy (season) tickets here, what price range per game are you interested in?
Ticket availability*		Have you ever attempted to buy a ticket to the game and couldn't find what you wanted?

Table 5.2 *Continued*

INCENTIVES	Score	Power Question
Involvement*		On a scale of 1 to 10, how much of a ____ fan are you?
Team loyalty		Across all sports, what is your favorite sport? Within this sport, who is your favorite team? On a scale of 1 to 10, how loyal would you say that you are to our team?
Identification		Who are some of the players on the team that you are familiar with? What players on the team do you follow?
Similarity		How do you feel about the players on this year's team?
*Factors most likely to predict ticket purchases.		

Although all are statistically significant differentiators between attenders and nonattenders (viz., see Table 5.1), our analysis of the NBA fan data for those fans that live in the area reveals that 12 of these factors are most likely to predict actual game attendance above the others. From all of the 21 factors on the scorecard, the 12 items that explain the most variance in game attendance over a two-year period are (in order of influence):

1. Radio listening
2. Age (older more likely)
3. Times going out per month and spending $25+ each time
4. Household income
5. Perceived ticket availability
6. Psychic costs
7. Involvement with sport
8. Game-talk: Frequency of talking about the game with others
9. Marital status (married more likely)
10. Hometown acclimation
11. Popularity with friends and family
12. Perceived ticket value

This does not mean that the other factors are unimportant. For instance, identification with the players is the underlying influence that drives radio listening, psychic costs, game-talk, and perceived ticket value. Yet, it is these consequences of identification that are the best predictors of game attendance. Consequently, given limited time, salespeople would be wise to prioritize the information they collect to those factors with the most direct impact on attendance.

Reducing Churn of Season Tickets

Churn refers to the turnover rate of season ticket accounts in a given year. Just as universities and every other service provider is concerned about retention, franchises are equally concerned about retaining season ticket holders. A franchise that experiences 20 percent churn in season tickets each year must find an equal number of new season ticket buyers just to maintain last year's level of season ticket sales.

Franchises can engage in three activities directed at reducing churn and increasing retention of season ticket holders. All three activities emphasize the role of proactive listening. Proactive listening means that you seek to maintain high levels of communication and interchange between clients and sales associates as an ongoing process throughout the season *after* the sale. The most successful salespeople in any business are those who are able to retain clients year after year—that's how salespeople build up a large base of commissions. It rarely does much good to engage in reactive listening after the ticket holder has already opted to not renew for the coming season—except to learn what not to do in the future.

Specific methods to employ proactive listening to retain season ticket holders include contacting nonattenders, executive communication with season ticket holders, and conducting focus groups with season ticket holders.

Contact Nonattenders

With respect to causing a fan to not renew season tickets, the worst thing that can happen is for the fan to look in the desk drawer at the end of the season and see a bunch of unused tickets. The obvious conclusion is that those tickets represent wasted money and a poor purchase decision. To prevent this from occurring, teams can proactively contact season ticket holders who don't attend games, shortly after the games, to find out why. Oftentimes the reason has more to do with being too busy rather than any disinclination to attend games. In these cases, the team can offer to assist in redistributing the tickets—either to charity or possibly to clients of the season ticket holder. Some teams actually employ at least one individual expressly to carry out the task of making sure that season tickets are used, contacting nonusers following consecutive absences to offer assistance.

For successful teams, the difficulty may be less in the selling and more in the using of the tickets. Even though the team receives the ticket revenue, unused tickets have four other deleterious effects for the franchise. First, the team loses the revenue for parking, concessions, and merchandise associated with each used ticket. The average per cap for these items is often around $15 at major league level games. Suppose that 10 percent of 10,000 season ticket holders did not use their tickets for 41 NBA home games. That amounts to $615,000 in lost revenue to the team. Second, when every seat—particularly in the lower bowl—is filled, it adds to the excitement of the game experience. Having the season ticket seats filled makes everything more valuable to everyone at the game. This leads to the third consequence. When seats are unused in the lower bowl seats, fans in the upper bowl perceive their tickets as less valuable. They are not as thankful to be able to get a seat in the upper bowl if they can look down and see that there are plenty of good seats that aren't being used. In fact, some of them will probably try to slip down into the lower bowl if at all possible—making the value of the lower bowl seat the same price as whatever they paid for the upper bowl seat. This is one reason that it is a good idea to provide barriers making this practice difficult. Even if they don't attempt to move down to the better seats, they will likely be disappointed that they have to sit in these crummy seats when so many good ones are available close to the field of play. Finally, when seats are sold in the lower level but fans are not seated in those sections, fans watching on TV may get the impression that attending the game isn't very exciting. To most people watching an event, empty seats send the clear signal that being there isn't worth it—even if you have already paid for the tickets.

Executive Communication

Most season ticket holders think of themselves as valuable contributors to the welfare of the franchise. Since many of them are executives in their own companies, they believe that their opinions are valuable and would like the opportunity to share them with the club executives. Rather than wait until issues become critical enough to prompt voluntary communications from season ticket holders—or more likely that may prompt nonrenewal without any communications—franchises can invite season ticket holders to special functions organized by the club executives. Special private lunches with the club president can feature a "no holds barred"[6] question and answer period that increases the feelings of ownership in the club by season ticket holders. Plus, it gives them special insider information that enhances their feelings of self-importance and contribution to the welfare of the club.

Other means of executive communication can come through targeted email communications that provide "inside" information regarding player transactions and other club-related news. Additionally, season ticket holder liaisons or service personnel can periodically call season ticket holders to ask if there are any opportunities for the club to assist them in obtaining more tickets for special outings, holding family or corporate events at the venue, providing team merchandise (e.g., commemorative clothing, autographed merchandise, etc.) for special people or occasions.

Season Ticket Focus Groups

Clubs do not have to wait until problems arise in order to seek out ways to improve services to season ticket holders. Periodic focus groups drawn from subsets of season ticket holders (individual/families, small corporate, large corporate) can be conducted to weed out any problems that might be cropping up. For example, teams may decide to implement new policies regarding ticket purchases. How do you think fans would react to the following policy changes?

---

[6]Have you ever wondered where the saying "no holds barred" came from? We had no clue, so we went to www.word-detective.com, which tells us: *"Hold" meaning "grasp" is a word we inherited from Old English, and can be traced back to a prehistoric Germanic root meaning "to watch or guard." The Oxford English Dictionary lists fourteen separate definitions "hold" has acquired over the years as a noun, and one of them, dating back to the early eighteenth century, is "a grip or tactic in wrestling." Real wrestling (as opposed to the WWF clown shows so popular today) has very strict rules, and certain "holds" are indeed "barred" or not permitted. Similar rules pertain in boxing. Thus an impromptu boxing or wrestling match (most likely in a barroom or other informal setting) where there were no rules of conduct imposed would be a "no holds barred" brawl. "No holds barred" in a figurative sense meaning "no restrictions" first appeared around 1942.*

Management action	Consequence
The University of Utah moved from an open seating policy for home soccer matches to reserved, assigned seating for the final game of the season (which was to determine the conference championship).	Faithful fans who had attended every other home game were not aware of the policy change and many were unable to sit in the same seats that they had occupied all season long.
In 2002, organizers for the FIFA World Cup in Seoul, South Korea, designated blocks of tickets for sale to specific global markets, so as to allow fans from all countries to attend the matches. Unfortunately, some markets did not respond and the tickets were not made available to other markets.	Matches were announced as sold out, despite the fact that TV camera shots showed entire lower bowl sections empty. As many as 20,000 seats went unused in the opening round. Japanese and South Korean fans were unable to purchase tickets to these matches.
Students who pay $135 for basketball season tickets at Michigan cannot miss more than two games and must wear an "Izzone" shirt to be eligible to use their own tickets. Students can avoid losing their seats if they have a doctor's note, death notice of a family member, or paperwork showing a class conflict.	Students have protested to the Student Alumni Association, written letters to the school newspaper, and started a Web site to oppose the policy.
When the Cincinnati Reds moved to the new Great American Ball Park, fans were only allowed to buy opening day tickets via phone or the Internet. No tickets were sold at the Reds' box office.	Phone and Internet sales allowed non-Reds' fans (including people from Great Britain) to buy up tickets online and resell them on eBay and ticket outlets at multiples of face value, leaving many locals out of luck.

Although not all of the examples listed above include season ticket holders, they do illustrate the fact that good-intentioned team management (a) sometimes demonstrates intelligence levels most often associated with common household appliances, and (b) potential negative consequences of policy decisions could possibly be avoided if management sought more interaction and feedback from fans before implementing such policies.

Focus groups do not provide the best feedback loop in all cases, due to the qualitative, exploratory nature of focus group research. However, periodic focus groups with season ticket holders each season can identify sore spots before they become infected or incurable. The common link between most fan-management conflicts (and most every other kind of relational conflict) is poor communication. Even if management believes it did communicate pertinent information to fans in a timely manner—which, by the way, was typically the view of management in the cases presented in the preceding table—communication did not occur if the fans did not effectively *receive* the information and have an opportunity to respond.

With respect to communicating policy changes to season ticket holders, the first step should be to gather information from them and include them as much as possible in the process leading up to the policy change. The worst scenario is a policy implementation that has negative consequences for some segment of ticket holders and where there has been no prior communication regarding the issue with the fans. Sometimes tough decisions must be made, but in these cases, it is better to follow the moral taught by the following true story:

One day Jerry and Elaine went to Boston to a Yankees-Red Sox series, leaving Jerry's cat and elderly mother in New York City under the care of Jerry's family friend, Kramer. While Jerry and Elaine were in Boston, Kramer called from New York to say that Jerry's cat had died. Jerry cried, "Kramer, you don't just call someone and say their cat died. You need to ease into it. It's better to call someone and say, 'The cat is on the roof and we can't get her down.' Then call the next day and say, 'I called the fire department and they are still trying to get the cat down.' Finally, after the third game in the series, you could call and say, 'As we were finally getting the cat down, she jumped and fell to her death off a ten-story apartment building.'" Taking this in, Kramer responded, "Okay. By the way, your mom is on the roof."

Despite the fact that you have heard this story many times, you must remember that the moral to the story is that most people would rather be eased into hearing unfavorable news. This can be accomplished by announcing that the team is considering making changes and providing ample opportunity and time for fans to provide input. Once adequate information has been gathered—even if the preliminary decision remains the same—fans are more likely to accept the policy change if they have been given prior notice and have had opportunity to respond. Furthermore, management would also be wise to communicate the policy changes in terms of benefits fans receive, rather than assume that they innately understand the logic or wisdom of the policy change.

Build Value

6

Sports organizations engage in pricing on at least five levels:

1. Tickets
2. Concessions and merchandise
3. Stadium advertising and signage
4. Naming rights of stadiums, Web pages, and/or events, and
5. Broadcast rights to events and games.

The first two categories generate revenues from spectators at the gate and the venue. The final three generate revenue through media and sponsors. Historical data provides the relative volume of these sources of revenue for the major leagues in the United States (see Figure 6.1). Media revenue clearly dominates for NFL teams. This is not surprising, since the NFL has maintained the highest television ratings of all spectator sports, followed by NASCAR. Interestingly, the average gate revenue for teams in each of these four major sports leagues is relatively similar. In fact, the average gate revenue per team for the NHL, MLB, and NBA are not significantly different from each other. The NFL, which has far fewer games, generates a slightly lower level of gate revenues. This is, of course, offset by massive media revenues. Based on this fact, one might deduce that having fewer games (where each game's outcome has relatively greater effects in league standings) helps maintain strong television ratings. Conversely, note the difficulty that MLB has had with TV ratings as televised games proliferated on super channels (WGN, TBS, etc.) and regional networks.

This chapter focuses primarily on prices offered to spectators. We first look at aggregate economic factors that explain the occurrence of

Figure 6.1

Sources of Revenue (1996)

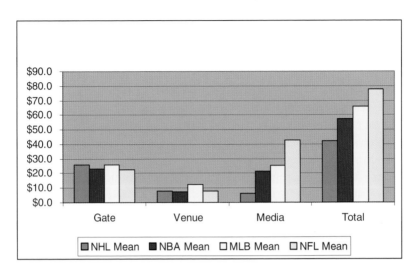

steadily increasing prices in virtually all professional sports. Next, we present theoretical and practical guidance in price setting for spectator events and related venue sales.

A Model of League Attendance and Price Setting (MLB)

Economic models explaining and predicting attendance at sporting events are plentiful. Most economic attendance models[1] include metropolitan population, team winning percentage (or other measure of performance), per capita income in the metro area, a dummy variable for a new stadium, a measure related to star players (BA, HR, RBI), and average team ticket price as independent variables predicting attendance.

Eckard's (2001)[2] study of MLB attendance from 1903 to 1993 finds that diminishing returns occur for those teams that have a streak of

---

[1]We trust that you have fond memories, and at least a bit of knowledge, of your statistics classes.

[2]Eckard, E. Woodrow. 2001. Baseball's Blue Ribbon Economic Report: Solutions in Search of a Problem. *Journal of Sports Economics* 2: 3, August 2001, 213–227.

three or more years where they contend for the title and when they win the title. Once the team achieves the goal (World Series Champions), fan expectations have been met and attendance drops the following year. Based on Eckard's model, if an MLB team averaged 3 million during streak years, attendance would be expected to drop 51,000 following a pennant year. As a contributing factor, the costs and benefits to free agency (since 1976) motivate MLB teams to do less to re-sign star players. The result has been greater competitive equity in the past 25 years. Eckard's study, however, does not attempt to account for the fact that teams may raise ticket prices following championship years, thereby dampening some of the excessive demand created by the previous year's performance.

Understanding aggregate predictors of attendance is important for price setting. While prior economic studies have modeled average ticket price as an independent variable explaining attendance, more recent market conditions suggest that professional sports attendance is more likely to predict prices. That is, successful teams build attendance as more fans are drawn to see a winning team. Due to rising payroll costs of superstars who led the team to the championship, high demand for tickets, and limited capacity, teams tend to raise prices following successful campaigns. Further, although it is well recognized that new stadiums have positive effects on attendance, one can observe that vintage stadiums with great traditions (e.g., Wrigley Field, Fenway Park) also attract fans. This suggests a curvilinear effect, such that fans appreciate older stadiums (pre-1950) and newer stadiums (post-1990), but are unlikely to highly value those stadiums constructed in the concrete dome era (1960s–80s).

We test a model analyzing data from MLB for one decade (1991–2000) to predict attendance, which in turn predicts ticket price. We use attendance figures based on each team's attendance as a percentage of stadium capacity as the dependent variable in the first stage of this equation. The independent variables predicting attendance in the model are the annual figures representing:

1. Team winning percentage: number of wins divided by total games played
2. Team player payroll: total salaries paid to players each year
3. Metropolitan population: annual extrapolations based on 1990 and 2000 census data
4. Post-season appearances: points awarded for each game played in post-season from previous season
5. Stadium quality: median of range of stadium construction minus year stadium built

To account for the value of old and new stadiums, we computed a stadium quality variable (#5 above) that is based on the absolute value of the year the stadium was built minus the median year of construction for all stadiums each season. Considering the attendance data for the 2000 season, this means that the oldest stadium, Boston's Fenway Park (built in 1912) has the same value (44) as Houston's Minute Maid Park built in 2000 (formerly Enron Field). The lowest stadium quality value (SQ = 3) for 2000 was Milwaukee's County Stadium, built in 1953 (note—County Stadium was replaced in 2001). With the exception of the metropolitan population (negative effect), each independent variable is expected to produce positive effects on attendance. The specific relationships are outlined below.

Relationship	Hypothesis
Fans are likely to be attracted to those teams that perform well.	winning → attendance
Player payroll acts as a surrogate for the presence of star players.	player payroll → attendance
Post-season appearances are expected to have a *lagged effect* on attendance. The team's winning percentage is likely to have an effect during the current season. However, since knowledge of playoff performance is after the season's conclusion, it is likely to have its greatest effect on attendance for the coming year.	prior postseason → attendance
Large metro areas are likely to have increased competition for sports and leisure dollars. In particular, the largest metro areas have more than one MLB team (Chicago, New York, Los Angeles, Oakland/San Francisco Bay area). So, larger populations should have a negative effect on attendance.	metro population → attendance
Attractive stadiums (vintage or newer) lead to higher attendance.	stadium quality → attendance

The resulting model (see below) explains 52.9 percent of the variance in MLB attendance during the 1990s. Each of the independent variables has a significant effect in the expected direction. Using the predicted value of attendance in a two-stage least squares regression model, attendance, in turn, explains 35.5 percent of the following season's ticket prices.

		Standardized Coefficients		
		Beta	t	Sig.
1	WINNING %	.213	4.599	.000
	PAYROLL	.331	6.471	.000
	POPULATION	−.103	−2.343	.020
	POST-SEASON	.108	2.434	.016
	STADIUM QUALITY	.420	9.690	.000

Running the regression model in the traditional economic sense with current price as an independent variable, predicting attendance produces no significant results (i.e., price has no significant influence on attendance). The results from this model have important implications for price setting.

Stadium quality. First, stadium quality explains the most variance in attendance (B = .420), which in turn allows the team to charge a higher price. This finding follows widely held beliefs by sports owners and marketers, as well as anecdotal evidence found in the media, regarding the need for sports teams to build new stadiums.

Milwaukee opened its new stadium in 2001, experiencing an increase in attendance of 74 percent, despite a .420 winning percentage. Ticket prices increased 50 percent over the prior year's prices, although largely fueled by high-end luxury boxes. Unfortunately, the increase in attendance was short-lived as the Brewers followed up with winning percentages (2002 = .346; 2003 = .410, 2004 = .416) that would try the patience of even the most comfortable fan.

One of the main reasons that the stadium is so important to baseball is that season tickets to an MLB team means that the ticket holder might spend upwards of three hours each at the venue for 81 games over the course of six months. That is a lot of time to spend in a place—so, it had better be more than just tolerable. The stadium may be less important for sports where fewer games are played (e.g., college football), but is still likely to play a prominent role in determining attendance.

The media often report on team owners demanding a new stadium or threatening to move the team. The data from MLB over the past decade supports team owners' convictions. "Build it and they will come" is more than just a famous line from Kevin Costner. It is the gospel truth in baseball. Of course, it never hurts to put good players and a good team on the field.

High payroll star players. The presence of high payroll star players (B = .331) is the second strongest influence on attendance in this model. This finding reinforces our view that attractive players have a significant effect on team identification. The Cincinnati Reds, operating at 48 percent of stadium capacity, saw attendance increase 25 percent in 2000 following the signing of Ken Griffey, Jr., despite the fact that the team performed worse with Griffey (.524) than the previous year without him (.589). Who knows what might have happened if Griffey had not slumped at the plate and whined about media coverage on ESPN and elsewhere (see http://www.cincypost.com/2001/mar/03/koch030301.html).

Similarly, the Rangers' signing of Alex Rodriguez was followed by an attendance increase of nearly 10 percent, despite the fact that Texas was already operating at 70 percent of stadium capacity. However, the revenue from the additional 31,000 fans at the Ballpark in Arlington hardly begins to cover the $22 million salary A-Rod received in 2001. Although other revenues are generated through star players via increased media coverage and merchandise sales, the presence of a star player like A-Rod in the absence of winning was apparently not enough to warrant keeping him on the team. Furthermore, with respect to their standing in the American League West Division, it was clear that the Rangers could not do any worse as a team than they did with A-Rod.

Winning and post-season performance. While many think that winning is everything, it apparently comes in third (B = .213) for MLB. Winning can make fans forgive a multitude of sins. However, the results of this model suggest that teams with new ownership like Montreal and Miami (in 2002) would be better off doing everything they can to get a new stadium and bring a few major stars to draw the fans. In particular, Miami owner Jeff Loria should recall what winning the World Series in 1997 (and then unloading high payroll players) did for the Marlins' attendance. Getting to the post-season almost always helps generate additional fans for the team and reinforces identification of current fans. But, just how many fans will go sit in an uncomfortable stadium with narrow seats and a bad view of a baseball game with few notable stars on the field in south Florida—which leads the league in humidity and mosquitoes? Apparently the answer is, on average, about 16,290 people during a championship season.[3] Interestingly, following

---

[3]Given the local market for intelligence, Loria reportedly considered renaming the team the Miami Chads following the 2000 elections.

their World Series Championship in 2003, the Marlins were only able to sell 5,000 season tickets by the following February (2004). So, winning will help attendance, but not independent of other factors.

Marlins' attendance	
1993	37,838
1994	33,695
1995	23,783
1996	21,565
1997	29,190
1998	21,363
1999	16,906
2000	15,134
2001	15,765
2002	10,038
2003	16,290
2004	22,091
2005	22,792

Population and competition. Cities with substantial population bases, but limited professional sports teams, are likely to offer good franchise opportunities due to the lack of direct competition from other professional sports team. Additionally, major cities such as New York and Los Angeles have plenty of other sources of entertainment apart from professional sports that provide indirect competition for leisure dollars. That a larger population leads to lower attendance is important for more than just MLB owners to understand. Obviously, the implication is not that major league teams should necessarily relocate to smaller and smaller towns. However, minor league teams that locate in cities of 100–200,000 can create focused interest in the local market, where fans have little other opportunity to identify with local sports teams. Similarly, NBA teams that relocate to medium-sized metro areas (e.g., Memphis, Oklahoma City, etc.) may be able to generate strong fan bases due to the lack of direct competition for the professional sports consumption dollar.

Pricing. This model explains factors that lead MLB teams to charge higher ticket prices. We also used this model to explain increases in

Team Marketing Report's Fan Cost Index (FCI), with similar results. The FCI includes additional venue prices for hot dogs, beer, sodas, and souvenirs. The implication is that as teams become more successful in building attendance, prices for all related consumption items tend to increase to take advantage of consumer surplus (see Chapter 1).

Why Do Teams Offer Discounts?

Sports organizations are able to charge higher prices when they have quality venues, star players, winning teams, recent post-season appearances, and limited direct competition. So, which organizations are bound to be charging lower prices? The short answer is: Organizations with lousy products in poor venues in highly competitive markets. Put differently, sports organizations offer frequent discounts due to poor strategic marketing planning. Strategic marketing planning includes:

- Analyzing the environment (competition, laws/regulations, society/culture, technology, and the economy)
- Determining target markets
- Designing marketing mixes (product, price, promotion, place) to meet the needs/wants of target markets

The core product for sports teams is the team and its players. The place is the event venue (stadium, racetrack, arena, etc.). The promotion positions the team in the minds of fans. Prices should be set consistent with the other marketing mix variables. Organizations that offer frequent discounts (or always have free tickets available) are basically telling the customer or fan, "We miscalculated the worth of our product." Obviously, the sports marketer's strategic marketing planning needs to ADD up.

Although sports marketing may differ in many respects to typical goods and services marketing (Chapter 1), the basic concepts that spell success for sports retailing are no different from other types of retailing. Consider local retailers (restaurants, clothing stores, etc.) that have failed or that attract few patrons. These retailers target undesirable segments, offer poor products or service, have inferior venues, poorly position themselves in the minds of consumers relative to competition, and are unable to attract enough patrons to at least break even at the prices offered. Hence, there is typically little mystery as to why sports organizations fail. Consider the XFL:

The Rise and Fall of the XFL

Television viewers showed up for the first Saturday night on NBC. Then the TV audience faded faster than Ricky Williams' NFL career. Why did the XFL fail? There is no mystery here. First, the XFL targeted a relatively narrow target market: Championship Wrestling Fans who were dissatisfied with NFL and NCAA football. Vince McMahon, owner and creator of the XFL, claimed that the XFL would go where the NFL was afraid to go. McMahon assumed that everyone agreed with his premise that the NFL was boring. Who knew that the NFL had and continues to have the highest TV ratings of any sport?

During the fall of each year, the NCAA dominates the airwaves on Saturday afternoons, followed by the NFL on Sundays and Mondays. The XFL clearly overestimated the demand for more football and miscalculated the competition. Second, and worse yet, the XFL offered an inferior product with misguided hype. Where perhaps the most entertaining aspect of the XFL product was players with nicknames on their jerseys like "He Hate Me," the play on the field was no better than the NCAA—despite the fact that uninformed announcers such as Jesse Ventura (Governor of Minnesota and ex-wrestling star) proclaimed *every* tackle as being a huge collision, fully supported by the on-field microphones turned to maximum volume. Third, promotional positioning of the XFL attempted to appeal to fans' more base desires. Apparently overlooked by the XFL was the fact that TV already offers a wide variety of scantily-clad women and salty language on other programming. At least they have the good taste to not mix those elements with bad football. Fourth, venues used by the XFL were located in either already saturated markets (like Los Angeles), weak markets (like Birmingham), or weak markets with bad stadiums (like Memphis). On the positive side, the XFL's failure indicates that you can only sell so much trash to Americans. Eventually we draw the line and say, "No more!" Of course, this does little to explain why Americans continue to watch *Survivor*, except that perhaps the competition is better.

Price Lining: The Key to Price Setting

Price lining refers to a common retail pricing policy that sets different prices for distinctly different levels of product quality (see Figure 6.2). Restaurants offer different price levels for appetizers, sandwiches, and entrees. Department stores offer different price levels for low-end to high-end dresses, blouses, and shirts. Each of these price levels appeal to segments with different price-sensitivity levels that value the product differently.

Apart from the quality of the team, players, and venue itself, it is likely no news to you that sports venues may offer different levels of quality with respect to:

1. Seats
   a. View
   b. Comfort
   c. Amenities
   d. Service
2. Participants
   a. Opponent teams
   b. Tournament or race entrants

Figure 6.2

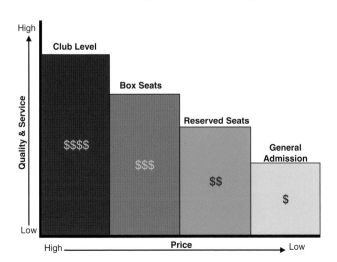

> With regard to discount ticket pricing, we would never consider it
> as an option. First, we are fortunate enough to sell out all games
> in advance. Second, we have PSL holders that pay a premium to
> get these seats and it would be tough to justify to them. Thirdly,
> I have always been of the mindset that you begin a slippery slide
> downward when you begin to discount your product. As the old
> saying goes . . . anyone can sell a bargain.
>
> Phil Thomas, Vice President of Sales and Marketing, St. Louis
> Rams

The quality level with respect to seats remains constant
across events or games throughout the season. The quality level with
respect to participants changes from event to event, dependent upon
the opponent or the entrants. Sports teams have a finite inventory
quantity at each pricing tier. Strategic marketing planning should
account for these differences in quantity and quality, such that
the team offers price lines consistent with market conditions,
market demand, product quality, venue quality and promotional
positioning.

Setting prices for each level of inventory is unlike pricing for goods
and many services. Most costs associated with a sporting event are
fixed. Whether 1,000 fans or 60,000 fans attend, the production costs
for the game itself remain relatively constant. Larger crowds mean
more game staff, but variable costs are minor compared to fixed costs
associated with the stadium, payroll, and event expenses that will be
incurred no matter the crowd size.

Seat inventory is perishable, meaning that once the game is played,
that inventory is lost. Unused seats also affect the volume of other
venue sales (viz., food, beverages, and souvenirs). Consequently, management is highly motivated to maximize capacity use. The temptation
is to offer ticket discounts to adjust for lower-than-expected performance with respect to the other marketing mix variables (i.e., the core
product, place, promotion). *Don't do it.*

Once you begin the walk down the slippery path of ticket discounts,
it is difficult to get back up the hill. David Stivers, Vice President of
Marketing for Pebble Beach Golf, outlines three key reasons that
sports organizations should never offer price discounts:

1. You run the risk of alienating your customers who are paying full
   price.

2. The discounts may become permanent (in the minds of consumers).

3. Discounts generate a negative connotation for your brand.

David goes on to state the importance of understanding how certain contexts or situations may influence the need to offer alternatives that *add* value, but that do not cut prices on the core product:

> Although Pebble Beach does not offer price discounts, we will during certain times of the year offer package deals that allow our guests to receive greater value for their dollars: A room and golf package; a room and spa package, etc. One thing we don't discount, ever, is Pebble Beach Golf.

Obviously, we would all like to be working or at least playing at a place like Pebble Beach. Since not all of us can, we need to understand situational price sensitivity so that we can effectively manage our price lines (i.e., set ticket prices).

Situational Price Sensitivity

Why do many people spend 50 to 65 cents on a 20 oz. soft drink at the grocery store, $1 from a vending machine at a university, $2 from a vending machine at a hotel, and $3 from a concession stand at a sporting event? Because many people are idiots. While this may be true, it is not necessarily tied to why people pay different amounts for the same thing in different situations.

The situational context influences your willingness to pay more or less for a good or service. How might the situational contexts in Table 6.1 affect how you would respond to differences in ticket prices?

Each of these situations may influence an individual fan to pay different prices for the same ticket. The key for the sports marketer is to understand the situation and manage pricing in a way that maximizes revenue. In effect, the team's losing or winning is a situational context (temporal perspective) that motivates teams to consider practicing price discrimination.

Consider the situation for many baseball teams—even those with generally strong performance records. Baseball is unique in that many teams play in large venues with excess capacity. Most new stadiums are designed with capacities (less than 40,000) similar to the successful older venues such as Wrigley and Fenway. But, in those cases where excess capacity exists, the key is not to offer unplanned, nonstrategic discounts. As Scott Brubaker, former Vice President of the Arizona Diamondbacks states,

Table 6.1

Situational Effects on Price Sensitivity		
Situational variable	**Context**	**Your price sensitivity**
Antecedent State	*Mood*: Bad vs. Good *Condition*: Out of money vs. Just got paid	
Physical Surroundings	*Weather:* Rainy/Cold forecast vs. Clear/ Pleasant forecast *Facilities*: Unattractive stadium vs. Attractive stadium *Event promotions*: Boring vs. Exciting game day activities	
Social Surroundings	*Social setting*: Alone vs. With others *Sales setting*: Online vs. Salesperson	
Task Definition	*Purpose*: Buy for self vs. Buy for others *Utility*: Functional (necessity) vs. Hedonic (pleasure; luxury)	
Temporal Perspective	*Season*: First game vs. Mid-year game vs. Last game *Time constraint*: Five minutes vs. Two weeks to decide on ticket purchase *Opponent*: Last place team vs. Archrival	

Strategic discount packages are a very important part of overall marketing plans. First of all, you have an inventory of over 4,000,000 seats for sale. Without some creativity, you would have great difficulty moving all the excess—particularly if the product is not performing well. All discount packages should be strategic in the sense that they 1) Are programmed and consistent (i.e., different discount or offer on different days of the week) and 2) They all are in some form of partnership with one or more of our sponsors who support each program promotionally and otherwise.

Discount programs are OK and necessary as long as they don't create the attitude, "Why buy a ticket for full price because there are always cheap or free tickets out there." You must walk the line of moving the most amount of product you can and still retaining the value of that product. Once you devalue your own product you can never go back.

The point here is that any form of price deals should be a part of a strategic plan and must consider the situation or context that drives some segments of fans to respond to price differentials. The end objective, of course, is to get to the point where demand exceeds supply and the sports organization is in the position of building value for its current (and future) customers, as is the case for some NFL teams who have sold out of all available season tickets. Such is less likely the case for teams in leagues that play long schedules with many games, such as MLB, the NHL, and the NBA. In any case, teams frequently practice some form of price discrimination to reduce inventory, and, if they are going to do it, they may as well do it right.

Price Discrimination

Marketers use price discrimination when different customer segments are willing to pay different prices for the same product. In one sense, the sports marketer sells tickets at different prices to view the same sporting event. However, given that the tickets represent seats from different views of the event, the sports marketer is actually selling tickets to experience the event at different quality levels. In that sense, the sports marketer is primarily just using price lining or tiered pricing. However, if a team sells the same ticket (e.g., reserved balcony seats) at different prices, then the team is using price discrimination. They may also just be disorganized. Sports marketers that offer discounts on tickets that simultaneously sell for higher prices without effectively planning and practicing price discrimination are likely to confuse and alienate fans.[4]

Organizations may seek to not maximize revenue due to other organizational goals. NBA teams all must make low-priced tickets available for low-income fans. In other cases, the community's local government may require the team to follow pricing guidelines in order to obtain public funding. Denver has required the Broncos to sell 2,000 tickets to the community at 50 percent off regular ticket prices for this reason. Unfortunately, this practice has turned into a public relations fiasco and management nightmare due to the fact that the team has had difficulty finding ways to fairly distribute these tickets to disadvantaged fans who are not also scalpers.

---

[4]A good (or bad) example of this is the frequent practice by airline and hotel operators who offer different prices—based primarily on customers' ability and willingness to search for low prices in advance (7–21 days) of purchase. Consequently, customer confusion and frustration is frequently high. Note: You can always save by using www.hotwire.com or www.priceline.com on hotels and car rentals. The best flight deals are often found at www.southwest.com, www.airtran.com, etc. or from the source—Delta Air emails.

Price discrimination can be planned and practiced when organizations are able to forecast that event capacity will not be maximized. Sports marketers can carve the market into SLICES for price discrimination if six conditions are met (see Table 6.2). Based upon these six conditions, when can organizations use price discrimination for tickets?

First, fan segments must differ in their price sensitivity. Price sensitivity refers to how people respond to changes in price. Lower-income consumers are often more price sensitive than others. Interestingly, these individuals are not always willing to search for low prices for leisure and entertainment. This suggests that, second, the segment must be large enough to warrant the different prices. Management must be careful to not overestimate the size of the price-sensitive segment for tickets. As you will recall, a survey that asks fans their opinions about current ticket prices will nearly always lead one to believe that a sizeable price-sensitive segment exists. However, such research should examine actual behaviors of those individuals who say they are price sensitive. Most folks prefer lower prices, but when it comes to sports tickets, a much smaller proportion may actually want to buy the lower priced ticket. Further, when it comes to spending on entertainment, even lower income fans may be willing to spend full price for tickets. They just aren't as likely to buy frequently.

Third, management must be able to identify the segments that are price sensitive. The best option for doing so is through effective database management. Individuals who fit price-sensitive profiles (low income, purchase lower priced tickets, attend infrequently, otherwise loyal/identified with team) may be selected to receive pertinent ticket information. The problem with a good deal of sports marketing pro-

Table 6.2

Conditions for Effective Price Discrimination	
Issue	**Price discrimination works when segments**
Sensitivity	have different levels of price **sensitivity** that motivates some fans to search for lower prices.
Large	are **large** enough to warrant different prices.
Identifiable	are **identifiable** so that they can be priced differently.
Confusion	are not **confused** by the different prices.
Economics	are **economically** profitable segments.
Separation	are **separate** enough so that those who pay one price can't exchange the product (or ticket) with those who paid higher prices.

motions targeting price-sensitive segments is that they are communicated through mass media communications (TV, radio, newspaper, etc.) that include wasted coverage, given the promotion and price objectives. Furthermore, offering different prices for the same ticket through such media may also lead to violating the fourth principle of effective price discrimination—confusion.

Accordingly, price discrimination methods should not confuse fans. In particular, offering discounts for some games/events and not others for the same ticket (e.g., reserved seating) may lead fans to become disillusioned as to the real value of the ticket. If fans find that seats on Tuesday's Ladies Night are priced at $7.00, but are $9.00 on other week nights, what is the perceived value of the ticket? The perceived value of the ticket is based upon what fans think they get for what they give. If a fan can get a ticket for $7 (or even get free tickets), what is the perceived value of the same ticket at $9? What is the bottom line? The more frequently discount or complimentary tickets are offered, the more fans' perceptions will shift toward the lower price.

Fifth, the segments targeted via price discrimination must be economically profitable. In the short term, offering lower ticket prices to price-sensitive segments are likely to be profitable in the sense that each additional ticket sold at the lower price brings in additional revenue with little incremental cost. Management must be certain, however, that they are not simply shifting demand from fans who would have purchased the higher priced tickets anyway. Sticking with our example of $9 reserved seats, a team may run a price promotion for the $7 discounted seats and sell 1,000 of these tickets. Does this mean that this price promotion produced $7,000 in additional revenue? Not necessarily, since some portion of these 1,000 would purchase regular priced tickets without a price promotion.

What if the team had not expended the resources to run the promotion and sold 800 tickets at the regular price? It is commonly known among sports marketers that individuals that receive cheap or free tickets also spend little or nothing at the event on concessions or other items. This question of trade-offs requires more in-depth quantitative marginal analysis, but one should be able to see the risks in simply shifting demand due to price discounts. Admittedly, any sports marketer worth his or her salt[5] would only run a promotion with the financial support of a sponsor that covers the potential loss of any revenue. However, the long-term cost of running the price promotion

---

[5]I don't really know what this means. Why would anyone price one's self relative to salt?

is likely to have the same effect that prevailing discounts have on fans' perceived value of the ticket.

Drawing from a different leisure setting, consider the perceived value of tickets to a Six Flags theme park. The following were prices for the 2002 season at Six Flags over Georgia:

2002 Pricing	
Regular Admission	$39.99
One Day Senior Citizens 55 and Older	$24.99
Junior Admission, Kids 48″ and Under	$24.99
Value Parking	$9.00
Premium Parking	$12.00

Six Flags effectively uses price discrimination for senior citizens and juniors. However, Six Flags also runs sponsored price deals throughout the season with Coke that allows a $4 weekend discount and an $8 weekday discount when you go to the park. The good thing about this promotion is that it targets price-sensitive segments that must do something to obtain the discount. The bad thing about this promotion is that it may move the perceived value of the ticket closer to $31.99 than $39.99 for many consumers.

It is not uncommon for visitors to arrive at the park to find extra discount coupons sitting outside the gates. Over time, customers learn that the actual value of the ticket is always at least $4 less than the listed price. In such cases, the marketing objective may be to target average ticket prices at the $32 level, such that fans feel like they are getting a deal when they get the discount. (The good news is that Six Flags also offers a great bargain on parking.[6]) The main point here is that any price discounting should be part of a strategic marketing planning process with clear objectives consistent with corporate goals.

Finally, marketers can use price discrimination if the price-sensitive segment can be effectively separated from those less price sensitive. If the cheaper ticket can be bought and transferred to others at a higher price, then the profits are simply shifted from the sports entity to middlemen known as scalpers or brokers. Clearly, the Denver Broncos' practice of selling 2,000 tickets at half price (to satisfy local government requirements to make tickets available to underprivileged segments) gives an excellent opportunity for individuals to purchase and

---

[6]Premium parking includes a bonus *Yosemite Sam Rootin' Tootin' Barf Bag*™ for up to four individuals per vehicle.

resell the tickets. To the extent that the team is forced to develop unusual systems to regulate the use and transfer of these tickets makes it clear that no economic need existed to offer these discounts. Another example of ineffective price discrimination due to the lack of separation also occurred in Denver. Fans attending a Denver Nuggets game received a free ski lift ticket to local ski areas. Within the week, attendees were selling these lift tickets on eBay at prices approaching the regular daily lift ticket prices.

But, what about being socially responsible for the poor fan who can't afford to go to a game? Social responsibility is an important reason for sports marketers to consider price discrimination. If members of the organization and the community agree that an important goal for the sports entity is to serve less affluent segments of the population, clearly management has a responsibility to seek ways to achieve this objective. Perhaps the easiest thing to do is to offer cheap tickets so that the club can claim it is doing what it can to reach out to all segments in the community. However, many of the "value tickets" to these events only give the fan the opportunity to get in the building at the same time a game is being played. Since the only thing they can really see well is the large video scoreboard, they would have been as well off watching on TV at home.

If sports entities really want to fulfill social responsibility objectives, they would be more effective if they used some of their profits to directly assist those less privileged. For example, the Memphis Redbirds AAA baseball team is set up as a nonprofit organization. Its profits are returned to the community via two programs, STRIPES (Sports Teams Returning in the Public Education System) and RBI (Returning Baseball in the Inner-city). These programs do three things.

1. They provide support for underprivileged children to participate in sports programs that they could not otherwise.
2. The nature of the programs is tied directly to building involvement in the sport, which should help build a long-term fan base among the participants.
3. These programs can provide the opportunity for participants to attend the team's baseball games. In this manner, individuals who really do need discounted or complimentary tickets are identified and served.

The overall point here is that anyone can run a price discount. It takes a good deal more planning and caring for sports marketers to actually achieve social responsibility objectives.

Adding Value

Successful teams today focus more on adding value to the event. Instead of thinking of ways to get fans to come to undesirable games, they emphasize making the game into an exciting event that offers fans far more than just a ballgame. Kerry Sewell, Vice President of Marketing for the Memphis Redbirds, explains their approach to building one of the most successful minor league baseball programs in the country:

> When we came into the market, one of the most difficult obstacles we faced was the access this community had to discounted or free tickets to see the previous franchise. We do not blanket the area with discounts or free tickets. Even when we package ticket promotions with a sponsor, the price of the tickets is factored into the sponsorship. As a rule, we never discount food concessions. Our predecessor themed nights by discounting concessions (e.g., dollar beer, quarter hot dog night, etc.). We would rather theme our promotions towards entertainment and giveaways than through concessions. In most cases, you end up discounting merchandise or concessions that would have been purchased at regular price and train fans to bargain shop. We do not believe that such discounts are sparking new buyers or traffic. We have always believed that frequent discounting cheapens the overall value of our product to our fans and our sponsors.

Source: Courtesy of Inman Images/Memphis Redbirds.

Build It and They Will Come

7

Proper management of facilities and services at the home field can provide a competitive advantage by attracting fans so that the team plays in front of a good home crowd. However, management sometimes has difficulty getting consistently good play from their employees and keeping the place in proper shape. A new stadium or arena can make things better in the short term, but it won't save bad management and a bad team in the long run.

Managing sports venues can be difficult for at least three reasons. First, the longer you work at a place, the more difficult it is to remember what it is like to be a customer. You can get accustomed to the cranky worker at the gate, not notice the paint peeling in the hallways, and ignore the mildewed tiles that ominously droop down from the restroom ceilings waiting to fall on an unsuspecting fan. This is unfortunate since, in today's tort-ridden climate, some fan is apt to sue you and the organization for mental anguish and suffering resulting from the foam tile dropping at an inopportune time.

Second, owners and managers are less likely to receive or even see the same service the average fan does. A good deal of time and effort may be (appropriately) expended in serving the needs and wants of those individuals and corporate sponsors who lease suites and sit in the expensive box seats. However, unless management purposely observes and controls all aspects of customer service, it is difficult for them to get the same picture the typical fan is getting.

Third, a certain proportion of sports fans lack social skills essential for functioning in modern society. Odds are you have recently had the profound displeasure of sitting next to one of these individuals at a sporting event, assuming that you are not one of these individuals yourself—in which case the annoying fan seated next to you at the game is likely your best friend or significant other.

Anyway, the point is that event management can be trying due to aberrant fan behavior. Particular situations at sporting events can be a recipe for disaster, sometimes minor and sometimes major. At the major disaster level, you might have these ingredients:

- an important rivalry game,
- two groups, each with tens of thousands of fans who mutually hate each other,
- in the same facility, supplied with a mass quantity of alcoholic beverages of their choice.

It is a foregone conclusion that the referee or umpire will blow a crucial call, causing each group of fans to behave in ways that the video of this behavior is repeated over and over again on Sportscenter, or at least on the "You've Gotta See This" sports program.[1] On a more minor, yet frequent, level there are still individuals who behave in ways that require them to be personally escorted from the game due to their enthusiastic support for the home team and an inability to avoid confrontations with the other fans sitting around them.

These three areas of difficulties in event management represent three critical aspects of sports marketing that hit close to home: facility management, service management, and fan management. The following sections outline pertinent issues from a marketing perspective and discuss effective methods to satisfy fans' needs and wants in each context.

Facility Management

The Sportscape

The sportscape includes the entire built and managed environment that the fan sees when attending a sporting event. Managing the place is particularly important in sportscapes because fans spend hours in the place. In fact, the more time fans spend in the place, the more

---

[1]This is a Fox Sports program that mainly features 17-year-old skateboarders knowing ahead of time that they are doing something incredibly stupid, otherwise they wouldn't have their buddies videotaping it.

important the facility is in determining fan attendance. The sportscape has the most influence on fans' feelings and behavior in baseball (70–82 home games), followed by basketball and hockey (40+ home games), and football (6–8 home games). The point is that the more hours that season ticket holders (or frequent fans) are paying to be in the place, the better the place has to be to attract and maintain fan attendance.

In today's sports marketplace, management cannot focus on the sports facility as merely a place to play a game. Today, it is more often a place that people go for entertainment throughout the year, as sports facility owners seek to hold events in the facility for social groups, weddings, birthdays, bar mitzvahs, multiple sports, concerts, and, hopefully, rodeos and monster truck shows. In any case (except perhaps rodeos), the attractiveness of the facility as a meeting place will influence the likelihood that others will want to spend time in the facility. Obviously, the quality of customer services (i.e., food service and catering) is also important, as we will see in the next section on service management. Overall, however, investments aimed at enhancing facility quality can be offset with increased usage both in-season and out-of-season.

Sportscape Factors

Because management becomes accustomed to the physical environment and the people they work with every day, it is important to be aware of the focal points that affect fans' perceptions of the place. The ten factors[2] listed on page 136 influence how (dis)pleasurable fans feel the place is. These feelings influence fans' willingness to stay in the stadium, spend money while in the stadium, and to return to the stadium in the future.

The following sections walk you through each aspect of the sportscape, noting its influence on fans and what management can do to manage each aspect of the sportscape.

Parking Access

When properly designed and managed, parking access (ingress and egress) may go almost unnoticed by fans as long as it does not hinder them from achieving their goals (i.e., to get to the game and then go elsewhere in the facility). However, improperly designed and poorly

---

[2]This is like the Big 10 Conference, which actually has 11 team members. Actually, #11 in the list is a consequence of some of the other factors and is not a structural component of the built environment.

	Sportscape factor	Description
1	Parking access	Ease of entry, ample parking, convenience and ease of exit
2	Architectural design and appearance	Attractive and interesting structural design, exterior appearance and landscaping
3	Interior decor	Color schemes, wall decor, lighting, and ambience
4	Facility layout	Visibility of layout and ease of going wherever you want to go
5	Wayfinding signage	Signage (including wayfinding markers) directing fans to seats, restrooms, services, and exits
6	Facility space	Enough space in restrooms, walkways, concessions, and seating areas to accommodate fans
7	Seat comfort	Knee room, elbow room, seat space and comfort; offers an unobstructed view
8	Equipment quality	Functionally and aesthetically pleasing; in good order and repair
9	Scoreboards and sound systems	Quality of information: exciting, interesting, timely, and complete. Sound quality: music selection, volume and clarity
10	Cleanliness	Restrooms, walkways, concessions, and seating areas
11	Perceived crowding	Feeling restricted, cramped, stuffy, and constrained due to facility layout; influenced by wayfinding signage and space

managed parking can have a significant negative effect on attendance and influence how long fans want to stay at the game before exiting to try to beat the traffic.

Since management personnel are rarely the ones trying to leave right after the game, traffic issues may not get enough attention until people complain. The problem is that people have difficulty letting management know about the problem because they are already out of the building. Further, people will complain if there are parking problems, but they frequently won't take the time to complain to management. They'll complain to other people and may just decide not to come back. Or, if they do come back, they may decide to leave early based upon their recall of previous problems.

Importantly, the less time that they are in the facility, the less chance they have to spend money on concessions and merchandise. This is not a trivial matter since in-game purchases are an important revenue stream for the team. Consequently, there are five things that organizations can do to facilitate parking access:

1. Employ enough personnel to (a) direct fans to open parking when entering and (b) to educate and direct fans to the most expedient exit routes.
2. Add routes that give fans more entrance and exit choices. It is important that management carefully evaluate physical routes and barriers that may inhibit proper traffic flow. If adding additional entrances/exits will save fans 10–20 minutes, it is probably worth the investment in the logistic infrastructure (roads).
3. Arrange traffic light management with local police. Sometimes the problem isn't in the parking lot—it could be problems down the road where traffic lights stall the free movement of traffic.
4. Offer entertainment or promotions before and/or after the game that encourage fans to come early and stay later. Having a concert or some other pre/post-game entertainment allows the crowd to not have to enter or disperse all at the same time.
5. Provide shuttle service from a more distant parking lot, free—by getting a sponsor who gains personal contact with the fans on the way to the facility. The sponsor can pass out samples or coupons and provide other brand/product information while also gaining the positive association with the team in the minds and hearts of fans.

Architectural Design

The first impression that fans get of a place is from its exterior appearance and its architectural design. HOK, the leading sports architectural design firm, has made its reputation based upon stadium designs that catch the emotion of the sport. Although most of us won't be deciding which architectural firm to use to build a stadium or arena or what the design will be, it is interesting to note that attractive stadium designs include mostly older stadiums (Wrigley Field or Fenway Park) and new stadiums that look like the old ones (Camden Yards, AT&T Park, Baylor Ballpark, and nearly all new minor league parks).

Stadiums that aren't very popular are those that have generally failed to capture the look and feel of vintage ballparks. For example, fans viewed Chicago's New Comisky Park built in 1991 (now U.S. Cellular Field) as something closer to an amusement park rather than a ballpark. Recognizing these problems, this field has undergone 9 renovations in the 15 years since it was built. Visit the link below to see the improvements that should help make the home of the White Sox more competitive with the Friendly Confines of Wrigley Field: http://chicago.whitesox.mlb.com/NASApp/mlb/cws/ballpark/cws_ballpark_cellularfield.jsp

While you may read editorials complaining about the rash of new stadiums and arenas and the accompanying drain on taxpayers, the fact of the matter is that facilities of all types (not just sports) require frequent renovation or entirely new facilities to maintain competitiveness. On the extreme, one can observe the frequency and expense with which casinos in Las Vegas renovate and rebuild in order to remain competitive. On the other end of the spectrum are government buildings housing Departments of Motor Vehicle Registration that are rarely renovated. Of course, this may explain why nearly all DMV employees are so depressed and then take it out on you when you wait until the last day of the month to renew your license.

Fan's E-Opinion of Pro Player Stadium in Miami

Having grown up in Miami, my family had Dolphins tickets for more than a decade. We enjoyed our experience at the Orange Bowl, but hated when they moved to what was then Joe Robbie Stadium.

I have very few compliments for Pro Player, a.k.a. JRS. When I used to go to the Orange Bowl, there was not much official parking. However, the local Cuban neighborhood made it very easy and inexpensive to park in their driveways and yards. Also, the Orange Bowl is near downtown. If they could only put a baseball stadium downtown!

Getting to JRS requires a long drive, but it is right off an expressway. The long drive is the easy part. Getting into the stadium parking lot is a nightmare that can take up to an hour to go a half mile or less. The staff has little control over who parks where, despite colored passes. They have only about 14,000 spaces for 73,000 people. I was very irritated to learn that despite having nine season tickets, I needed ten to get two passes.

Once inside you go to your seats. When we were in the OB, we had seats on the 35 yard line lower level, but due to Joe Robbie's arbitrary seating policy, we were now in the corner of the end zone, but thankfully in row 3 in front of the cheerleaders! You really do not have any good sightlines in this stadium. Even sitting on the sidelines, you are very far back from even the team's sidelines. Plus, the sun creates bad shadows during certain times of the day, leaving you with bad sunburns.

The food is atrocious and pricey, enough said. This is true even in the club seating area. Would you like a $5 mini-Perrier bottle? However, if you sit in the club seating area, you have cover from the rain, and cold or hot air blowing down on you depending on the time of year.

Since the Dolphins play in basically a stone stadium, the Dolphins crowd cannot drown out the QB like they did in the OB. I like to think of JRS as a crappy country club, if that is possible.

I still love the Dolphins, but I hate JRS, now Pro Player.

Recommended: No
Parking Availability: What A Nightmare
Seat Location: Lower Level

Virtually all categories of public facilities go through cycles requiring expensive renovation or rebuilding. In particular, many public sports facilities were built decades ago and are in need of replacement. With the need to augment revenue through multiple-use facilities, owners (whether public or private) must have facilities that can accommodate more than just sporting events.

Interior Decor

One of the most common sports facility interior design concepts of the 1970s and 1980s was to rely upon the clever color scheme of gray. Concrete walls and facades with gray concrete steps and walkways were used to create the perception that these are the same people who design our prisons, only with less attention to detail and style (at the stadiums). Although less frequent today, fans may still encounter sportscapes that make design decisions based upon cost factors. Such venues make fans feel like they want to leave as soon as (a) the game is decided, (b) they stop serving beer, and/or (c) they recover from walking around the seemingly endless winding walkways to their seats in the upper deck.

Some organizations with older facilities have improved the interior decor and have been able to build or maintain fan attendance. In St. Louis, the Cardinals painted the outfield facade walls in team colors, hung colorful banners, redesigned seating and concessions (viz., outfield concessions and seating areas overlooking the field), replaced Astroturf with real grass, and installed decorative centerfield landscaping to deal with the concrete dome (circa 1970s) nature of their stadium. (Nonetheless, even these efforts were insufficient, as the Cardinals opened their new Busch III Stadium in 2006.)

During the same time period (1970–2003), working with a facility and downtown location very similar to the Cardinals, the Cincinnati Reds did virtually nothing to Riverfront Stadium, and saw fan attendance drop and remain relatively low even when the team performed well.

The key issue here is that management must periodically assess the relative attractiveness of the interior decor of the facility and seek ways to improve it, just as the White Sox have done. In particular, if management is a bunch of guys, it is also a good idea to gain insight from someone who doesn't decorate their own home with velvet pictures of Elvis or dogs playing poker.

Layout and Wayfinding Signage

A frequent problem encountered by new fans visiting a stadium is finding their way around. Again, management already knows where to go, so they often overlook the fact that the layout of the facility can be confusing and that clear wayfinding signage is needed.

Visualization and markers. An important advantage of most of the new stadiums is that they are designed so that fans can see through the facility to be able to visualize where they are, where they want to go, and what's happening on the field. For example, fans at some stadiums can search for seats, stand in line for concessions, or enter restrooms from the field side rather than facing an exterior wall. If fans can see where they are with respect to the field, finding locations in the facility is far easier than without the visual reference point.

Better interior designs provide wayfinding markers that may include landmarks (e.g., sculptures, displays, etc.), differentiated wall design (e.g., wall colors, pictures, etc.) or differentiated facilities (e.g., concessions with different storefronts) to enable fans to separate one part of the large facility from another. An important disadvantage of many older facilities constructed with a large quantity of concrete blocks or similar materials (with no visualization) is that fans can easily become lost or disoriented. In these facilities, the upper deck level looks exactly the same as the lower deck level, each of which looks exactly like the adjoining seat sections, making it difficult to determine where you are. Making it worse, some of these same facilities use identical seat section numbers on different levels (e.g., you can find a Section 203 on both the lower level and the upper level).

If the facility lacks visualization, a new stadium or remodeling (e.g., removing walls) will help. Obviously, the less extensive and less expensive alternative is to add wayfinding markers, signage, and differentiating color schemes.

Good concourse with signage and visualization.

Poor concourse with no signage and no visualization.

Signage. Lacking effective interior layout and design, wayfinding signage becomes critical in helping fans find seats, services, and exits. "You-Are-Here" signs are useful in larger facilities. However, these signs can cause more confusion than they are worth if they are not properly positioned from the viewer's perspective. For example, some of these signs are placed with respect to North-South-East-West, but the fan is not standing at a position facing north when looking at the sign.

Seat sections should be clearly marked with signs visible from a distance, as with signs extended from the wall or ceiling (see picture above). Merely marking the seat sections on the wall makes it difficult for the individual to see, particularly in crowded situations where fans may be blocking the signage. Some facilities err by placing seat section numbers on the back wall of the sections—which is fine until people actually sit in the back row seats and block the numbers. The point is that management must view things from the fans' perspective and consider situations that occur when the stadium is occupied and when new fans are attending.

After fans find their seats, they will likely seek directions to food service, restrooms, shops, and other services (such as first aid, ticket offices for future sales, etc.). In the case of food service and restrooms, it can be particularly useful if directions are available communicating alternative locations (viz., "Expanded restrooms are also located behind the first and third baselines and outfield bleachers.").

Finally, exits should be clearly marked; but fans would also benefit from knowing the best ways to exit. Announcements and informational pamphlets can communicate some of this information. However, having personnel available to answer questions and direct fans as they exit is also an important responsibility of attendants and security personnel.

Facility Space and Perceived Crowding

The amount of space available given the number of people in that space has a direct psychological and physiological effect on fans. Perceived crowding in its strictest sense refers to the negative psychological reaction that an individual has when the number of people in a given space exceeds an acceptable comfort level for that individual.

A visually open layout and clear wayfinding signage can alleviate the perception of space problems. However, the lack of space available for fans to easily navigate the facility in a timely manner can lead to feelings of frustration. For anyone but maybe the most committed fan, cramped walkways, stuffy concession areas with long lines, and long narrow rows of seats lead to negative affective responses (read: they don't like it) and ultimately to exit (read: they leave and don't come back).

It is no surprise that some fan segments are particularly disadvantaged at sporting events due to the lack of equitable restroom space. To combat this problem, the new American Airlines Center in Dallas has nearly 9,832 stalls in the women's restrooms to accommodate fans. Unfortunately, to accommodate the space requirements, the men's restrooms are now located outside the arena. Seriously, the American Airlines Center was specifically designed to have a disproportionate share of restroom space for women to meet their needs—despite the fact that such space problems could be reduced by nearly 50 percent if women were willing to go to the restroom by themselves.

Crowding is a two-edged sword in the sportscape. On the one hand, the team wants a large crowd. The large crowd means greater excitement in the stands, more revenue to the organization, and home field advantage for the team. On the other hand, a large crowd without ample space will lead some to exit early and not return due to perceived crowding. Like Yogi Berra once said, "No one goes there anymore. It's too crowded."

The key is to be able to draw a large crowd that is comfortable despite the large crowd. In addition to improving layouts to have a more open feeling and providing clear signage to properly distribute the crowds, two constructive ways to improving space include smaller (new) venues and making space.

Smaller venues. Interestingly, to combat crowding problems, nearly all new baseball stadiums over the past decade actually seat fewer fans than their predecessors. Rather than cram more people into uncomfortable spaces, they have chosen to make cozier facilities for fewer—but more satisfied—fans. Having 40,000 relatively good seats (including suites) compared to 60,000 seats of which only 20,000 are decent seats (as in some old stadiums) allows the organization to charge higher prices for the better value afforded by the seats. Further, new facilities have purposely brought fans even closer to the action, placing prime seats closer to the playing field and placing even the cheap seats in relatively good view of the event. This also leads to greater risks of fan injury, as we will discuss later.

Make space. Some facilities have attempted to deal with cramped space by removing seats and expanding the width and number of aisles and walkways. The Chicago White Sox actually eliminated the top dozen rows of seats that were at the top of the stadium at a high incline and modified other seating to be more spacious and closer to the action.

Other venues with limited attendance have shifted pricing policies to encourage or allow fans to get closer to the action (and out of the cramped upper level seats). Some teams offer seat upgrades for a small fee that move fans to unused lower level seats after the beginning of the game. Others have changed prices such that lower level (better) seats are available at what were formerly upper level seat prices.

In addition to the benefit in reducing negative responses to cramped spaces, providing spacious areas to allow fans to easily navigate the venue is likely to have a positive effect on food service revenues. Difficulty in exiting the seating section due to long, narrow rows hinders fans' willingness to obtain food and drinks, as they are unlikely to enjoy whacking the knees of everyone on the way to the food service areas. Also, if fans know that the food service line is also crowded, they will be less likely to want to miss 15 to 30 minutes of the game just to get food. Even if food vendors are available in the stands, poor layout and space makes service difficult (viz., passing food and change down a row of 20 people).

Seat Comfort, Equipment Quality, Scoreboards and Sound Systems

The most important aspect of seats, equipment, and scoreboards is that they function properly. You can have the highest quality seats, service equipment (e.g., including things like air conditioning), scoreboards, and sound systems in the country, but if they do not work they are of little use at the time. Fans are likely to attribute the malfunctioning to management. Why? Because it is management's job to make sure that someone prior to every game examines and immediately fixes everything, including:

1. Seats (ticketed and toileted)
2. Video displays and monitors around the facility
3. Electronic signage and sponsor boards
4. Scoreboards (all boards, all functions)
5. Sound system volume (adjusted for expected crowd level)
6. Roof leaks, retractable mechanisms—if available (e.g., Miller Park's roof leaked in a downpour in the first year)
7. Light fixtures
8. Stadium/arena lights
9. Glass panels and windows
10. Railings (aisle, walkway, etc.)
11. Self-service machines

Fans are not appeased if you announce or put a sign up to say that something is broken. The point is that you should have realized the problem with enough lead time to get it fixed. This means that replacements must be stocked and that technicians are contracted to provide immediate repair.

Scoreboards and sound systems. The quality of the scoreboard and sound system limits or affords opportunities to entertain and inform fans. Since most sports organizations should be able to obtain decent systems through sponsorship deals, the only reason for lousy scoreboards is likely to be because someone has not effectively presented a package deal to the appropriate sponsor(s).

Given that capable systems are available, management must take the fans' perspective as to what they want to see on the scoreboard. What fans want are:

1. *Complete team and player stats*: Real sports fans eat up statistics about players and teams. Why else would Jerry Seinfeld say, "I'd read the sports page if my hair was on fire."? It's because most

guys would rather miss the birth of their firstborn than to miss a day reading the sports page. Knowing this, scoreboards should be managed to provide complete up-to-the-minute stats on the team and player. I think it is safe to say that teams cannot supply too much player information. OK, there are a few players that we know a bit too much about. But, mostly, it's a good idea to provide as much information as possible so that fans feel like they really know a great deal about each player so that they build an attachment and identify with the players on the team.

2. *Emotion-driven entertainment*: While highly identified fans want plenty of stats, fans of all identification levels are likely to enjoy video entertainment that sparks emotion. Fans come to the game for the emotion (excitement, pleasure, and relaxation) of the event. Showing movie clips and playing songs related to the sport has become a staple at most venues. The key is in maintaining continuity while also providing variety. A good [local] example of this is the "Happy Dance" video played at Baylor Baseball games. Some of the funny video clips are changed from time to time, but the music stays the same from game to game. Fans want to know what to expect, but they don't want to be bored either.

3. *Replays*: Show them. Teams may have a policy of not showing replays of opposing team's good plays. But, there is no excuse for not having replays available for when the team wants to pump up the fans, since the costs of the equipment and personnel can be covered by a sponsoring corporation who desires the frequent exposure (viz., Alltel Instant Replays).

Cleanliness

Keeping a facility clean is much like maintaining seats and equipment. Individuals must be assigned to clean every aspect of the facility before, during, and after the event. Since cleanliness is entirely up to the personnel managing the place, fans will make attributions regarding management if the place is not clean. They will assume that management lacks:

1. Organizational skills and attention to detail,
2. Concern for fans' needs, and/or
3. Finances (due to poor attendance) to pay janitorial staff.

None of these assumptions about management are beneficial. Part of the problem at the major league level is that janitorial and food service work may be contracted with a unionized service supplier. Consequently, management has no direct control over the quality of service except for when they sign the contract. So, it is critical that (a) such suppliers are very carefully evaluated, and (b) the contract be written in a way that allows for control mechanisms (read: cancellation of contract).

To the extent that management does have direct control over these services, personnel should be assigned to complete cleaning assignments at every customer contact point (halls, aisles, restrooms, etc.). A few easy ways to alleviate some of the burden is to enlist the fans' help by:

1. Informing fans of the need to keep "their stadium" clean, via signs and announcements.
2. Supplying ample garbage disposal units (trash cans). Most fans will throw stuff away if there is a repository close by. If not, they will simply deposit it below their seat or in the aisle.
3. Conducting mid-game clean-up by having attendants pass through each section with trash bags asking for and collecting all trash.

Service Management

In this section we consider four keys to effective service management at sporting events.

Key 1　Food Service Is Not Just Hotdogs, Popcorn, and Beer

Fans do not compare the food service at the game with food service at other sporting events. Fans compare food service at the park to food service they can get outside of the park. Due to the upper income levels of frequent fans and how often they are there, price is less critical than high quality and variety.

If it means eating the same thing every night then it means they aren't going to eat there. Most individuals who are season ticket holders are unlikely to want to survive on a diet of hot dogs (82+% fat content), French fries (46+% fat content), hamburgers (52+% fat content) and beer (no comment). Although we admit that we have seen a few that appear to have tried.

Most new facilities are investing in high-end food service with large scale variety. Consider Invesco Field, home of the Denver Broncos (76,125 seats):

- 79 permanent food service stands
- 101 portable kiosks

- 560 points of sale (1 for each 135 customers)
- catering service for parties up to 2,500 guests
- 15,000 employees and volunteers work per game
- 20 merchandise locations

See http://www.invescofieldatmilehigh.com/stadium/concess.html

The point is that if teams want to have high per caps on concessions, then they must provide high quality and variety. The average per capita concessions at pro sporting events and shows (concerts, etc.) at places like American Airlines Center is $4–$7.50. In order to keep fans spending food service dollars at the game, teams can improve food service in one or more of the following ways:

1. Recruit and retain quality employees, with an emphasis on retention.
2. Use not-for-profit groups as a solid and consistent source of workers who are motivated to serve if they obtain a percentage of the revenue (frequently done at NCAA venues).
3. Designate high-end seating and employ specially trained concierge service for premium seat holders.
4. Encourage advance call-in orders (cell phone or online) to increase revenue and service quality.

Key 2   Develop a Signature Food Item

Whatever the quality of service, the menu, and variety of items, you must have a signature item that fans actually prefer over other food offered outside of the park. Consider the following examples:

- BBQ Rendevous Nachos (AutoZone Park, Memphis, TN)
- Hand-rolled pretzels (Pretzelry, Busch Stadium, St. Louis, MO)
- Pierogies (Jacobs Field, Cleveland, OH)
- Clam chowder (Fenway Park, Boston, MA)

An increasingly popular trend is to develop a partnership with fan favorites. Examples:

- Krispy Kreme at Qualcomm Park (San Diego)
- Outback Steakhouse at PNC Park (Pittsburgh)
- Wolfgang Puck at Dodger Stadium (LA)

The bottom line is that if you want to have high per caps on concessions, you must realize that you are primarily selling to an upper-scale clientele willing to pay for good food. Alternately, they are willing to plan ahead to avoid bad food. Having a signature item justifies the expense to the fan, assures the fan of reliable food quality, and adds to the value of the overall experience at the game.

Key 3   Think High-Tech Customer Service

The future in sports venue technology will change the way fans view the game over the next decade. Air-Grid Networks now offers live in-game video and instant replay feeds to spectators via wireless LANS to wireless handheld devices such as PDAs or laptops. Fans at Indiana Pacers' games can rent these devices for $25 a game, allowing them to review every blown or questionable call at will. A 10-second broadcast delay lets users access their device on replays from multiple camera angles. In the future, expect to see more venues like AT&T Park with these systems available in seats, including, among other things:

- Live broadcasts of other sporting events
- Web access
- Games for kids
- Services to order concessions without leaving the seat

The pay-off from these systems is not likely to be immediately viable. However, teams that can find corporate sponsors that are also vendors may find it worthwhile to provide the technology. For example, an electronics firm (retailers like Best Buy, or manufacturers such as Dell or Sony) may be interested in having fans use their technology and to also provide commercial information to the user while at the game.

Key 4   Customer Service Must Focus on Families

The principal target demographic of sporting events is families. Fans attend games with others and most often with their families. Facilities and services must be geared toward satisfying families' needs and building involvement and identification among all members of the family. Most of the newer facilities take this into account. The AT&T Center in San Antonio has devoted a large entertainment section for kids and their parents that could have otherwise been used as a seating area. This FANFiesta area is sponsored by the HEB grocery chain and is complete with a kids' merchandise store and interactive games for the entire family. Another good example is the San Francisco Giant's Coca-Cola Fan Lot (see below).

Source: Courtesy of Kirk L. Wakefield.

Fan Management

Spectator liability is a reality that cannot be ignored. Virtually everything else we deal with in sports and venue marketing has some entertainment value to it. Controlling fans and protecting fans, however, is no laughing matter. Some of the worst case scenarios:

- Hockey: Brittanie Cecil (NHL, Columbus, OH, 2002) died from a hockey puck shot to the head. The NHL installed 30-foot screens around the rinks in 2002–2003.
- Car racing: 29 died and 70 injured by race cars and flying parts at U.S. auto racing events since 1999.
- Golf: Six spectators were struck by lightning at the 1991 Open at Hazeltine National Golf Course (Minneapolis), including one fatality.
- Soccer: 39 people died and 375 others were injured in a crowd panic during a soccer game in Brussells, Belgium (1985).

NHL Hockey Death

> Sitting behind the goal, Brittanie Cecil, 13, was struck in the forehead by a puck deflected into the stands by defenseman Derek Morris off a shot by center Espen Knutsen at Nationwide Arena. The puck caromed off another spectator before hitting Cecil, whose seat was more than 100 feet behind the glass. Cecil died two days later, the first spectator fatality in the NHL's long history.

These examples illustrate that all teams must have ample commercial property insurance, which has been going up about 30 percent a year in recent years. (FYI, you probably can't get covered for terrorism.) Also, event cancellation is also becoming so expensive that insurance firms aren't even offering that coverage any more. In order to manage the risk involved with fans at sporting events, management can be proactive to prevent fan injury and employ appropriate personnel for crowd control.

Be proactive to prevent fan injury. While the precise nature of harmful events cannot always be foreseen, most can be anticipated and measures can be taken to prevent injury. The following are but a few of the steps teams should take to protect their fans:

1. Provide written and announced warnings (e.g., warn fans of the danger of balls flying from field). Fact: Approximately 35–40 balls go into the stands per each MLB game. The most often injured are fans along the first and third base lines.
2. Train attendants to look for potential injurious situations, including disruptive fans. Attendants should never be facing away from the fans (viz., watching the game)—they should always be facing the fans (and not leaning on railing).
3. Inspect premises for dangerous walkways—slips and falls at golf tournaments outnumber the claims from being hit by balls.

In short, each team should consider every possible contingency so that fans are protected. Obviously, liability insurance should be incurred, but it is even better to proactively seek out ways to prevent injuries to fans.

Do background checks on security and service personnel. In these post 9–11 days, you just never know. While most sports organizations do background checks on full-time employees, about a third don't check backgrounds of part-timers who are more likely to be candidates for terrorist activities or at least give terrible service. You should do background checks (call past employer and check residence) on *all* employees if you are a manager at a large sports venue.

Conclusion

So what have we learned about facility and event management? First, fan management is a tough job, but one that cannot be overlooked in today's volatile and litigious society. Second, every detail of the facility sportscape must be managed with an eye toward customer comfort and satisfaction. Third, effective food service management requires innovation and variety to satisfy today's upscale fan base. Finally, crowd control and fan safety are vital elements of event marketing management. Sports organizations that effectively manage the experience in the stands can be successful despite whatever quality of play occurs on the field.

Create Sponsorship Partners

8

The process of selling sponsorships is not all that dissimilar from other selling processes. It is similar to selling media (e.g., radio and TV advertising), as corporations are considering sponsorships among competing media vehicles in their overall media and marketing plans. Successful sponsorship salespeople often start their careers in media sales, giving them a deeper understanding of how sponsorships integrate into an overall corporate marketing communications plan. What makes sponsorships different is the high need for creative selling—in the truest sense of the word. The needs of corporate sponsors may require you to sell something that you hadn't even thought of before, let alone sold before. Creative selling in sponsorships might include the creation of a live marketing event such as the Red Bull Flugtag, wherein participants strap "themselves to totally outrageous home-made, human

Source: Courtesy of Red Bull Flugtag USA.

powered flying machines and launch themselves off a 30-foot ramp into the wild blue yonder, or alternatively straight into the water" (www.redbullflugtagusa.com). Conversely, other corporate sponsors may be pleased with a large sign on the outfield wall at a baseball game. But not very many.

Sales executives of successful properties realize that they are really doing much more than just selling sponsorships. David Stivers, executive vice president of Pebble Beach Golf, explains the critical elements of what Pebble Beach does to attract and select sponsors:

> Our marketing arm acts as an agency for the sponsor to help them activate. We are creative and find ways to expose our guests to the sponsor's product or services. And, we are flexible. Every sponsor has a different need and different strategy for connecting with their customers. We provide a venue to help facilitate that connection and we have a customer base that is a very attractive target group to sponsors.
>
> The most important terms in a sponsorship are cash, brand fit, ability for the sponsor to enhance our guest experience (e.g., luxury cars, quality golf equipment, etc.), good fit with the people (i.e., they understand golf and how Pebble Beach works), and committed funds to activate the sponsorship. This last point is key because the sponsorship will fail if the sponsor does not spend to support the program.

As the Pebble Beach example illustrates, your primary task in selling and managing a sponsorship is to help the sponsor activate the brand in the minds of consumers. Activation refers to putting the sponsorship into action. Sponsorships are not static (e.g., signs/billboards). Fans looking at signs or ads is *not* activation. Activation occurs when fans recognize and make the connection between the sponsor and the property, allowing for fan identification and affinity with the property to transfer to the sponsor. Activation plays an integral role in the sponsor's leveraging the sponsorship tie-in within the sponsor's overall advertising or promotional campaign. The role of the property is to activate the benefits offered by the sponsor in the minds of the property's customers (the fans).

This chapter provides an in-depth examination of the five P's of creative selling that differentiate the context and content of selling sponsorships from the context and content of selling other types of products and services.[1] We begin by explaining the importance of a

---

[1]If you are not familiar with the basic steps in professional selling covered in introductory marketing and sales courses, these are easily accessed elsewhere (cf., http://www.sba.gov/library/pubs/mt-1.pdf).

partnership approach to sponsorship sales, followed by the remaining four P's of creative sponsorship sales: Prospecting, Preparing, Personalizing, and Problem solving.

Partnering

Truly successful sponsorships occur when both the property and the sponsor achieve their objectives. Although some sponsorship deals are still made on the whim of corporate executives without clearly specified corporate objectives, the vast majority of corporate sponsorships today are based on the ability of the property to deliver value equal to or exceeding the level required in the marketing plans of the sponsor. Sports properties are less frequently developing preconceived sponsorship packages to sell to sponsors, as if they were taking a package or product right off the shelf ("OK, we've got the gold, silver, and bronze sponsorships. Would you like fries with that?"). Rather, successful properties are taking more of a partnership approach to selling sponsorships that seeks to offer packages of benefits suited specifically to the needs of the sponsor.

In the not too distant past, properties approached sponsorship sales with a relatively generic value proposition. Sponsorships may still be sold in this manner. However, the use of a generic value proposition is transactional in nature and is primarily production-oriented or selling-oriented ("Let me sell you one of these here sponsorships . . .") rather than customer or partner-oriented. Too often these types of sponsorships are really looking for donations out of a public service commitment or other noneconomic motivation (such as the CEO is loyal to the team or the event). For instance, the Madison, Wisconsin Race for the Cure (www.madisonraceforthecure.com) has the following sponsorship levels:

PRESENTING SPONSOR	$40,000+
PLATINUM	$20,000
DIAMOND	$10,000
GOLD	$5,000
SILVER	$2,500
BRONZE	$1,000
PASTA DINNER	$500

The platinum sponsor receives a corporate logo on race t-shirts (8,000) and bibs, race applications (25,000), event posters, advertising media (radio, TV, print), ½ page newspaper ad in the special feature section of local paper, logo and links on race Web site, 15 free race admissions, sampling opportunities at registration site, recognition at dinner and ceremonies, signage at water stops, 10 company banners and a booth at the race site, complimentary on-site breast health workshop, and opportunities for volunteers to work the race. How do you suppose this standardized offering of media and hospitality services is suitable to the needs of a given sponsor?

Suppose that the local Whole Foods Market (a 2005 Platinum sponsor) is most interested in driving traffic to its natural and organic foods supermarket stores by acquiring the names of race entrants and sending them direct-response emails with coupons to its stores. Where is the opportunity to accomplish that objective within this package? Is the value of that service worth $20,000? It may be worth more if Whole Foods is allowed to be the exclusive sponsor of the give-away goodie-bags provided to all runners and attendees at the race site and the expected return of the sponsored event exceeds $20,000 for Whole Foods Market. The sponsor may have no interest in having signage at water stops or some of the other features of the package—thereby costing the property more by promising features that are not necessary to make the deal. The point is that a generic value proposition doesn't recognize the fact that sponsors have different objectives with different means necessary to reach those objectives.

Figure 8.1 illustrates the differences in perceptions between properties and sponsors.[2] The Madison Race for the Cure offers a generic value proposition to sponsors. The extent to which they are willing to adapt the sponsorship package to the needs of the sponsor may mean that they are less transaction-oriented and more partner-oriented in their approach. Yet, their starting point is that sponsors have generic needs (such as brand awareness) and they have designed their packages accordingly.

In contrast, a partnership approach recognizes the unique need of the sponsor as its starting point for developing a sponsorship package that offers a unique value proposition suited specifically to the sponsor. Such an approach requires adaptive or consultative selling that relies upon extensive research and spending time with the sponsor inquiring, listening, and understanding how the sponsorship can be integrated into the sponsor's overall marketing communications plan.

[2]Model adapted from Pels, J., Coviello, N.E., and Brodie, R.J. 2000. Integrating Transactional and Relational Marketing Exchange: A Pluralistic Perspective. *Journal of Marketing Theory and Practice* 8 (Summer): 11–20.

Figure 8.1

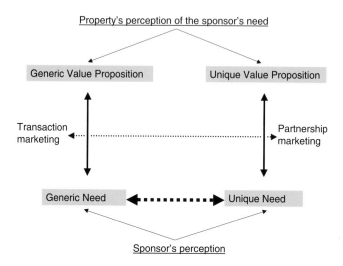

Sponsorship Selling Dyad

So, what makes a good partner? A good partnership is based on trust that is determined by your long-term commitment, honesty, benevolence, and the special relational benefits you provide the sponsor.[3] Interestingly, these are pretty much the same characteristics that make good friends or good marriages.

Long-Term Commitment

A partnership approach takes a long-term perspective because the sponsorship is meant to become part of the long-term marketing communications program of the sponsor. The property is not just interested in selling this year's sponsorship packages (viz., a transactional approach). Instead, the intent is to develop a partnership that lasts through year-after-year renewals of the sponsorship. In fact, prominent properties (e.g., Major League Baseball teams) typically sign sponsorship deals for three years at a time. Title sponsorships are likely to be much longer (e.g., Invesco Field at Mile High Stadium in Denver, $120 million over 20 years). Corporate sponsors develop integrated marketing communications plans that are intended to extend for

[3]See Roberts, Keith, Varki, Sajeev, and Brodie, Rod. 2003. Measuring the Quality of Relationships in Consumer Services: An Empirical Study. *European Journal of Marketing* 37 (1/2): 169–196.

years—not just the three or four months of one given sports season. Further, it typically takes more than just one season or one event for fans to make a strong connection between the property and the sponsor. Consequently, successful properties must develop sponsorship opportunities that can be an integral part of the corporation's media and marketing spending plan.

At the heart of a partnership approach is the notion that you are willing to put the needs of the partner at least at an equal level as your own. Your first objective is to meet their needs, dealing with them in the same way you would like to be treated if you were in their position. Some quick-witted readers will recognize that this is not an original idea. However, following the Golden Rule in sponsorship sales is relatively new, as the nebulous nature of what one gets for one's sponsorship dollars has made it relatively easy for the seller to take advantage of the buyer in the short term. Yet, the properties that hope to get sponsorship renewals at the end of the contract will want to make sure that sponsors are completely satisfied with their investments. If you see a frequent turnover in major sponsorships of a sporting event, you can bet that the property is not living up to its end of the bargain—either by overselling or underservicing the sponsor.

Sponsors are more likely to agree to long-term relationships when the property provides an offer of exclusivity, which is typically offered to anchor (also called dominant or primary) sponsors. Exclusivity means that the property will only accept one sponsorship within a given product/service category, as when the San Antonio Spurs opted to have only one telecommunications company as a sponsor (AT&T) and excluded others (Verizon, Alltel, etc.). Some properties modify the exclusivity such that they have exclusive anchor sponsors, but have secondary or lower tier sponsors within the same category. Obviously, this is not as attractive to anchor sponsors, as it dilutes the advantage they have as a primary sponsor of the property. Consequently, nonexclusive deals will not be able to maximize the revenue from an individual anchor sponsor.

Properties may be able to generate more total revenue from multiple nonexclusive deals (e.g., the Spurs' sponsors include McDonald's, Pizza Hut, and What-A-Burger in the food service category). However, the real difficulty lies in activating these brands in a meaningful way to fans. Sponsors within the same category of the same property find themselves competing with each other for retail participation and undermining the value of each other's offers in the consumer's mind. As a result, the property may be able to offer only limited periods during the season for a given sponsor's promotion (e.g., McDonald's,

Pizza Hut, and What-A-Burger each get 4 weeks during the season to run a tie-in promotion with the Spurs and their respective stores). While some properties may be able to handle such polygamous relationships, it clearly creates a strain with multiple partners competing directly with each other for the limited time and attention available from the property.

Properties typically have an exclusivity threshold that requires that any exclusive sponsorship deals include a minimal sponsorship investment. For most professional franchises, that threshold is one million dollars. Sponsors will nearly always want to have exclusive rights to market through the property, but are not necessarily willing to pay the price to play at that level. You must be prepared to handle this objection from potential sponsors, as they will want to know who the competing sponsors are and what kinds of deals they have with the property. It is important to understand that a motivating factor for many sponsors is the desire to block out or preempt competitors. At the end of the day, the sponsor wants to know how it has gained a competitive advantage by engaging in this partnership.

Honesty

The second mark of a good partnership is that your partner has trust in your honesty. That means that you can be trusted to be honest about problems, you have high integrity, you are sincere, and what you say is trustworthy. When trust erodes due to a partner not being able to believe in the words spoken (or printed in the contract), then you have a break-up waiting to happen.

From the sponsor's perspective, you need to be certain that you can trust in the honesty of the property to perform the contract. World-caliber speed skater Shani Davis did not remove the logo of a former sponsor from the leg of his racing suit and replace it with Qwest, the official sponsor of U.S. speed skating, despite warnings of the violation. Qwest terminated the contract. Obviously, the dishonesty of the skater did nothing to help Qwest's reputation or brand image, not to speak of their ability to make wise sponsorship decisions.

From the property's perspective, you must be careful to not be overly optimistic on your ability to deliver as a salesperson—particularly when it comes to promising such things as player appearances or other features over which you have limited control. In fact, most team properties avoid including player appearances and endorsements due to the difficulty of fulfillment. Such deals are typically made separately with the player's agent. The bottom line is that people want to deal with others who are honest. Besides, research has consistently shown that honest salespeople are more successful than those who are not.[4]

Benevolence

The third mark of a good partnership is that your partner trusts in your benevolence. Your partner knows that you are concerned first for his or her welfare, even before your own. They know that when they share their problems with you that you will respond with understanding and seek to help them solve their problems (rather than stand on or demand your own rights). Your partners know that they can count on you to only take actions that will be to their benefit. This also means that you will take actions beneficial to the partner even when something new comes up that you didn't originally plan for or that both partners overlooked.

Sport is by its very nature full of unexpected occurrences. Winners become losers from one season to the next. Players get injured. Players perform poorly. Players do stupid things ("I used a clear substance the trainer gave me. I didn't know it was steroids."). Sponsorship contracts often (and should) include stipulations regarding marketing performance, such as guaranteed television ratings or other objective measures, that may be affected by how well the player or team may be playing that season.

As partners, the property and sponsor will need to adjust aspects of the contract as unforeseen changes occur. Some parties make formal changes or accommodations in the contract. Others provide make-goods to the satisfaction of the sponsor in a less formal manner. In either case, the partners must be able to trust in the benevolence of the other. Good corporate partners typically recognize that the occasional bad year is offset by other good years and are willing to take a long-term view of the relationship. As an example, Pizza Hut decided to stick with Baylor University as a major sports sponsor in 2003 following hardships in the basketball program (i.e., a recruiting scandal was uncovered in the aftermath of a shooting death of a player by his teammate). Had Pizza Hut terminated its contract at that time, it would have forgone the benefits it received from its sponsorship deals during Baylor's winning the NCAA national cham-

---

[4]See Brooks, Bill. 2000. How Important Is Trust in Making a Sale? *The American Salesman* 45 (April): 21–24; and Dion, Paul A. and Banting, Peter. 1988. Industrial Supplier-Buyer Negotiations. *Industrial Marketing Management* 17 (February): 43–47.

pionship in women's basketball and men's tennis in the following year.

Relational Benefits

When a corporate salesperson acts in a manner to generate trust, the individuals responsible for making the corporate sponsorship decisions will feel an emotional attachment with the sports property due to their relationship with the salesperson. They will desire to continue the sponsorship deal because they like being associated with the people they work with when they correspond with the sports property. In fact, they genuinely enjoy the relationships they have with the sales and marketing executives of the sports property. This is no different than in any relationship. We enjoy being with those people we can trust. We avoid being with those people who seem to only want to use us.

Sponsors, or the people representing the sponsor, benefit from positive relationships in at least three ways:[5]

1. *Confidence benefits*—the sponsor has comfort in knowing what to expect from the property and has no anxiety when meeting with you.
2. *Social benefits*—the sponsor becomes emotionally attached to the people working for the property; employees of the sponsor and the property are comfortable and familiar with each other; and close friendships are created.
3. *Special treatment benefits*—the sponsor receives better prices or concessions, faster service, and individualized attention.

Your goal as a salesperson is to generate close personal relationships with corporate sponsors that enable effective partnerships. When you do that, you will excel in building relationships that last and succeed for both you and the corporate partner. In interviews with executives from professional sports franchises (e.g., Dallas Cowboys, Houston Texans, San Antonio Spurs, Dallas Mavericks, Texas Rangers, Dallas Stars, etc.) who thrive on generating sponsorship revenue, each one makes it clear that successful partnerships develop because the primary individual responsible for the corporate account has generated trust

---

[5]Hennig-Thurau, Thorsten, Gwinner, Kevin P., and Gremler, Dwayne D. 2002. Understanding Relationship Marketing Outcomes: An Integration of Relational Benefits and Relationship Quality. *Journal of Service Research* 4 (February): 230–247.

through a personal social relationship with the corporate client. The personal relationship enables sponsors to work through the myriad of issues that are bound to arise in activation and fulfillment. Absent this relationship, sponsors are unwilling to invest in sponsorship deals in any substantive way. Corporate executives are putting their own necks on the line when they invest in sponsorships (i.e., they have to report to superiors or stockholders) and they want to know that you have their best interests at heart.

In summary, partnerships are strengthened to the degree that they are characterized as having (1) long-term exclusive commitment, (2) honesty, (3) benevolence, and (4) special relational benefits accorded to each party in the partnership. That means that no matter which side of the property-sponsor (husband-wife) equation you represent, you should exhibit these qualities as well as look for partners (a partner) with similar qualities. This leads us to the second step in selling sponsorships—prospecting.

Prospecting

When considering prospective sponsors, properties must consider selectivity/fit criteria and the product/service categories most likely to be interested in sponsoring sporting events.

Selectivity

Scott Brubaker, former VP of Marketing with the Arizona Diamondbacks noted that you should look for "partners that can help you move the product [Diamondbacks baseball] forward in the eyes of the marketplace. Sports organizations should look to build, and be careful not to dilute, their own value and brand equity through sponsorships." The Diamondbacks evaluate potential sponsors on the basis of these three questions:

1. Who is prominent in the community?
2. In what other ways (besides sponsorships) do they market, advertise, and promote their products?
3. How will they use our relationship to sell their products?

Your objective in prospecting is to find sponsors who not only help the property through a cash infusion, but who also positively position the property's brand in the minds of fans. You may be tempted to make a sponsorship deal that brings in needed revenue but that does not represent a good brand fit with the property. The point is that as you search for partners, you should have at least some standards. You're not easy; rather, you are willing to be selective in building up your good name and your property's as well.

The potential brand fit of the sponsor with the property is determined on the basis of three dimensions:

1. Relatedness
2. Image
3. Prominence

Relatedness refers to the extent to which the sponsor and property are perceived as belonging together. Fans will recognize and recall sponsors more easily if there is a natural connection between the sponsor's brand and the property. For instance, Gatorade is a natural sponsor for the NFL because of its high relatedness. Levitra, on the other hand, is a less obvious sponsor for the NFL, despite the fact that Levitra claims to be "committed to generating awareness of men's health issues and excitement in the NFL."[6] Due to its relatedness, odds are that you would have recalled or guessed that Gatorade is an NFL sponsor and had little or no recall of Levitra's NFL sponsorship. In fact, even if Levitra spent as much money as Gatorade does leveraging their official sponsorship of the NFL, relatively few fans would make the connection between Levitra and the NFL (compared to Gatorade and the NFL).

The managerial practicality is that you will have a much better chance of implementing a successful sponsorship package with a brand that is somehow related to the property or the event. Importantly, relatedness can be created for brands that are not inherently related. The corporate marketing executives of the Memphis Redbirds produced high sponsorship recall for Hunter Fans with creative sponsorship activation. The sponsorship package included an in-game presentation of the "Hunter Fan of the Game," wherein a fan was selected to receive a ceiling fan. At the same point in each home game, a fan was announced and shown receiving a Hunter ceiling fan on the digital scoreboard by the roaming game MC. Through this creative activation to increase the perceived relatedness of the sponsor to the property, Hunter Fans achieved very high recall of its sponsorship by Redbirds fans. So it is possible to create relatedness, but you are

---

[6]Please see http://www.levitra.com/consumer/promo.htm

fighting an uphill battle if the brand has no natural association with the property.

Image. Virtually every sports property relies upon families as a primary target audience. OK, maybe not roller derby, the defunct XFL, or the WWE; but every major sports property relies upon families as a major target market. Sports properties project the image of a place where families can enjoy entertainment together. The images of some sponsors are not appropriate fits with the image of a family atmosphere. Given your innate intelligence, you are quick enough to deduce some of the more obvious examples of sponsors that would generate potential image problems. However, what may not be a particular image problem at some venues may be problems elsewhere. For example, at the college level, many universities refuse alcohol sponsors because it would indicate that the sponsor is targeting underage drinkers (most college students are under 21).

Failure to be selective in the property's sponsors may lead to difficult ethical dilemmas that could have been preempted with more selective screening and prospecting of sponsors. Because of a lack of care at this stage, as well as a vague sponsorship contract, one corporate marketing executive found his organization spending an undue amount of time regulating a sponsor's advertising copy that did not fit with the desired image of the property. The sponsor, a maker of hair and body care products containing hemp and cannabis, wanted to run ads in the game program with a graphic of a hemp leaf and the tagline, "A higher state of hair care." While we agree that this is a clever ad, we agree with the property that such an ad would likely send the wrong signal to its family-oriented audience. We also agree that people who are willing to spend upwards of $40 for this brand's sun-tanning lotion containing natural cannabis sativa hemp seed extract may have been using variants of the ingredients for prolonged time periods.

Prominence. The more prominent the brand name of the sponsor in the minds of consumers, the more likely it is that they will be able to correctly identify the brand as a sponsor. Prominent brand names (e.g., VISA, FedEx, McDonald's, etc.) are familiar to consumers and are thus easier for them to recognize and recall as sponsors. Further, fans are aware that prominent brands are frequent sports sponsors, so it makes sense for them to be a sponsor of a given sports property. Conversely, unfamiliar brand names, such as Shamrock Farms (official MLB online sponsor) are more difficult for fans to process and recall. In the case of Shamrock Farms, it also suffers from a lack of relevance, making it doubly difficult for fans to make the association with MLB. So, Shamrock Farms may benefit if it is able to sell its ice cream at MLB parks, but is unlikely to get much of a return in terms of increased brand awareness or loyalty because fans are unlikely to make the connection.

As you prospect and profile potential sponsors, you must recognize your potential obligation as a partner to help fulfill their marketing objectives. Sponsors that are less prominent in the marketplace (and/or less related) require extra effort just to get fans familiar with who they are and what they offer—let alone to build the association between the property and the sponsor that allows for a transfer of fan affinity from the property to the sponsoring brand. Such sponsorship deals can succeed with creative approaches that rely upon increasing the relatedness (e.g., Goody's Fast Relief Zone at NASCAR events), but the task would be even easier with a prominent brand (i.e., Excedrin's Fast Relief Zone). Goody's, by the way, makes a headache powder—which we presume is applied topically.

Product/Service Categories

From the property's perspective, your better sponsorship prospects will fit in terms of relatedness, image, and prominence (RIP). From the sponsor's perspective, sports properties tend to be good media and promotion vehicles for companies that produce

1. frequently purchased packaged goods and services, that are
2. mass-marketed to consumers in highly competitive markets, and are
3. frequently consumed at sporting events.

Frequently consumed and mass-marketed products are well-suited for retail promotions, facilitated through tie-ins with the sports property and its corporate partners. Primary sponsors of sports properties typically have some or all of these attributes. Secondary categories tend to include more services, as well as other retailers, that have upscale clientele similar to those attending professional sports. Often services such as these are interested in obtaining customer prospect data via the sponsorship. Ameriquest, an aggressive home mortgage company, has become a major sports sponsor for this reason, as frequent attenders of sporting events are more likely to be homeowners than are nonattenders.

The table below contains the primary and secondary product/service categories likely to be involved in sports sponsorships. A good starting point in prospecting is to list (potential) sponsors in each of these categories to determine any obvious holes in the sponsorship line-up.

Primary categories	Secondary categories
Auto	Grocery Markets
Beer	Quick Service Restaurants (QSR)
Candy/Snacks	Airlines
Soda	Media
Telecom	Office Supplies/Overnight Delivery
Home Improvement	Mass Market Retailers
Banks/Financial	Local Corporations
Sporting Goods and Retailers	Insurance

Food (snacks) and beverages (beer, soft drinks) are always good prospects because they can increase sales volume by obtaining the distribution or pouring rights at the stadium or arena as part of the sponsorship agreement. These products are also highly related in the minds of fans, because they associate going to the sporting event with what they eat and drink at the game.

Home improvement centers such as Lowe's or Home Depot and automobile dealers are typically interested in sports properties due to the demographics of frequent game attenders (middle-to-upper income, middle-aged, home and car owners). Banks, financial institutions (like Ameriquest or MBNA), and telecommunication companies (like AT&T, Nextel, Verizon, or Qwest) have substantial advertising and promotion budgets that allow them to leverage their investment, most often by offering customer incentives (backpacks or shirts with team logo) to sign-ups for new accounts at sporting events.

Sporting goods manufacturers (Nike, Adidas, Reebok, etc.) are primary sponsors, often at the league level as well as the team level. Sporting goods retailers, compared to other retailers, are primary sponsors due to the high relatedness to the sports property. Sports fans attending sporting events have very similar psychographics to buyers of sporting goods, making it easy for a company like the Sports Authority to reach their target market and get their attention via the sports property.

Secondary categories tend to be either less frequently consumed and/or have more segmented markets. Many of those in the secondary categories are regional brands or operate primarily in limited geographic regions. HEB grocery stores dominate the southwest and are good sponsorship prospects in that region, but not elsewhere. In this case, HEB sponsors sporting events as a way to foster good marketing relationships with their vendors and to drive traffic to their stores. HEB, for instance, offers hospitality to build relationships with its vendors (e.g., Frito-Lay) at Houston Texans games while also giving the vendors opportunities for joint marketing programs at those games (HEB tailgate events).

Other secondary categories likely to sponsor sporting events include airlines, quick service restaurants, media, office supplies, mass market retailers, insurance companies, and local corporations. Airlines have major hubs in given regions and will likely be a title sponsor for one property, but will only do lower-level deals in other markets. While Wendy's, Burger King, McDonald's, and Pizza Hut are frequent sports sponsors at upper and mid-tier levels, other regional chains may be good prospects for mid- and lower-level sponsorship deals. Media, such as local newspapers and TV or radio stations that broadcast or report on the events are obvious sponsors—but are unlikely to be anchor sponsors. Corporations, legal offices, and the like make up a large proportion of suite and season ticket holders, thereby offering office supplies stores like OfficeMax or Staples a well-defined and reachable target audience. Mass market retailers of less-frequently consumed products, such as Circuit City or Target, frequently eye sports properties as good promotional vehicles because selected product categories (e.g., big screen TVs) are purchased more frequently by 25–49-year-old males. Local corporations, including the regional offices of national insurance firms (e.g., State Farm), may be interested in sponsorships that facilitate hospitality opportunities and events for its salespeople. State Farm agents can use their allotment of tickets to invite clients to a pregame event and a game to get to know clients and to solidify relationships.

Now that you understand the partnership approach to sponsorship sales and have developed a prospect list, you must prepare before making the sales call on the prospect.

Preparing

All sales training programs begin with knowing everything you can about the product or service you are selling. In that sense, sponsorship sales are no different. You must understand the inventory your property has to offer. However, unlike selling a car, appliances or other manufactured goods, you must keep in mind that you are free to modify or create new inventory to meet the needs of your sponsor. Properties often have lists of common sponsorship inventory (e.g., visit http://www.nashvillesounds.com/stadium/sponsorship.asp), along

Table 8.1

Sponsorship Components	
Visual/Audio Media	**Product/Business Promotion**
Presenting or naming rights	Cross promotions—networked promotions
Signage/venue branding exposure	Events-within-events
Licensing/right to use of trademarks/logos	High profile pre-event marketing
ID in promotional materials	Customer recruitment (database building)
Program ads	Exhibiting
Broadcast media ads or mentions	Trial/sampling/product launch
PA announcements or scoreboard zip ads	
Client Entertainment/Hospitality	**Research**
Parties	Pre-event research
Lunches	Event surveys
Special dinners (including athletes)	Postevent research
Private meeting facilities	
Skyboxes/seats/tickets	

with associated media numbers for sponsors to review. Traditional sponsorship inventory encompasses at least four primary categories (see Table 8.1): Visual/Audio Media, Client Entertainment/Hospitality, Product/Business Promotion, and Research.

Visual/Audio Media. If you are thinking about what you can offer potential sponsors primarily in terms of how you can get their company name in front of people's eyeballs, then you are probably trying to sell signage for the local little league field. If you understand that your objective is to help the sponsor reach the sponsor's marketing objective, then you recognize that the visual/audio media elements available to sponsors must be presented as a vehicle that complements (or even drives) the other elements in the sponsor's marketing communication strategy. For example, the marketing objective of Southwest Airlines is to increase customer traffic to www.southwest.com. Southwest sees sports sponsorships as a way to leverage their media dollars to reach a footprint (or target audience) similar to that of the properties it sponsors (i.e., upscale, frequent fliers). Southwest also realizes that fan affinity for sports teams offers a good opportunity to connect with their customers at an emotional level. To reach their objective and their audience, Southwest Airlines seeks four basic things in a sponsorship deal:

1. Broadcast rights during game telecasts (with guaranteed ratings), to air their unique ("Want to get away?") commercials
2. Camera-visible signage within the venue
3. Game-day (a) communications and (b) promotions
4. The right to use league/team logos in their advertising (to connect with fan affinity)

How could you sell a sponsorship package to Southwest if you didn't know this? Answer: You couldn't. So, how could you discover this information in the preparation stage? First, you research the current marketing efforts of the prospective client. For larger companies like Southwest, a quick trip online will likely turn up examples and articles regarding their advertising campaign (e.g., "Want to Get Away?"). You can even learn about their ad campaign history on their Web site (http://www.southwest.com/about_swa/netads.html). Other sources include corporate reports you can obtain from the company. Second, make appointments or calls to visit with other properties that are sponsored by the prospective sponsor. In the case of Southwest Airlines, you could visit with corporate marketing executives with the Baltimore Orioles, Texas Rangers, Houston Astros, Dallas Stars, Buffalo Sabres, Houston Rockets, Orlando Magic, and San Antonio Spurs, to learn about Southwest's approach to sports sponsorship deals. Third, after you've done the first two steps, you make your first call to visit with individuals at Southwest Airlines sports marketing agency (Camelot Communications) to get to know the principals in the decision-making process for sponsorships. During this conversation you might learn that Southwest has no interest in naming rights (unlike its competitors Delta, American, US Airways, American West, Continental, and even Midwest Airlines Center in Milwaukee), due to the fact that (a) it is not the way Southwest wants to build an emotional bond with its customers and (b) naming rights aren't seen as helping reach their objective given the necessary financial commitment.

The point to remember here is that you are preparing—preparing for a partnership relationship, not just a one-night stand. Your prospective partner will appreciate the fact that you cared enough to find out about the company's marketing history, interests, and current corporate relationships and are now willing to listen to the plans they have in order to discern how your property's assets or inventory could be integrated to facilitate the reaching of their marketing goals. Showing up at a prospective sponsor's doorstep without proper preparation is like asking for a date at 6:30 p.m. on Saturday night—for 7 p.m. Saturday. My guess is that you're not that good and they aren't that desperate.

Client Entertainment/Hospitality. One of the most important elements of your sponsorship inventory for business-to-business customers is hospitality and entertainment. For business to business companies, the motivation for the sponsorship has more to do with enabling and developing business relationships, including between the sponsor and other corporate partners with the property. For instance, the UPS brand is well known ("What can Brown do for you?"), so increasing brand-awareness is not the primary objective of its sponsorships. Rather, UPS sponsors the San Antonio Spurs because they are interested in opportunities for (a) UPS salespeople to invite clients to a Spurs game to develop relationships, and (b) partnering with other corporate partners of the Spurs who might currently be using other overnight delivery services. Consequently, the availability of quality season ticket seats and suites are important to these sponsors, as well as opportunities to meet and network with other corporate partners of the property.

Properties can facilitate the use of hospitality services in the sales programs of sponsors by hosting parties, lunches, and dinners in the property's facilities. Private meetings or parties can be held at the stadium or arena for sponsors, as when the Houston Texans hosted Miller Lite's "Cheerleaders Halloween Bash." The newest sports facilities are designed to accommodate corporate meetings and other creative facility use, allowing expensive facilities to be used beyond game day and increasing the availability of valuable inventory desired by sponsors.

Source: Courtesy of Houston Texans.

Product/Business Promotion. Corporate sponsors with a high interest in hospitality are also likely to be interested in developing cross-promotions or networked promotions. As sponsors develop relationships between themselves, they are able to create memorable and effective cross-promotions. Cross-promotions occur when two or more sponsors promote each other via the property. For example, Coca-Cola partners with HEB grocery stores to promote its game to be an "Honorary Team Captain" of the Houston Texans. Fans can only register by going to HEB and down the aisle to the special Coca-Cola display in the store. Cross-promotions of this kind tend to get more bang for the buck, because fans are attracted to the promotion at multiple interest points (e.g., soft drinks, grocery shopping, love for the team, etc.) that would be difficult to achieve on the merit of a single corporate identity in the advertisement. This promotion can be networked across partners and their media buys, such that the ads appear in game-day programs and scoreboards, in-store at HEB, online for all participating entities, and other traditional media. Such deals are typically a win-win solution for the partners, as the Texans also benefit from the promotion of the team that is a by-product of the advertising campaigns of each of the sponsors.

Source: Courtesy of Houston Texans.

Corporate marketers are increasingly turning toward an event within an event or "live marketing" to break through all the clutter of messages pelted at consumers via traditional media. Combined with the emotional impact of fan affinity with the team, sponsors increase their ability to prompt consumers to immediately try or buy the sponsor's product at well-executed live marketing events. The week prior to the Super Bowl, and including the Super Bowl (e.g., halftime), is nothing but one live-marketing event after another (see http:// firstcoastphotos.com/tusuperbowl/ for examples). More realistic for most properties are events such as post-game concerts or competitions held at the sports venue, combining fan interests (e.g., rock bands and sports) into one event. For instance, Krispy Kreme might be interested in sponsoring a concert by the "Bag of Donuts" band (www. bagofdonuts.com) at a New Orleans Hornets game to promote its latest new flavor, wherein fans can get special game/concert tickets at Krispy Kreme stores. An interesting pre-game event might be a donut-eating contest. Or not. Anyway, I think you get the point. Properties can help meet sponsors' needs to break through the advertising clutter when introducing new products or services with live marketing.

Live marketing events hosted by sports properties are often part of a large-scale pre-event marketing campaign wherein the sporting event (and the event within the event) provides an attractive focal point to reach the sponsor's desired target audience. Pre-event and event marketing campaigns can be designed as a customer recruitment tool and as a means to build the database of prospective customers for both the sponsor and the property. Sponsors frequently host tailgate parties prior to football games that are heavily promoted prior to the event. Interested fans may register for more information online prior to the event or register at the event. Such registrations should include the opportunity to collect pertinent customer information for the sponsor and the property. For example, Verizon Wireless could collect information from customers regarding current cell phone usage and perceptions when fans attend the tailgate party they host with the Houston Texans.

Research. The majority of professional sports properties do not spend a great deal of time or money providing research for sponsors to measure outcomes for at least three reasons. First, those corporate sponsors truly interested in measuring the results from their sponsorships are likely to be conducting their own research to evaluate their sponsorship deals. Second, measuring outcomes or effects of sponsorships is a tricky business for properties. If research is conducted for the sponsor, the property is obligated to communicate the results. Unflattering research results for the sponsor may lead to renegotiation

Source: Courtesy of Houston Texans.

or canceling of the sponsorship. Third, few professional properties have the in-house expertise to measure sponsorship results.

Nonetheless, for those sponsors interested in measuring something besides TV rating points or sales volume, carefully planned pre-event, event, and post-event research can reveal areas needed to improve the sponsorship deal from year to year. If the property and sponsor indeed see themselves as partners, then conducting valuation research on the sponsorship becomes easier because both parties want to know the results so that the sponsor can continually find ways to better reach their objectives. The next chapter outlines methods to capture sponsorship results. At this point, suffice it to say that if a sponsor is spending millions of dollars on an anchor sponsor, it follows that the sponsor would want to work with the property to ascertain the return on this investment. Increasingly, sponsorship executives are being held accountable for expenditures and are required to present reliable financial data to back up what they are doing. The more that the property can do to facilitate this research, the more valuable the property is in the partnership.

In addition to valuation-type research, properties can offer the opportunity for the sponsor to conduct research before, during, or after the event on issues unrelated to the sponsorship. Dr. Pepper may be interested in finding out what customers think of its Cherry-Vanilla Diet Dr. Pepper, either through taste tests and/or other attitudinal measures. Sporting events, such as the AT&T Cotton Bowl, make such research easy to conduct as fans are easily accessible before and after the event.

Personalizing

If you have been paying attention so far in this chapter, then you realize that anyone who comes to a corporate sponsor with a prepackaged sponsorship deal off the shelf is about as intellectually challenged as the folks that tried to sell us Harley Davidson Perfume, Colgate Kitchen Entrees, or Earring Magic Ken—Barbie's once-significant other[7] (which is still available on eBay as of this writing).

As we discussed regarding preparation, you do need to have an idea of the inventory you have to offer. However, the inventory value of a property is completely in the eyes of the beholder. Inventory value depends upon what it can achieve for the sponsor. Siemens, who provides communications technology and other business infrastructure needs, is an anchor sponsor of the Houston Texans. The sponsorship included $26 million of construction business at Reliant Stadium, as well as the opportunity to bring prospective clients on tours of the stadium to see Siemens' quality work firsthand. Siemens estimates that it brings in over $20 million annually due to its relationship with the Texans. How much does Siemens value this sponsorship? What if you offered to sell an anchor sponsorship to them for $1 million when they were willing to pay more?

Offering a prepackaged sponsorship assumes that you know the sponsor's objectives and how the sponsor wants to achieve them. Consequently, as a good partner, following prospecting and preparing, you must personalize the sponsorship package to reach the sponsor's marketing objectives. In order to personalize the sponsorship package, you must understand the objectives of the sponsor and then find creative activation means to achieve the objective with the inventory you have or can make available. At times, the sponsor may have difficulty ver-

---

[7]For more badly conceived products, see Haig, Matt. 2003. *Brand Failures: The Truth About the 100 Biggest Branding Mistakes of All Time*. UK: Kogan Page.

balizing or knowing the precise objectives of the sponsorship—particularly if motivated by personal goals (viz., association with pro sports, tickets, suites, etc.). This means that you must be familiar with common marketing objectives and may need to help the sponsor clarify the purpose and benefits sought from the sponsorship. Sooner or later, for instance, someone at corporate headquarters is going to ask who and why someone decided to spend £100 million for Emirates Airlines to sponsor Arsenal's new football (soccer) stadium in the U.K. Odds are that it will be Sheikh Ahmed bin Saeed Al-Maktoum, Chairman of Emirates, who was the one who agreed to the deal. At that point, particularly if you are Keith Edelman (Managing Director of the Arsenal Football Club), you will want to have a clear explanation of the objectives and measurable results that allow you to maintain the sponsorship.

Sponsorship Objectives

Research from IEG, Inc. (www.sponsorship.com, 2001) reveals that sponsors are most likely to sponsor events to increase brand loyalty (68%), create brand awareness or visibility (65%), or to change/reinforce brand image (59%). Figure 8.2 reveals other likely sponsorship goals. Not surprisingly, then, sponsors are most likely to be interested in exclusivity (68%), signage (53%), and other means to communicate their selling message to fans (see Figure 8.3). Some sponsoring companies have a very clear set of objectives and an associated sponsorship plan to activate the brand to achieve these objectives. Unfortunately, many do not. Let's start with how to deal with those who do not have clear sponsorship plans.

Figure 8.2

Sponsorship Objectives. *Source:* IEG, Inc.

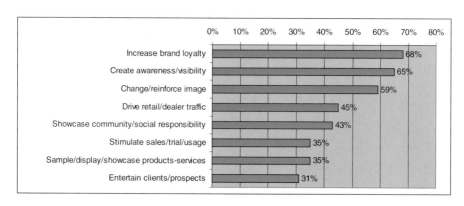

Figure 8.3

Importance of Sponsorship Components. *Source:* IEG, Inc.

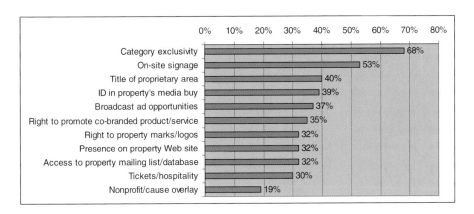

Some properties, such as the Dallas Cowboys, work with an advertising agency to integrate or develop a cohesive sponsorship plan for all of its sponsors. The Cowboys act as a marketing agency to ensure that the sponsor is getting all it desires from the sponsorship. The expense for the ad agency is incorporated into the sponsorship contract and is standard for all sponsors who would like to be associated with the Cowboys. The Cowboys produce a high-quality personalized end-of-season report for each sponsor (on multi-media CD and yearbook) containing proof-of-performance (pictures of all signage, magazine/program ads, in-game activities, etc.) of the sponsorship contract. In this way, the partners are assured that proper planning occurs on the front end and that fulfillment of the contract was executed as planned on the back end.

Communication

Your property may or may not have the resources comparable to the Cowboys. However, your primary task to communicate before, during, and after the fulfillment of the sponsorship is the same. Successful communication in a sponsorship context means that you do three things over the course of the sponsorship each year:

1. Before: Set measurable goals.
2. During: Measure performance.
3. After: Report, review, and revise.

You can add perceived value to the partnership through communication and planning. Sponsors will perceive the value of the sponsorship in direct relationship to the amount of communication and interaction they have with you. The property may execute the sponsorship plan in exact accordance with the contract. However, if you don't maintain communication with the sponsor before, during, and after the sponsorship fulfillment, the sponsor is unlikely to perceive that it has received its money's worth. Practically speaking, you should schedule update appointments with key sponsors (e.g., put these on your Outlook calendar to call the sponsor every few weeks) throughout the fulfillment period.

Other efficient ways to increase communication with sponsors are to hold frequent (quarterly) partner summits and networking events to get sponsors together. At partnership summits, the goals are to update and refine sponsorship goals and to confirm activation plans. Networking events are useful for developing co-branded sponsorship events and promotions, such as when Wendy's and Coca-Cola got together to offer a free Texans' schedule cup with any "Biggie Size" combo meal.

Source: Courtesy of Houston Texans.

Problem Solving

No matter how good a job you do partnering, prospecting, preparing, and personalizing, problems crop up in sponsorship relationships. Successful sponsorship salespeople must have creative problem-solving skills. Compared to those account executives who are less resourceful and creative in resolving issues, salespeople with creative problem-solving skills are more likely to perform well within the organization, sell more, and be more satisfied with their jobs.[8]

The best way to solve problems, of course, is to prevent them with effective, ongoing communication with sponsorship partners. Partnerships are rarely dissolved if the two parties have frequently communicated, know each other well, and have developed a long-standing trust. Like many marriages, however, problems are more likely to arise in the early years of the relationship. Curiously, the ten most common causes of marital discord are alarmingly applicable to sponsor partnerships (with the likely exception of #6, see Box below). Whereas we'd like to help you resolve any marital difficulties you may (or will) be experiencing, we'll stick with helping you identify common problems sponsorships encounter.

Top 10 Causes of Divorce

1. Lack of interdependence
2. Premature partnership
3. Economic factors
4. Poor communication skills
5. Ease of legal exit
6. Sexual incompatibility
7. Role conflicts
8. Personal problems (alcoholism and substance abuse)
9. Differences in risk-taking behavior
10. Personality/value differences

Note: Not in particular order.
Source: Lowenstein, Ludwig F. (2005). Causes and associated features of divorce as seen by recent research. *Journal of Divorce and Remarriage* 42 (3–4): 153–171.

---

[8]Wang, Guangping, and Netemeyer, Richard G. 2004. Salesperson creative performance: Conceptualization, measurement, and nomological validity. *Journal of Business Research* 57 (August): 805–812.

IEG (www.sponsorship.com) has identified several problem areas[9] that lead to sponsorship failure. Let's look at five of these and how the property might help to resolve or prevent such problems.

1. Signing the Check and Dropping the Ball

Some sponsors may sign a sponsorship contract, assuming that the value of the sponsorship is derived solely on the basis of the performance of the contract. Sponsors who believe that they are buying signage or media space on a cost-per-thousand basis are unlikely to get the return they seek unless they are leveraging the sponsorship with additional commercialization. Sponsorships targeted only at those attending the event are likely to fail. The total audience must include a much broader audience than those at the event or attending the games.

The average spending on activation of a sponsorship is 2.4-to-1. That means that when Vodofone committed to spending £36 million over four years (2004–2008) to sponsor Manchester United, we would expect that they are also likely to spend around £86.4 million (or more) on advertising and promotional efforts to activate the sponsorship. Why would Vodofone be willing to spend that kind of money? In addition to keeping their current customers, getting new ones, and building their brand, they are able to introduce new services such as sports videos for G3 cell phones specifically for fans of the lads who play for Manchester United (go to www.manutd.com and click on "mobile" to see how Vodofone activates this sponsorship). The popularity of the United team provides an excellent platform for introducing these features and products as sponsor of the most popular sports team in the U.K., if not the world.

Partners like Vodofone do not sign the check and then drop the ball. On the other hand, less experienced or less sophisticated sponsorship partners may not anticipate or understand the magnitude of what is financially required to activate the sponsorship. Your responsibility is to understand the marketing plans of the sponsor well enough to know whether or not the funds committed to support the level of sponsorship they have bought is sufficient. Again, a good rule of thumb is that they should be spending at least as much on activation as they're spending on the sponsorship (1:1), but that the norm is two to three times as much (i.e., 2:4 to 1).

---

[9]The five problem areas identified in the text are found in "Why Sponsors Fail," 2002, IEG, Inc. All Rights Reserved. For more information about IEG's products and services, please visit www.sponsorship.com or call 312/944-1727.

2. Due Diligence Overlooked

The second type of problem encountered between partners occurs because the features of the sponsorship contract are not explicit. The sponsor should know not only what they get, but what they do *not* get. The following are key questions that sponsors and properties should review during the due diligence phase of sponsorship evaluations:

1. *Restrictions.* Are there any restrictions to the sponsor's rights to use the property's marks, logos, images, likenesses, and personalities in the sponsor's advertising and promotion?
2. *Exclusivity.* If exclusivity is offered, what is the definition of the business category covered in the exclusivity? How does exclusivity extend to the host venue, event signage, event broadcast, and event publications?
3. *Exclusivity of ad sales.* What is the exclusivity policy regarding ad sales to nonsponsors? Can the property sell ads to other companies in the same category who are not sponsors?
4. *Customer databases.* Does the sponsor have access to the property's database(s)? Are there any limitations to access?
5. *Online rights.* Does the sponsor have access to online rights? What online capabilities are available to the sponsor?
6. *Audience profile.* What exactly are the audience profiles and ratings for the various media and collateral (print, etc.) offered by the property? What ratings are guaranteed?
7. *On-site capabilities.* What opportunities are available for on-site sampling, booths, tables, surveys, etc.? How many of these opportunities are included in the package?
8. *Hospitality.* What is the number and value associated with the package's season tickets, other tickets, suites, parking spaces, venue uses (nonevent), invitations to events, and personal appearances by players/talent? Are there any restrictions on the use of any of these for promotional purposes?
9. *Concessions.* Who controls the concession rights? What concession rights does the sponsor have?
10. *Licensing/merchandising.* What licensing or merchandising opportunities does the sponsor have? Any restrictions?

Disputes arise when sponsors assume or believe that they have rights that were not made explicit in the sponsorship contract. A sponsor might assume that it will be no problem to get a star player to make an appearance at the sponsor's car dealership without paying any extra fees. (Player appearances are often negotiated directly with the player's agent.) Each of the questions listed above should be discussed and the answers incorporated into the written sponsorship contract. If you each follow due diligence in the details of the contract, you will be less likely to arrive at a point where one feels that the other is taking advantage of their partnership.

3. Insufficient Staffing and Fulfillment

You've probably heard it said that the "devil is in the details." We're not sure what that means, but we're fairly certain that it has something to do with what breaks loose when someone overlooks important details in sponsorship fulfillment. When the Altoona Curve (Pirates AA affiliate) plan one of its "Awful Nights" sponsored by Dodge (see Box below), someone has to make sure that all elements of the sponsorship are carried out by individuals as assigned. For instance, someone has to actually watch the Ben Affleck movies and select the most awful scenes. To make sure that details like these are managed, in addition to account representatives, the San Antonio Spurs have at least four individuals on staff serving as liaisons with team sponsors to make sure that sponsorship plans are fulfilled. In addition, title sponsors may have a full-time employee working with the team.

Awful Night at the Park

The first 1,000 fans through the gates (open @ 6 p.m.) will receive an "awful" noisemaker, consisting of a souvenir plastic cup with duct tape covering the top and a penny inside the cup. (Previous Awful Night giveaways have featured bubble wrap and bottomless cups.) Other highlights of "Awful Night" at Blair Country Ballpark (2005) include:

- Clips from Ben Affleck movies.
- Awful music from artists such as Mr. T, David Hasselhoff, and William Shatner.
- An awful post-game video board fireworks display.
- A look at the "Five Most Awful Moments in Sports" since last year.

- Awful between-inning contests such as "Helium Balloon Toss," "One-Person Hamster Ball Race," and "Dry Water Slide Contest."
- Non-celebrity autograph sessions.
- Display of awful foods, such as peanut butter and jelly sandwiches with red onions, chicken livers, sardines and stale crackers, pickled pigs feet, and liver and onions with Brussels sprouts. Also, fans will be able to purchase spam and cheese sandwiches for $2 and Tang for $1.

In addition, one unlucky grand prized winner will receive two (2) tickets to an independent minor league game of their choice.

Sponsors may develop activation plans that look good on paper, but that require significant manpower to pull off. You might agree to allow the sponsor to pass out product information cards to fans as they enter the stadium. At a large stadium, this might require 20 workers. Who is going to supply the labor? The point is that for every sponsorship component, you need to specify the following—in writing:

1. Who will perform the work?
2. Who will recruit, contact, and oversee the workers?
3. When will these workers be recruited and in place?
4. What are the responsibilities and rights (e.g., game access) of the workers?
5. Who will the contact person be at the property?
6. Are there any conflicting promotions or events on the date planned that will make fulfillment of this component difficult to carry out?

Managing these details will allow the sponsor to have a good grasp of the requirements to activate the sponsorship. The bottom line is that you don't want the sponsors to have any surprises when it comes to fulfillment—particularly surprises that cost them more money than they had budgeted.

4. Failure to Sell Internally

A potential problem in selling sponsorships to an executive or group of executives in a company is that the executives are completely behind the sponsorship, but the rest of the company and its related vendors do not see the benefits of engaging in the sponsorship. Senior executives, who most frequently review and agree to major sponsorships, have been known to make sponsorship decisions more on the basis of personal interest.[10]

The critical element required from the sponsor's side is a clear internal marketing plan that identifies key targets (employees, vendors, or other stakeholders) and incorporates sponsorship components that offer real benefits to identified targets. Xerox's 2004 Olympic sponsorship included the opportunity for 20 employees to carry the torch in Athens, as well as an advertising campaign that included employees as a target audience.[11]

Sponsorships can be a means to encourage employees and to help them identify with and take pride in the company. Other internal marketing plans are likely to include hospitality (tickets, invitations to events, etc.) as a means to include key employees and vendors/suppliers that are critical to the overall success of the sponsorship. As a good partner, your responsibility is to aid the sponsor in developing internal marketing plans that garner the support of those responsible for carrying out the practical aspects of the sponsorship. This may mean offering to host events at the property venue to plan the execution of the sponsorship or to generate enthusiasm among stakeholders (as when the Houston Texans host HEB's grocery suppliers at Reliant Stadium).

5. Overlooking the Fans

Have you ever been to a sporting event and wondered who in the world thought up that dumb idea? When sponsors come up with inane promotions that are actually carried out, it not only does not meet their sponsorship objectives, it makes the property look equally bad. A number of years ago, the Arena Football League (AFL) teamed up with Tinactin, maker of a leading foot spray for athletes, in a sponsorship deal. In general, the prominence, relatedness, and image of Tinactin make it a reasonable fit for the AFL. However, the promotion developed for activation was a bit less fitting. AFL teams were mandated at halftime to hold a tug of war on the field, with the teams asking fans on one side to yell "Tough Actin' " and the other side to holler "Tinactin." We'll give you a minute just to picture this exciting

---

[10]Burton, Rick, Quester, Pascale G., and Farrelly, Francis J. 1998. Organizational power games. *Marketing Management* 7 (1): 27–36.

[11]Callahan, Sean. 2004. Sponsors reach for Olympic gold. *B to B* 89 (Aug. 9): 1–2.

halftime extravaganza. . . . Can you picture yourself in the stands yelling either of these upon command? If so, you are probably one of those in the accompanying picture. However, most people sat on their hands and did not participate in this ingenious promotion.

Source: Courtesy of San Jose Sabercats.

When it comes to sponsored promotions, your job is to protect your fans, the experience at your venue, and the sponsor. Assume that you were responsible for negotiating the Tinactin contract with the AFL. Assume also that you were intelligent enough to recognize this promotion as a disaster waiting to happen. You could have either (a) been direct in your evaluation with the sponsor, or (b) suggested a focus group or other third party to evaluate the quality of the recommended promotions. The direct or indirect method may be more appropriate, dependent upon the nature of your relationship with the sponsor.

Careful consideration of the fans means more than just making sure that they are not offended or unamused by promotions. Not overlooking the fans also means that as partners, the property and sponsor are seeking ways to accomplish the underlying goal of affinity transfer through the sponsorship. Affinity transfer means that fans understand that as a result of the sponsorship, they are getting events or services that would not otherwise be available to them. The goal of the San Antonio Spurs is for fans to recognize that if it weren't for the support of AT&T as title sponsor, then they wouldn't have it as good as they do at the arena.

Fans must make the connection between what they are receiving and who is responsible for providing it. A mistake made by many sponsored events, contests, and the like is that fans do not perceive any tangible benefits associated with the sponsorship for themselves. A contest that only has one winner, for the most part, only benefits that one winner. A solution to that dilemma is to create sections of fans that win, based on the outcome of the contest. Another solution is to offer a promotion that generates fan excitement, but that draws attention to an offer or other benefit provided by the sponsor. Fans are reminded that this promotion is "brought to you by . . ." and then are given a tangible reminder, such as a coupon passed through the stands at a predefined juncture in the game. The Texas Rangers are sponsored by Ozarka Natural Spring Water, who sponsors a dot race that includes coupons passed out to every fan during the inning the dot race is run. Of course, the fact that many fans continue to get excited about their ability to select the random winning color dot in these races gives some credence to the philosophical belief that sports fans are intellectually incapable of achieving feats beyond the mastery of an eight-button remote control. We don't even want to talk about those who get emotionally distraught when they do not ever seem to be able to pick the winning dot.

The point is that a frequent problem for sponsors is that they spend large sums of money for a title or anchor sponsorship and affinity transfer does not occur because fans do not see the sponsor as adding anything tangible for fans of the event or the team. Your responsibility is to review the sponsor's plans to see that it includes some tangible benefit to fans in a way that fans will be able to identify the sponsor as bringing something to the event that fans would otherwise not receive.

Source: Courtesy of Southwest Airlines.

Source: Courtesy of Southwest Airlines.

Create Sponsorship Value

9

A full 78 percent [of] companies do not have an ongoing budget dedicated to sponsorship research. Specifically, 72 percent . . . allocate either nothing or no more than 1 percent of their sponsorship budget to concurrent or post-event research, even though tracking ROI is the industry's war cry. And, pre-event research fares no better: More than three-quarters spend $5,000 or less per deal on external research prior to making sponsorship decisions—33 percent spend nothing and 44 percent spend less than $5,000.[1]

Tracking Return on Investment (ROI) is the war cry in the sponsorship industry. However, it's been mostly crying and not much real war breaking out. The future, however, is likely to include far more quantification of the value of sponsorships. The buzzword in corporations worldwide is marketing metrics—which simply means that firms measure the effectiveness of marketing expenditures. Corporate marketing managers investing in sponsorships are not getting a free pass—just because all the executives get to sit in the suite at the stadium.

Ideally, properties and sponsors work together to help each reach their organizational objectives. Some teams, such as the Houston Texans, work closely with anchor partners to assure that they achieve their marketing objectives by providing them with key marketing metrics such as sponsorship recall, brand preference, and brand usage

---

[1]IEG Sponsorship Report, 2002, "Performance Research/IEG Study Highlights What Sponsors Want," www.sponsorship.com.

among Texans' fan segments. In contrast, executives at some teams rely on the notion that sponsorships are often bought on the basis of what is known to be an emotional buy[2] and that measurement of such emotional returns is difficult to capture. For instance, in the same Houston market, the success of the Houston Astros (who in 2005 made it to the World Series for the first time in franchise history) have led many corporate sponsors to be willing to invest in the team in 2006 and forward. It is safe to assume that not all such decisions are based on clear marketing objectives and careful presponsorship research.

In this chapter we take the perspective of the corporate sponsor. Sports properties need to have an understanding of how corporations are measuring the effectiveness of their marketing expenditures so that the property can be an effective partner in achieving corporate sponsorship objectives. If the title sponsor of an NBA arena regularly tracks consumers' brand preference, it would be a good idea if the executives of the team knew how the sponsor measures brand preference and how the sponsor uses the data in making marketing decisions.

We first examine how to valuate the media portion of a sponsorship package. Understanding the media value of a sponsorship provides the baseline for what the sponsorship package would be worth if the sponsor merely wanted to buy media exposure on the open market. We then turn to determining the value of the sponsorship in terms of its reaching organizational objectives beyond mere exposure.

Media Valuation

Traditionally, major sponsorship packages have focused on signage and media exposure. Corporations have been attracted by the opportunity to reach a large, well-defined, captive target audience offered by sports venues and game broadcasts. Oddly, most companies would not make a media buy from a major TV network or outdoor advertising company without knowing the comparative CPM (cost per thousand), yet have been willing to plunk down in excess of seven figures for team sponsorship deals to reach these same audiences.

The goal in determining the media value of sponsorship packages is to estimate the total number of audience exposures across the different media included in the sponsorship package. Standard or average

---

[2]The buy is emotional both on the part of the corporate sponsors as well as the individual fans.

costs per exposure are available for the various media to calculate the value. The relevant average cost per exposure selected to calculate the value is up to the researcher, dependent upon the comparable media offered by the sponsorship. For instance, an anchor sponsor of the Dallas Mavericks may have the opportunity to gain exposure via a 4-color, full-page ad in the team's program. What type of media buy would gain comparable exposure to a similar target audience? Few comparable publications exist on a local level. However, on a national level, a sponsor might run an ad in *ESPN The Magazine*, which costs an average of $0.09 per exposure for the same ad for one issue.[3] If the team distributes the program to 45 home games (including pre-season) to an average of 10,000 fans, the value of that exposure could be calculated as $40,500[4] ($0.09 × 45 × 10,000).

To gain a better understanding of the media value of a sponsorship, let's examine a typical sponsorship package for an anchor sponsor of a Major League Baseball team. The components of the sponsorship are presented in Table 9.1. The task is to determine the equivalent media value of the sponsorship that will serve as a baseline for negotiations with the team. Progressive teams could actually help the sponsor by placing verifiable media value on the components—as opposed to the asking price—although we are unaware of properties actually doing so. For this example, we will use the city of Houston, Texas as the relevant media market.

Signage. The basic unit of measure for "out-of-home" or outdoor advertising is the Daily Effective Circulation (DEC). The DEC is the number of people 18 and over who have the chance to view the sign on a daily basis. Billboards are sold according to the number of standard-sized sheets it takes to create the sign. Typical sizes are 8-sheet posters, which measure 5 feet high and 11 feet wide, and 30-sheet posters, which measure 9½ feet high by 21'7" wide.

The cost for an 8-sheet poster in Houston via Clear Channel Outdoor for a 4-week period is $104,220 with a 4-week circulation (or exposure) of 102,060,000, giving an average cost of $0.001 per exposure. Similarly, the average cost of a 30-sheet poster is slightly higher at $0.0016 per exposure. How many exposures would a similar sign receive at the ballpark? What would a 30-sheet poster be worth at a stadium? The answer lies in your assumptions.

---

[3] *Source: Marketer's Guide to Media* (2004), Mitch Tebo, ed., New York, NY: VNU Business Media, 2004. Based on ad cost of $148,750.00 with a circulation of 1,650,000. All rates used in this chapter are based on data from this media guide.

[4] For ease of discussion we hold the pass-along rates for print media as constant. To the extent that such rates vary, calculations could be adjusted accordingly.

Table 9.1

Example of a Major League Baseball Anchor Sponsorship Package

1. Signage
   a. One scoreboard sign
   b. One ramp sign
   c. One main concourse sign

2. Print advertising
   a. Team magazine (FP,[1] 4-C ad)
   b. Team media guide (IFC[2])
   c. Team pocket schedules

3. Game tickets/parking passes/hospitality
   a. Four field box season tickets
   b. Four dugout box season tickets
   c. Four season parking passes
   d. Luxury suite for three games: 10 tickets/seats, includes food and beverage
   e. Luxury suite for one promo game: 10 tickets/seats, includes food and beverage
   f. Allotment of 100 tickets for one promo date
   g. Pregame party for 100 people on one promo date
   h. Allotment of 100 tickets for one game
   i. Pregame party for 110 people
   j. Ceremonial first pitch

4. Scoreboard feature
   Sponsor of video feature (e.g., replays, contest, "Kiss-me Cam," etc.) for each game

5. Promotions and sampling
   a. Magnet schedule giveaway
   b. Other product giveaways (vouchers, coupons, etc.) at two games
   c. At least three "theme games" (can incorporate with giveaways)

6. Sponsored events
   a. Sponsor of team golf tournament
   b. Sponsor fantasy baseball camp

[1]FP = Full Page.
[2]IFC = Inside Front Cover; IBC = Inside Back Cover.

Assumption #1: Scoreboard signs are seen by all attending fans. Total attendance at the Houston Astros Minute Maid Park in 2004 was 3,087,872. Of those attending, however, about 80 percent are likely to be adults aged 18 or over. Hence, dependent upon the size of the scoreboard sign, the total value of a sign that is equal to a 30-sheet poster would be worth at least $3,952.48 (3,087,872 × .80 × $0.0016).

Assumption #2: Fans are viewing the scoreboard throughout the game, but diminishing returns occur after repeated exposures. Advertising agencies frequently use three exposures per four-week period as the effective frequency for TV ads to communicate the message. However, that number goes up to something closer to a dozen exposures (per month) for less intrusive media like billboards. For most sporting events, it is safe to say that fans will view the scoreboard and surrounding signs at least one dozen times (e.g., even the least attentive fan is likely to view the scoreboard at an MLB game every half inning).[5] Consequently, the value of the sign based upon effective frequency could be calculated at $47,429.76 ($3,952.48 × 12).

In general, a good plug value for signage exposure at most venues across the United States will be in the neighborhood of $0.011 per exposure for an 8-sheet poster and $0.022 per exposure for a 30-sheet poster. These figures are based upon averages for billboard signage costs across major media markets in the United States in 2004 and the assumption that fans will be exposed to the signage at least 12 times. Other assumptions could be made and the value adjusted upward or downward, as we now discuss.

First, some might suggest that *fans' senses are elevated at sporting events*, thereby increasing the extent to which fans pay attention to and process information relevant to the event and the team. For instance, if you are a season ticket holder you probably have a fairly clear picture of the team's scoreboard and its surrounding signs. Whether or not this picture is any more clearly implanted in your head than the billboard you pass every day going to work is uncertain, but odds are that you have more positive attitudes toward the sponsors located on the team scoreboard than you do toward the advertiser on the roadside billboard you stare at while stuck in city traffic.

Second, the audience of the home team may be *more tightly targeted* to a sponsor's intended market, such as males, 21–49 years old, who consume large quantities of alcoholic beverages. In that case, the out-of-home (OOH) media buy at the MLB park is more effective than most other OOH alternatives. Assumptions such as these, however, point to the need to determine (a) the value of the sponsorship that is not directly tied to media value, and (b) the achievement of different

---

[5]Since we are primarily interested in the number of adults exposed to the media, we do not consider the behavior of children—who most likely are spending most of their time asking for funnel cakes, ice cream, soft drinks, hot dogs, souvenirs, and the like before they are ready to leave in the top of the second inning.

marketing metrics apart from awareness and exposure (e.g., brand liking or brand preference) which may differ across various fan segments. We address such issues in the second half of the chapter.

Other signs. Similar calculations could be made regarding the other signage offered in the sponsorship package. A major determinant of assigning *any* value to the other signs is the assumption made regarding any additional impact on fans. For sponsors with dominant signage on the scoreboard or field level, additional signs will generate little additional awareness impact since fans have already been exposed beyond the effective frequency rate (i.e., 12). However, the prevalence of signage around the venue with the same sponsor's message may lead to other attributions (e.g., "Pizza Hut *must* be a major sponsor of the team.") that enhance the value of the media buy. Highly identified fans that make this connection between the property and the sponsor could have more positive attitudes toward the brand. Once again, the extent to which fans make such evaluations points to the need to measure outcomes beyond exposures.

Print. As discussed earlier, sponsors receiving four-color print ads in team magazines or media guides can be evaluated on the same basis as if advertising space were bought in comparable magazines targeted to the same audience (e.g., *ESPN The Magazine* or *Sports Illustrated*). In those cases, the value per exposure is in the range of seven to nine cents per exposure. The problem is that the credibility one gains by placing an ad in *Sports Illustrated* or the like may not be directly comparable to team magazine productions. Alternatively, media valuation could be based on either local magazines or newspaper media rates.

Local four-color magazines. Local print media options are the better comparison point for media guides and game programs. Unfortunately, rarely do local options exist with similar target audience exposure. In such cases, local magazines distributed either by newspapers or other sources could be considered the low-cost alternative. In Houston, advertising in the city's "002+" magazine costs $200 for a full-page ad and has a stated circulation of 70,000, yielding a cost per exposure of approximately $0.003. The wasted coverage of such magazines will be very high, as the majority of readers will be outside of the intended target audience for the sponsor. If one assumes that only 10 percent of the readership is in the target audience (team fans, regular game attenders, etc.), then the relevant cost per exposure would be about $0.03.

Local newspaper. Others might believe that the exposure is not much different from having an ad in the sports section in the Houston *Chronicle*. The newspaper cost for a quarter-page, black/white ad is roughly $0.03 per exposure in the Houston *Chronicle.*[6] What you are probably beginning to notice is something of a pattern with regard to the going price for print exposure. Table 9.2 contains the average cost per exposure for a quarter-page ad in the top 15 U.S. media markets. As can be seen, some publishers in some markets are a bit more proud of their work (e.g., Chicago *Sun-Times* at a nickel per exposure), but

Table 9.2

	City	Newspaper	Circulation	Cost per square inch	Average cost per exposure
1	New York City	*Times*	1,118,600	$975.00	$0.03
		Daily News	729,100	$615.50	$0.03
		Post	652,400	$388.76	$0.02
2	Los Angeles	*LA Times*	892,900	$786.00	$0.03
		Newspaper Grp	581,900	$517.00	$0.03
3	Chicago	*Sun-Times*	708,700	$1,134.56	$0.05
		Tribune	680,900	$580.00	$0.03
4	San Francisco	*Chronicle*	512,600	$533.00	$0.03
5	Philadelphia	*Inquirer*	520,700	$586.00	$0.04
6	Dallas	*Morning News*	510,100	$462.00	$0.03
7	Boston	*Globe*	450,500	$443.00	$0.03
8	Miami	*Herald*	315,900	$379.25	$0.04
9	Detroit	*Free Press*	580,100	$576.00	$0.03
10	Washington, DC	*Post*	732,900	$617.00	$0.03
11	Houston	*Chronicle*	552,000	$577.00	$0.03
12	Atlanta	*Journal-Constitution*	371,900	$478.50	$0.04
13	Phoenix	*Arizona Republic*	432,300	$353.00	$0.03
14	Seattle	*Times*	231,500	$232.03	$0.03
15	Minneapolis	*Star-Tribune*	380,400	$257.06	$0.02 $0.03

Average Cost per Print Exposure in Major U.S. Markets

Overall average based on 2004 figures for a quarter-page ad.

Source: Courtesy of Marketer's Guide to Media.

---

[6]The Houston *Chronicle* circulation is 552,000 and the cost per column inch is $577. A quarter-page ad is equal to 32 column inches. That makes the cost per exposure equal to about three cents: ($577 × 32)/552,000 = $0.033.

a good rule of thumb is that print exposures for a standard-sized ad will cost about three cents per exposure.

Other print items. Teams often offer anchor sponsors the opportunity to be promoted on pocket schedules or magnet schedules, as well as other handouts with the sponsor logo or identification. You can compare the relative value of the distribution of a pocket schedule to a free-standing insert (FSI) in the local newspaper. The typical CPM for targeted FSI's range from $9 to $12, which can be rounded to about one cent per exposure.

Hospitality

The value of the game tickets, suites, parking passes, and parties can be priced at face value. For our example given in Table 9.3, the value would be $52,340.[7]

Each of these could be purchased without sponsoring the property. Consequently, if the sponsor is primarily interested in the benefits associated with hospitality, then purchasing tickets and suites a la carte may suffice. In those cases where the target audience is more business-to-business with well-defined client prospects, corporations

Table 9.3

Hospitality Valuation			
Item	Value	Quantity	Total
Four field box season tickets	$2,405	4	$9,620
Four dugout season tickets	$3,055	4	$12,220
Four season parking passes (part of season ticket package)	—	—	—
Luxury suite for 3 games (10 tickets)	$125	10 × 3	$3,750
Luxury suite for 1 promo game	$125	10	$1,250
100 tickets for promo date	$15	100	$1,500
100 tickets for one regular date	$20	100	$2,000
Pregame party for 100 (regular and promo)	$110	100 × 2	$22,000
Ceremonial first pitch	—	—	—
			$52,340

---

[7]Ticket and suite prices are from the 2006 season.

may be more cost-effective using personal selling versus mass media. In other words, it is a debatable question if having the corporate name on a billboard sign in center field adds any value to having prime seats or suites in which to do business between corporate employees and clients.

On the other hand, it is a researchable question as to whether or not the client may make positive attributions about the brand due to its anchor sponsorship. Research we conducted on the opinions of 127 C-level (chief executive) officers indicates that the majority believe potential business partners who are title sponsors of a sports venue are perceived as winners (50.4%) rather than losers[8] (16.5%). Similarly, companies who are title sponsors are seen as distinctive from competitors by 44.9 percent of CXO's, versus being "just like the other brands" in the market (18.1%). Finally, 60.6 percent of CXO's believe that attending a sponsored event (as a guest of the sponsor) helps build relationships that benefit the company. Again, such data suggests the need to look at the value of sponsorships beyond the mere unit cost of the inventory (e.g., tickets, suites, etc.) delivered.

In-Game Spots

In-game mentions (10 seconds) and in-game spots (15 s or 30 s) can be priced according to local radio or TV spots with similar audience exposure. Radio spots may run for less than $20 for local spots to around $40 in major cities (or on Sirius radio) and multiples of those rates during prime drive times.

Promotions and Sponsored Games and Events

Samples given away at sporting events are comparable to other in-store trial or distribution methods, which typically cost about six cents per item ($60 cpm) if done cooperatively (e.g., in a bag along with other companies' items) or between 8–16 cents per item if done solo (i.e., only the company's products). Hence, the value of sampling 20,000 fans would be between $1,200 and $3,200. Similarly, coupons can be distributed on-site in stores or malls for only approximately $15 cpm (or 1.5 cents per coupon).

---

[8]The remainder (33.1%) are indifferent.

Most often samples are limited to early arrivers (e.g., first 20,000 fans). In that sense, giveaways may be biased toward infrequent fans, as season ticket holders are less likely to arrive early. To combat that problem, some properties have taken the unusual position of guaranteeing that all season ticket holders will receive promotional items. Doing so helps the sponsor reach the desired target audience and also rewards loyal fans who may believe that the team is more interested in getting new fans to the park than honoring or rewarding those who have already proven their allegiance to the team.

Sponsored games and events. Properties allow sponsors to theme games, often combined with sampling or giveaways with the sponsor's logo imprinted on the giveaway. Coca-Cola sponsors the Coca-Cola Value Night at Minute Maid Park on multiple Fridays throughout the season for the Houston Astros (see Box below). Coke promotes the Value Night on its products through grocery stores, driving sales of 24-packs of Coke or Diet Coke. In keeping with the theory that price discounts should require an effort on the part of those customers who are price sensitive, fans must purchase Coke products and redeem the on-package coupon online to purchase the tickets. Once fans arrive at the game, they may redeem a printable coupon for free cokes (viz., samples). What is the value of a theme night like this to Coke?

Coca-Cola Value Nights

A $127 value for just $55. *Tickets may be purchased beginning one week prior to the "Value Night" game date you have selected.* Subject to ticket availability.

Offer is available on 24-packs of Coca-Cola classic and Diet Coke specially marked with the Coca-Cola "Value Nights" offer, available at participating Coca-Cola retailers from 4/3/2006– 7/22/2006 or while supplies last.

Step 1
With the purchase of any specially-marked 24-pack of Coca-Cola classic or Diet Coke, you can qualify for savings during Coca-Cola "Value Nights" with the Houston Astros at Minute Maid Park.

Step 2
Select which of the 11 Coca-Cola "Value Nights" you wish to attend with family and/or friends. Offer is subject to availability.

Step 3
Visit **astros.com/valuenights**, and follow the instructions for redeeming your seven-digit code found on your discount coupon to purchase the "Value Pack." **Tickets may be purchased beginning one week prior to the "Value Night" game date you want to attend.**

- Four (4) Mezzanine level tickets to one of the Coca-Cola "Value Nights" games
- One coupon redeemable for four (4) hot dogs, four (4) 20 oz. bottles of any available Coca-Cola product
- One coupon redeemable for two Astros branded baseball caps.

Step 4
Arrive on your game date, and proceed to your seats located in the Mezzanine Level. Once there you can redeem your coupons for Astros Caps at mezzanine home plate supply company or fan accommodations at section 323.

First, Coke derives revenue from the sale of the 24-packs at the grocery store—which compensates for the value of the free drinks offered at the game. Second, fans of the home team should be able to see that Coke is providing them with a great value for something they really care about (viz., going to Astros' games). Third, if the Astros caps received at the game are co-branded with the Coca-Cola logo, then Coke extends its reach outside of the realm of the game experience. Fourth, given that Coca-Cola products are sold through HEB grocery stores (another anchor sponsor of the Astros), this kind of deal keeps Coca-Cola's distributors and retailers happy. Yet, the question still remains, how much is this worth in dollars? What should Coke pay for this opportunity?

Theme nights at sporting events are essentially live-marketing events that would be difficult to achieve without the property. Similarly, sponsoring team golf tournaments or other team events are live-marketing events that cater to the team's fan base. Alternatives do exist in the form of sponsoring other live events such as concerts or initiating live events built around special interests (which Coke does; see http://www.youthdevelopment.coca-cola.com/). However, all present the same ROI dilemma. The cost to the company is in (a) leveraging the event through other media, and (b) running the activities associated with the event. In the case of a sporting event or concert, the event will go on with or without a sponsored theme night—and the marginal cost of fulfilling a sponsor's theme night is minimal compared to the costs a sponsor would incur for a self-initiated event. So, the question for the company is: Is it worth the asking price of the anchor sponsorship to be able to gain access to the sporting event with a captive live-marketing audience?

The answer lies in the extent to which those in attendance at the event transfer their affinity with the property (e.g., the home team) to the sponsor—and consequently are more inclined to purchase from the sponsor compared to those who do not attend the event.

Measuring Affinity Transfer

Communications models represent a hierarchy of effects aimed at achieving adoption:

$$\text{Awareness} \rightarrow \text{Interest} \rightarrow \text{Preference} \rightarrow \text{Liking} \rightarrow$$
$$\text{Trial} \rightarrow \text{Adoption}$$

The traditional media outlined in the first half of this chapter (outdoor, print, video/audio) are suitable for achieving awareness promotion goals, but are less appropriate for higher level communication objectives. Measuring the achievement of awareness goals is often thought of as being primarily a function of exposure. Hence, some sponsors are primarily concerned with how many sets of eyeballs are exposed to the media. However, exposure does not guarantee attention or recall that the brand is a sponsor of the property. Consequently, merely counting exposures assumes effectiveness—and almost everyone knows what it says about you and me when we assume. So, how do sponsors know that the media exposure translates into actual recognition or recall of the sponsor's brand? Sponsors can measure either unaided or aided recall.

Awareness. Unaided recall questions can be administered on and off-site by asking consumers: "When you think of companies that provide ____ services (products), what is the first brand that comes to mind?" (What is the second brand that comes to mind? What is the third?) Awareness levels can be compared between consumers who are nonattenders, infrequent attenders, and frequent attenders to determine whether or not the sponsorship has a differentiating effect on brand awareness.

Recall. Aided recall can measure the extent to which fans are making the association between the property and the sponsoring brand. Since we know that individuals will infer prominent (e.g.,

VISA, FedEx, etc.) and related (e.g., Nike, Budweiser, etc.) brands are sponsors, a method must be employed that accounts for this bias.

Subjects can be asked to indicate which brands are (not) property sponsors from a list of the brands that include the property's sponsors together with a mixture of (non)prominent and (un)related brands that are not sponsors. For example, along with the actual sponsors, foils could be interspersed as follows:

NFL team sponsors	Sponsor?	Prominence	Relatedness
Budweiser	Actual	Prominent	Related
Heineken	Foil	Less prominent	Related
Reebok	Actual	Prominent	Related
Nike	Foil	Prominent	Related
Play-it-Again Sports	Actual	Less prominent	Related
Sports Authority	Foil	Prominent	Related
Geico	Actual	Less prominent	Unrelated
State Farm	Foil	Prominent	Unrelated
1st Providian Bank	Actual	Less prominent	Unrelated
Bank of America	Foil	Prominent	Unrelated
Wells Fargo	Actual	Prominent	Unrelated
Independent Bank	Foil	Less prominent	Unrelated

Compared to simply asking if individuals recall whether or not a brand is a sponsor of the property (as done with traditional aided recall methods), using this approach guards against respondents guessing based on prominence and relatedness.[9] Further analysis can compare sponsorship recognition rates between those that are infrequent versus frequent attenders to determine the effectiveness of the sponsorship in achieving increasing recall as exposure increases. Figure 9.1 demonstrates results from anchor and upper-tier sponsors of an NFL team.

Results such as these indicate that fans are making the association between the team and its anchor sponsors, albeit not for all sponsors. Individual analyses can be conducted to determine the specific effects

---

[9]It is important to clean the data before analysis by deleting those cases where subjects were yea-saying (marking all as sponsors) or nay-saying (marking none as sponsors).

Figure 9.1

Sponsor Recall as a Function of Attendance

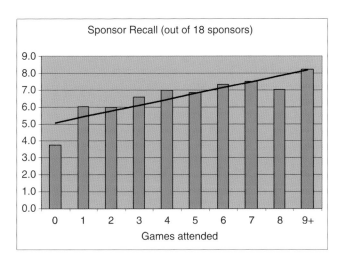

for each sponsor, but we can promise you that the brands that aren't recognized are less prominent and unrelated to the event.[10] However, even knowing that fans make the association between the property and sponsor does not mean that fans prefer, like, or want to use the brand. Admittedly, it's a pretty good start since it's hard to prefer a brand you aren't aware of.[11]

Higher level goals. Assessing ROI implies that we are interested in measuring the effect the sponsorship has on adoption (viz., purchases). Yet, before the audience adopts (tries or buys), they must prefer and have an affinity (liking) of the brand. This understanding of the hierarchy of effects forms the basis for the steps to affinity transfer (see Figure 9.2). We first explain each step before explaining how sponsors can determine their Return on Sponsorship Investment (ROSI).

Brand activation and leverage through other media is the crucial determinant of sponsorship effectiveness at all five stages. Sponsors must measure and assess the extent to which fans perceive that the sponsor "PACES":

1. is *Prominently* displayed at the event
2. provides memorable game day *Activities*

---

[10]Unless special efforts have been made to activate and relate the brand as discussed in previous chapters.

[11]Please excuse the preposition in search of an object.

Figure 9.2

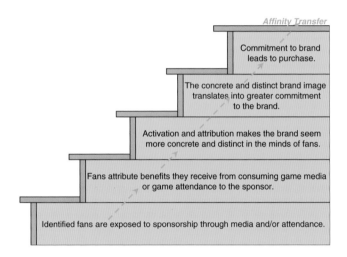

Steps to Affinity Transfer

Affinity Transfer

Commitment to brand leads to purchase.

The concrete and distinct brand image translates into greater commitment to the brand.

Activation and attribution makes the brand seem more concrete and distinct in the minds of fans.

Fans attribute benefits they receive from consuming game media or game attendance to the sponsor.

Identified fans are exposed to sponsorship through media and/or attendance.

3. *Communicates* ways fans can do business with them
4. *Enlightens* and informs fans about their products/services
5. *Stands* out among the other sponsors of the event.

Without effective activation, fans will not process or deeply elaborate on the meaning of the sponsorship to the team or to its fans. If the sponsor's brand gets lost in the clutter of the event and the plethora of other sponsors, there is little chance that fans will transfer their affinity and love for the team to the brand.

Step 1. Fans must first be *exposed* to the sponsorship through media consumption (TV, radio, or Internet) and/or event attendance. The more frequently fans consume games via TV, radio, Internet, or in person, the higher the likelihood that they will make the *association* between the event and the sponsor. An increasingly important avenue to reach fans is through the team's Web site, as active fans will frequently visit the team Web site and are likely to be relatively attentive to everything on the site—as they are there to explore and consume team-related information. If fans can actually *interact* directly with the brand (as they do when they click on the sponsor's link on the team Web site), the more likely it is that the brand will be stored as a distinct sponsor.

Step 2. Once fans are cognizant of the sponsorship and make the connection with the property, the critical step is for fans to make positive *attributions* about the sponsor. The objective is for fans to believe that the game experience is better off in some way because of the support of the sponsor. Brand activation that makes it clear the property is better off because of the sponsorship (e.g., "The Spurs would like to thank AT&T for its sponsorship of the team and making all we do at the AT&T Center possible.") will prompt fans to acknowledge the benefits provided to the team and its fans. In short, fans should believe that games wouldn't be as good if it weren't for the support of the sponsor (through exciting game activities, funded facilities, social welfare programs, etc.).

Not all attributions are positive. Image congruency is an important determinant of whether or not activation leads to positive attributions. Image congruency means that the values and image of the sponsor are seen as similar to those of the property. The more fans see the image of the sponsor and the property as similar, the more they will think good things about the sponsor—assuming the property has a positive image. The reason a sponsor wants to sponsor the property is because the property enjoys a position of prestige in the community. To the extent this is not true, it is important to see that the brand image of the property could tarnish the image of the sponsor, if fans make attributions about the kinds of companies that sponsor losers (either on or off the field).

Step 3. With proper activation, the activation and attribution that take place in the first two steps lead fans to see the brand as *distinct and concrete* compared to its competitors. A chief reason for the growth in sponsorships versus traditional mass media is the opportunity to make a unique imprint on the minds of consumers. We may see an entertaining advertisement on TV for a brand, but the odds that we freely recall any ad we saw yesterday is lower than the likelihood that we'll remember the deal we got from a Coca-Cola Value Night or some other sponsored event which we consciously chose to attend, interact, and respond. In any case, appropriate activation *differentiates* the sponsor's brand from others in the marketplace—all of which are already players in the traditional media, but typically aren't competing head-to-head at the sports venue due to exclusivity deals. Well-designed and integrated sponsorship plans such as Southwest Airlines actually uses its other media (re: their entertaining seasonal sports advertising) to leverage its sports sponsorships. Consequently, Southwest has a clear positioning as a sponsor of professional sports, despite the fact that it is the only airline without a title sponsorship of a sports facility.

Brands are seen as more *concrete* in the minds of fans due to activation and attribution. This means that when fans think of the sponsor's brand, they see a clear image or representation of the brand, including its logo and what the brand stands for in the marketplace and the community. Brands most likely to benefit from sponsorships, then, would be those that have a vague brand image that can implement a sponsorship strategy that elucidates clear brand attributes. Services, which by nature are intangible, and particularly those more difficult to understand (e.g., telecommunications vs. groceries) can communicate service products or characteristics to customers that otherwise may not be willing to learn. Thus, Ameriquest may make strong gains in fans having a concrete understanding of their mortgage business through their sponsorship of the Texas Rangers stadium. Conversely, American Airlines may get less lift from a title sponsorship since most people understand the concept of air travel and are aware of American Airlines services.

Step 4. When the brand becomes distinct from its competitors and has a concrete image in the minds of fans, they become willing to *commit* to the brand. Brand commitment means that individuals will remain with the brand, even if it requires some small sacrifices to do so. Because of the affinity transfer that occurs through activation and attribution, fans now see the brand as distinctly better than its competitors. Their commitment translates into a willingness to put forth more effort to purchase the brand (e.g., expending search and psychic effort; remember Chapter 1?). High levels of commitment are obtained when customers no longer feel the need to search for or even consider other brands within the product/service category.

Step 5. The payoff is that individual customers with high brand commitment are significantly better customers than those with low commitment. Those who are highly committed to Coke will consistently spend more on Coke than those with low commitment. If you are a committed Coke customer, you don't choose between Coke and Pepsi. You choose among Coke products. If you have a low commitment to Coke, you may buy Coke products occasionally, but it is only one of several alternatives. You get the point.

But, just in case you don't, we now return to the question of the hour, or at least this chapter. How can you use this knowledge for yourself to make more money? Or, put differently, how can companies measure ROSI?

ROSI. The first action is to measure *both* fans' and nonfans' perceptions of each of the dimensions outlined in each of the five steps above:

1. Activation*
2. Attribution*

---

*These two factors can only be captured for fans who consume game media or attend games, as nonfans will have no exposure to sponsorship activation accompanying the game.

3. Image congruency
4. Brand distinctiveness
5. Brand concreteness
6. Brand commitment
7. Purchases

Comparisons can be made to determine if highly identified fans differ in their perceptions and behaviors from those who are not exposed to the sponsorship. The results provide diagnostic help to the sponsor to determine whether or not the implementation of the sponsorship strategy has been successful in changing brand attitudes and purchase behavior.

The second action to measuring ROSI is to estimate the bottom line effects for the sponsor. Through additional research (both secondary and primary) the company can determine the market size, the number of customers it has in the market, and—with the information gained in the first step above—estimate the differential effects on purchases for those who are exposed to the sponsorship (game fans) and those who are not (nonattenders). While not presented here, our research indicates that effective sponsorships can generate significantly more customers with high commitment to the brand (compared to those who are not exposed to the sponsorship) that can be directly translated into increased profit margin for each highly committed fan.

Conclusion

The role of the property and the sponsor is to correctly value the sponsorship package so that each achieves its objectives as partners. The first part of this chapter provides ballpark figures to estimate media values. The calculation and summation of media values from the package (viz., Table 9.1) is the starting point for understanding the value of the package. The second part discusses the process by which affinity for the property transfers to sponsors. To fully understand the value of the package, sophisticated analytics are required to compare the impact of the sponsorship on fans that are exposed to the property's sponsorship versus those who have no exposure. To simplify, however, we can understand that sponsorship activation for a company like Southwest Airlines should improve brand perceptions among fans (vs. non-fans) such that fans will be more likely to be committed to Southwest (compared to non-fans) and more frequently fly on Southwest as a result.

Move Merchandise 10

The NFL generates over $3 billion annually in merchandise sales. Going into the 2005 season, Randy Moss' new Raiders jersey was the top seller, followed by Michael Vick, Tom Brady, Donovan McNabb, Ben Roethlisberger, LaDainian Tomlinson, Byron Leftwich, Ricky Williams, Jeremy Shockey, and Tiki Barber. Following their 2005 Super Bowl appearance, the Eagles sold the most NFL merchandise. Next in teams sales were the 2005 Super Bowl champs New England, followed by Pittsburgh, Oakland, Green Bay, Dallas, Denver, Chicago, New York Giants, and Kansas City.

Do you notice anything interesting about these two lists?

1. No linemen are in the top 10.
2. No defensive players are in the top 10.
3. Quarterbacks dominate the list (6 of 10).
4. Team sales are led by the most recent Super Bowl participants, but note the following 2004 records: #4 Oakland (5–11), #6 Dallas (6–10), #8 Chicago (5–11), #9 Giants (6–10), and #10 Kansas City (7–9).
5. In 2004, Williams[1] didn't even play and Randy Moss[2] missed three games and most of two other games.

---

[1]Upon his return to the NFL in 2005, Williams wanted to change his number to 27, since it is a derivative of nine, which according to numerology is the "perfect" number. One can only speculate as to why he didn't want to change it to "9," which was available. Reportedly, the NFL did not allow the change because of the merchandising opportunities associated with his No. 34. *Source:* Cole, Jason (August 15, 2005), "Ricky runs on a new path," www.miamiherald.com.

[2]In addition to admitting the use of marijuana during his NFL career, Moss has experienced a string of expensive incidents on and off the field. He has been fined for over $100,000 by the NFL for his behavior, including $10,000 for pretending to moon Green Bay Packer fans in a playoff game, squirting a referee with a water bottle, and cussing out corporate sponsors sitting on the team bus.

This list demonstrates some of the realities of sports merchandising. First, fans identify with leaders. Most teams will focus their merchandising efforts on only a few jerseys and these are unlikely to include the starting right guard on the offensive line. If you ask most fans, "Who's right guard?" most are likely to say, "Not mine. I use Old Spice." Quarterbacks, and sometimes other skill position players, are seen as the guys who lead the teams to victory, overcoming all odds to succeed. Fans identify with those leaders who overcome. Of course, one can question how Moss, Williams, and Shockey are seen as leaders. However, they are likely to be perceived as leaders to a relatively large counter-culture segment that values individualistic behavior, among other things. This leads to the next reality of successful sports merchandising.

Each of the top 10 jerseys represent players who have well-defined, concrete, individualistic, interesting personalities that separate them from other players. Although success on the field generally helps, these players are not the best at their positions. None of the quarterbacks was one of the top five passers in the most recent year. Shockey and Moss were not among the top 30 receivers in 2004. Barber was fifth in the league in rushing in 2004 and Tomlinson was seventh. Fans flock to guys like Ben Roethlisberger, who came out of nowhere (Miami of Ohio) as a kind of ordinary, unassuming guy, to take the Steelers to 11 straight wins in his first year and the Super Bowl championship in his second. His personality fits well with the Steeler's team personality and the team's working class fan base. You can check out his personal Web site (www.br-7.com) to understand more about his fan following.

Third, the leaders in team sales represent teams with the highest brand equity in the league. Over the years, through championships and effective marketing, these teams have developed a large fan base that identifies itself with the persona of the team. If you were asked to picture something about the top-selling teams, clear images are likely to emerge. You might imagine the Cheeseheads of Green Bay, Oakland's fans wearing Darth Vader helmets, the sea of red jerseys on the fans at Chiefs' games, or the big blue star of the Dallas Cowboys' helmets. Often building upon fan-initiated traditions or rituals, these teams have invested in building the value of being associated with the brand in a way that differentiates them from other teams and their fans.

Teams with high brand equity can enhance the value of merchandise beyond its functional worth. If the Raiders are your favorite team, what would you pay for a cap with the Raiders' logo on it versus just another black cap? Is a Raiders' cap really worth the $23.99 the NFL (www.nflshop.com) wants for it? The difference between what they are able to receive for that logo cap versus an otherwise identical cap is one way of understanding the value of brand equity. In this sense, it is similar to the branding efforts of recognizable fashion names, such as Polo, Armani, D&G, or John Deere.[3] Individuals are willing to pay more for clothing with those brand marks than for similar clothing with a less visible or less prestigious brand name.

In a practical sense, responsibility for building the brand for the purpose of merchandising in sports is developmentally different from brand management in typical goods and services. Teams have traditionally treated merchandising and brand promotion as an afterthought. Companies with similar levels of revenue devote considerable resources to brand management, merchandise strategy, and sales. Sports teams, on the other hand, are likely to have only one individual responsible for merchandising—likely just to oversee the team's one or two stores. An exception to this rule is the Dallas Cowboys, who develop and distribute their own merchandise, run over 30 company-owned retail stores (plus five licensed shops located in selected JC Penney's stores), and have expanded into international markets.

Sports marketers have a special opportunity to capitalize on the level of fan identification with their team and associated brand marks. Packaged goods manufacturers must often generate demand for a category and selective demand for an individual brand. Kellogg's must not only make customers aware that they *should* eat breakfast and make them aware of their latest brand of cereal—Scooby Doo Berry Bones—but also persuade kids (and parents) that they (the kids) should eat the "bone-shaped cereal that tastes like berries." Sports teams, on the other hand, are more likely to be in something closer to a monopoly position in the local market. The task of merchandise sales strategies is to take advantage of the demand that is generated by the team, since selective demand for the brand has already occurred among those that are even interested in the category in the first place.

The purpose of the remainder of this chapter is to provide team marketers with methods to maximize merchandising revenue for the team. The overarching principle in maximizing revenue is to take strategic steps to build brand equity through merchandising. This perspective focuses on a proactive, rather than a reactive, approach to building brand equity through merchandising strategies. Too many sports teams react with merchandise after demand surfaces, such as after the team wins a championship. Teams can, however, enhance the

---

[3]If you think we're kidding, go to www.johndeeregifts.com

value of the brand through aggressive, proactive methods, thereby driving demand rather than letting demand drive them.

We initially examine the importance of distribution and positioning strategy in selling team merchandise, followed by creative merchandising tactics within bricks-and-mortar stores. The chapter concludes by outlining ways to increase fans' impulse purchases of merchandise at sporting events.

Distribution and Positioning

The most obvious necessity for selling merchandise is that the product must be available in the right place at the right time. Selling merchandise over the Internet is one solution to the time-place-availability issue for linking the team with fans who initiate the contact with the team to purchase merchandise. However, the design and management of the bricks-and-mortar distribution channel influences the positioning of the brand in the minds of fans, even if they end up going to the team's Web site to purchase merchandise.

We recognize that teams also choose licensees who will use the team logos and marks in the distribution and sale of team merchandise. With respect to determining appropriate distribution channels and positioning, we do not differentiate between licensed distribution and direct distribution because consumers perceive the source of the products to be the same, namely the team.

Retail positioning is not a concept original to sports merchandising. The principles are the same for sports as they are for other product marketers. The intensity of the distribution channels selected influences seven key merchandise-related factors (see Figure 10.1) that largely determine your retail positioning: service level, product assortment, retail control, brand image, brand equity, profit margin, and market share. If you want your brand to be perceived as high quality, you must limit supply through exclusive distribution. If you expand distribution to the point that consumers see it as nothing special—because they see team merchandise displayed next to $12.99 NASCAR's *Git'r Done*[4] t-shirts in multiple sporting goods retailers, or maybe even in mass market stores like Wal-Mart—then consumers' perceptions of the brand generally deteriorate.

---

[4]We actually like the *Git'r Done* t-shirts. We are also amazed that its originator, Larry the Cable Guy, is apparently capable of putting complete sentences together in his new tell-all book *Git-R-Done*. See http://www.larrythecableguy.com/ for more details.

Figure 10.1

Distribution Intensity and Retail Positioning

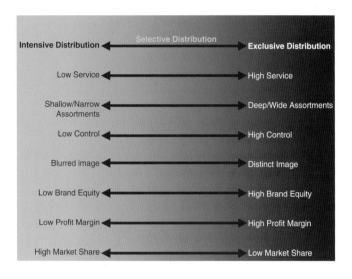

As distribution expands, the service level is reduced as you move from exclusive, to selective, to intensive distribution. Consumers associate higher service levels with higher quality, which also influences the brand image. Exclusive distribution provides more control over the merchandise mix and display, and over the service provided to customers. For instance, if a fan buys a jersey from a team-owned retail store, the fan is likely to find a broad and deep selection of team merchandise. Team-owned fan stores usually include all available apparel sizes and a wide variety of other team-related merchandise. The service people are focused on the team's merchandise and therefore tend to know something about the merchandise they are selling, such as knowing information about players, jersey types, and price lines. If anything goes wrong with the product, the fan knows he can return it and receive excellent service from the team store.

Conversely, customers are unlikely to get the same service at a sporting goods store, let alone a mass retailer. Sales and service people at these stores, if you can find any, are likely to be unfamiliar with specific customer needs. Employees are responsible for too many product lines, have too little training, and likely have the service motivation most often associated with stray felines. Furthermore, a given sporting goods store or mass retailer will not necessarily have the breadth of team-related product lines to meet the needs/wants of fans. Consequently, a fan watching Monday night football could see the NFL-licensed merchandise on the sidelines, go to the sporting goods store later that week searching for the Reebok NFL mid-weight pullover jacket of his favorite team, and not find it. Furthermore, service personnel in the store may have no idea what item he's looking for. The odds that this fan will ever get around to actually buying this item are greatly reduced.

Offering licensed merchandise in a more intensive distribution strategy can increase the team's market share, as more units are sold through more outlets. However, as merchandise moves to selective distribution through sporting goods stores and department stores, and then intensive distribution through mass (Target, K-Mart, Wal-Mart) and scrambled (convenience stores) retailers, profit margins are reduced due to increased price pressure through those outlets. Worse still, some of these retailers might use the team's merchandise as loss-leaders (e.g., "NFL team jerseys sold elsewhere for $74.99, now on sale—yours for only $19.99 when you shop at Grandpa Pigeon's") or promotional items (e.g., buy a DVD-player and get a free team cap) that devalue the brand. Increasing distribution intensity and market share also implies that the team is licensing the merchandise sold through these outlets, thereby receiving only a percentage of the total sales revenue. The sum effect of the more intensive distribution strategy is that you are aligning your brand with that of the retailer and the brands it carries. The further distribution is extended through other channels, the higher the likelihood that brand equity is reduced for team merchandise.

The solution is to find the appropriate middle ground that increases market share while not diluting brand equity. Due to the demand generated from success on the field during the 1990s, the Dallas Cowboys increased its distribution and market share, but lacked the control over its own merchandise and brand image. Consequently, the Cowboys took command over its own merchandising strategy, including design, outsourcing production, and distribution of its merchandise. The Cowboys withdrew distribution and refused to sell through Wal-Mart,[5] despite the guaranteed large volume. Distribution was

---

[5]Why not sell through Wal-Mart? Consider the Vlasic Pickle case. Vlasic agreed to distribute a 12 pound jar of pickles through Wal-Mart. Twelve pounds of pickles is a year's supply for most households—or more than a lifetime's supply at our house. Wal-Mart priced it at $2.97, which is about what most grocers charge for a quart of pickles. Vlasic spent decades convincing consumers that Vlasic means premium pickles and in one fell swoop Wal-Mart reduced Vlasic to a commodity.

limited to team-owned Dallas Cowboys Pro Shops and five Cowboys' specialty shops inside JC Penney's stores in Texas. This strategy enabled the Cowboys to position their merchandise as high quality. Fans knew where to go to find a complete line of all Cowboys' merchandise and received quality service. Distribution to sporting goods stores was dramatically cut back, so that fans were motivated to go to the Cowboys' shops. Since regaining control over their distribution channels, the Cowboys have slowly eased back into sporting goods stores— now more interested in getting Cowboys' merchandise after not being able to get any. This situation favors the Cowboys in terms of maintaining channel power, particularly when compared to the past when the Cowboys' retail fortunes were dictated by the merchandise strategies of its distributors.

Creative Merchandising

The previous section illustrated traditional means of distribution that influence brand positioning and brand equity. After the team has established its distribution intensity strategy, innovative merchandising tactics may be employed that get the brand to customers while also building brand equity. We address one dozen merchandising tactics that have been successful in other retailing contexts[6] and apply these concepts to sports team merchandising.

1. Training

Sports teams should provide an extensive training program for all team store managers and employees on all product categories and retailing practices.

What is the difference between shopping at a New Balance company store versus buying running shoes at other sporting goods stores that carry multiple athletic shoe brands? A salesperson at the New Balance store can guess your foot size and width at a glance, then tell you what shoes are best for your feet given your training program.[7] New Balance

---

[6]These merchandising tactics are largely derived from best practices in packaged goods marketing. See Dowdell, Stephen, Goldschmidt, Bridget, Major, Meg, McTaggart, Jenny, and Tarnowski, Joe. 2004. "Center store," *Progressive Grocer* 83 (November 15): 40–51.

[7]Palm reading is an extra $5.

employees are familiar with all of the stock that the store carries. Salespeople at many sporting goods chain stores (with the exception of The Athlete's Foot) will be lucky to differentiate a running shoe from a cross-training shoe. However, they often compensate by playing excellent hip-hop music in the store.

Training merchandise outlet employees provides better opportunities of selling and upselling merchandise. Well-trained employees can answer customer questions and provide excellent service that instills confidence in customers that customers are making a good choice when they spend upwards of $150 on an authentic game jersey versus a replica jersey for $59.99.[8]

2. Merchandise Display

Merchandise sales may be increased by grouping products by demographic profile (highest to lowest income) and high product interaction (e.g., pennants and other souvenirs) to make shopping easier. Shoppers will scan the merchandise displays to locate acceptable price lines. Arranging items from highest to lowest priced follows a logical pattern for consumer decision making, as consumers are likely to choose between two closely priced items rather than two disparately priced items.

Grouping complementary products together also takes advantage of the way people shop by placing similar alternatives in the same aisles. For instance, someone looking for a pennant is likely looking for a souvenir. So, it makes more sense to have the pennants located next to other gifts that might be substituted or added to the pennant purchase.

Scrambled merchandise displays that simply locate merchandise wherever space allows increases the psychic costs of shopping. We have been in some team pro shops where it appears as though the merchandise was displayed at the point closest to wherever it happened to get unloaded on delivery. In any case, if the merchandise displays and store layout make it taxing on the consumer to search for information and to evaluate product alternatives (e.g., jerseys are located in multiple areas in the store), consumers may instead opt to exit the store.

---

[8]While they are at it, maybe they can explain to us the difference between an authentic and a replica jersey besides the price. Perhaps the authentic jerseys are made with polyester harvested from only the highest grade of recycled milk bottles. If you think we're kidding again, you can read more at http://www.guvswd.org/symbols.

3. Service Level Modification

Sports organizations should identify why, how, where, and when consumers purchase and be prepared to offer appropriate service levels in different contexts. Specific shopping segments have different shopping modes and store sections can be designed to accommodate. For instance, product assortment, shelf space, and promotional events can be designed to attract speed seekers (in search of convenience) and empty nesters (high end gifts for selves and family members). To meet the needs of the speed seekers, high-volume items (e.g., Top Sellers Display) with an express check-out lane would likely increase sales to that segment. Conversely, elegant merchandise displays with ample sales assistance might attract the empty nesters.

At issue here is that not everyone shops in the same way with the same objectives. Wal-Mart has self-checkout areas for speed shoppers, express lanes for semi-speed shoppers and people who cannot count, and regular slow checkout counters for people with three kids hanging off the sides of the shopping basket whacking each other with Pixie Stix. In a similar fashion, sports merchandise outlets can be organized to cater to these segments. This would seem particularly useful for in-game arena/stadium outlets where shoppers are nearly always in a hurry (e.g., immediately before, during, and after the game).

4. Shelf Space Allocation

Shelf space allocation is a critical determinant of merchandise sales. Retail outlets must analyze the category dollar volume relative to shelf space to determine the appropriate allocation for key products. For example, one store found that its best-selling product in one category produced 34 percent of the volume but only had 11 percent of the shelf space, creating out-of-stock problems and reducing sales potential.[9]

Team merchandise outlets are likely to recognize their biggest sellers and will devote relatively large shelf space to these. However, shelf space analysis will enable you to know if too much space is being allocated to the top sellers and if other top sellers within categories are given too little space. For instance, if an NFL pro shop sold merchandise representing other teams, you might expect to sell large quantities of Michael Vick's jersey. What you might not expect is that rookies who haven't even played a down in the NFL are hot-

---

[9]Dowdell, Stephen, Goldschmidt, Bridget, Major, Meg, McTaggart, Jenny, Tarnowski, Joe. Center store. *Progressive Grocer* 83 (17): 40–51.

selling items that deserve more space.[10] Consequently, analysis of sales relative to shelf space might indicate that these jerseys receive more prominence in the bricks-and-mortar store, as well as on the online store.

5. Occasion Platforms

Team merchandise outlets can design special occasion platforms to spur purchase. Some of the obvious platforms are gift-giving holidays such as Father's Day (created by well-known fathers Calvin Coolidge and Richard Nixon[11]), Christmas,[12] and Talk Like a Pirate Day.[13]

Occasion platforms can increase sales because you are taking advantage of the sports fan's motivation to share his or her love for the team with others through gift-giving. This increases per cap sales for those individuals, as well as strengthening fan identification in the recipient of the gift. Further, individuals see the expenditure on the gift as an investment in their relationship with the recipient that has long-term benefits.[14] So, it's not necessarily allocated in the same personal budget that one has for spending on one's self. Research shows that individuals are willing to spend more money on gifts for one's (presented in order of expenditures):

1. Romantic partner,
2. Close family members,

---

[10]Among the top 25 selling jerseys in the NFL in September 2005 were four rookies: Tampa Bay running back Carnell Williams (eighth), San Francisco's Alex Smith (twelfth), Cleveland's Braylon Edwards (thirteenth), and Miami's Ronnie Brown (fifteenth).

[11]Father's Day was first supported by President Calvin Coolidge in 1924, as a result of an appeal for equity with Mother's Day. In 1972, President Richard Milhouse Nixon declared the third Sunday in June as the permanent date to honor Father's Day—really.

[12]Or Winter Solstice Holiday, for those whose institutions have a *Christ*mas break, but are censored from acknowledging anything remotely connected to the reason everyone gets to have a Christmas holiday.

[13]See http://www.talklikeapirate.com/. If in Great Britain, go to http://www.yarr.org.uk/. We personally think this would be a great promotional tie-in for the Pittsburgh Pirates, Tampa Bay Buccaneers and other assorted Pirates teams around the country. Whilst we arrgh against the likes of Captain Morgan Rum as a sponsor of said event, ye would do thee well to consider the notion.

[14]See Belk, Russell, and Coon, Gregory. 1993. Gift giving as agapic love: An alternative to the exchange paradigm based on dating experiences. *Journal of Consumer Research* 20 (4): 393–415.

3. Closest friend, and
4. More distant family and stepfamily members.[15]

Given these findings, Valentine's Day should be a great opportunity to target female fans to give team merchandise to their loved ones. Email offers, store displays, and event promotions can target the date with specific merchandise items, such as his and her jerseys. Promotions can be integrated into community service efforts that promote the merchandise while offering assistance to those in need. The New York Jets and Santana Moss offered his and her jerseys and four game tickets in an auction to raise money for needy individuals, helping raise over $100,000. Events like these can correspond to in-store promotions offering similar gifts for the occasion.

6. Purchase Situations

Merchandise displays can be designed to cater to specific recurring purchase situations. Whereas occasion platforms tend to be based on one-time annual events, arranging merchandise displays for specific purchase situations focuses on recurring or persistent shopping contexts. Examples of recurring purchase situations include (a) parents and grandparents buying souvenirs for kids or (b) highly identified fans buying authentic, personalized jerseys and fitted caps for themselves. Consequently, the Houston Texans could dedicate special display areas to the "Real Texans Fan" or "Texans Grandparents." Such areas allow shopping fans to quickly identify where they should shop to find products fitting their needs. Well-trained salespeople can steer fans to appropriate areas by asking, "Who are you shopping for today?"

7. Limited-Edition Product Promotions

Limited-edition products are not a new idea to pro teams and leagues, but can be more fully utilized as a means to increase merchandise sales. Souvenir buyers are primarily looking for a product that is unique—that relatively few others are likely to have—that bear special meaning and value to the owner. Tourists (i.e., infrequent out-of-town game attenders) are likely to have more interest in a unique,

---

[15]Genetic kin get much higher-valued gifts than nongenetic kin (i.e., step-children and step-parents receive cheaper gifts). See Saad, Gad, and Gill, Tripat. 2003. An evolutionary psychology perspective on gift giving among young adults. *Psychology & Marketing* 20 (9): 765–784.

high-quality, limited-edition souvenir than a common, lower-quality product.[16] Combining special-edition products with occasion platforms provides the opportunity to sell upscale merchandise. For example, the Boston Red Sox licensees sell a limited-edition opening day jersey that can be promoted heavily during early April each year.

Scarcity of a quality product increases fans' preferences for the product.[17] Product versions that are hard to find have more value to highly identified fans. Casual observation of sports card or coin collectors illustrates this phenomenon. Consequently, teams should select product lines and product editions that have limited production or supply that allow for higher profit margins. Teams can, however, produce too many special edition versions of merchandise such that fans start to see even the special editions as commonplace due to the frequency of their offerings. This implies that teams should develop an annual strategy of limited-edition productions with appropriate time intervals between introductions and clear conclusions to the selling period for the limited-edition items.

8. Growth Markets

Merchandise can be designed and promoted to be targeted at growing markets that previously did not warrant special attention. The growth of the Hispanic market in the southwestern United States, as well as other areas, led the Dallas Cowboys to design soccer jerseys emblazoned with the Cowboys' logo.

Consumer spending in the Hispanic market is expected to continue growing at significantly faster rates than overall U.S. consumer spending, reaching $1 trillion by 2010.[18] However, care should be taken in targeting Hispanics as a homogeneous market. For instance, while 20 percent of Cubans are 65 or older, only 4 percent of Mexicans are in the same age bracket. In contrast, 37 percent of Mexicans and 31 percent of Puerto Ricans are under 18 years old. The median age of individuals of Mexican descent in the United States is 24.7, compared to the overall U.S. median of 35.9 years. This suggests different merchandising approaches in the southwest (predominantly Mexican descent) and southeast (greater mix of Cuban descent). The merchan-

---

[16]See Swanson, Kristen K. 2004. Tourists' and retailers' perceptions of souvenirs. *Journal of Vacation Marketing* 10 (September): 363–377.

[17]See Lynn, Michael. 1991. Scarcity effects on value: A quantitative review of the commodity theory literature. *Psychology and Marketing* 8 (1): 45–57.

[18]www.csgis.com

dise mix in the southwest would need to appeal predominantly to the youth and young adult market, while the southeast could offer more products suitable for middle-age and older adults.

9. Frequent Shopper Cards

Supplying fans with frequent shopper cards allows teams to analyze price elasticities and to target customer offers based on buying behavior. Incentives to participate can be provided, such as cumulative discounts, so that the more they buy the greater the discount available (e.g., for every fourth purchase/visit, get a free team t-shirt of your choice).

The objective of frequent shopper cards is to collect individual purchase data each time a fan purchases a product. Combined with buyer profiles (income, ethnicity, age, attendance, media consumption, etc.), the team can determine what products at what prices are most frequently purchased by specific segments. Given that teams also have the buyer's email or mailing address, the team can offer personalized deals for individuals that meet specific segment criteria.

Retailers such as Barnes & Noble offer frequent buyer club memberships, requiring $25 to join and then offering 10 percent off of all purchases. Such a membership may be valuable for high volume bookworms who spend substantially more than $250 annually. The advantage to this program is that it is very simple for customers to understand ("I get 10% every time I shop at Barnes & Noble"). However, the $25 barrier to joining misses the point of being able to gather customer buying data for those that are not in the high-volume segment. Rather than giving customers an easy opportunity to opt out ("Would you like to join Barnes & Noble's Member Club today?"), teams might consider offering an initial deal (10% discount or bonus gift) to join the club. The upside of being able to track and target is worth the initial cost of such an offer if the team can more effectively merchandise and market.

10. Fresh Graphics Displays

Due to high fan involvement, sports teams frequently assume that buyers need no information or motivation to purchase their merchandise. If you go to the MLB.Com shopping sites, you can find frequent instances of apparel displays with no description of the product (except maybe the product name and jersey number). Most team's brick-and-mortar pro shops have little product description or promotional information accompanying the product. A crowded store layout and design exacerbates the problem as managers have little freedom to be creative when apparel hangs side-by-side or is stacked high in bins.

Individuals highly involved in a product category—in this case, your sport and your team where you work—will actually want to read more, not less, detail about merchandise. For instance, if you are a car nut[19] with a special bent toward Jaguars, you want to read everything there is to know about the new 2007 Jaguar XK. In the same way, if a fan is considering which team jacket or cap to buy, he or she will be willing to read all about it, providing the team with the opportunity to influence or reinforce the purchase choice (see Box on p. 218). The more information you provide fans about the quality of your merchandise and how it fits their lifestyle, the greater the likelihood that they will see the value of the merchandise as significantly better than similar items bought elsewhere.

Well-designed promotion graphics get shoppers' attention and allow for more in-depth mental and emotional elaboration related to the merchandise. As an extreme example, consider Niketown stores. Niketown stores are designed primarily as promotional vehicles more so than retail space designed to maximize sales per square foot. The graphic design engages shoppers who spend more time with the product and can evaluate specific features of the product. Team sports can use some of the same attention-grabbing techniques in graphic design used by Niketown while also providing shoppers with extensive product information that allows them to absorb and elaborate on the information—making it more deeply embedded in the minds of shoppers.

11. Electronic Product/Information Kiosks

Electronic kiosks can be used to expand the selling space available at sports venues, as well as speed up search, shopping, and purchasing for fans. Kiosks also reduce the need for employees to answer customer questions for those that are comfortable using the devices. Fans can scan products and instantly receive information ranging from prices of comparable or complementary products to interesting sports trivia associated with the product.

A critical problem faced by shops at peak selling periods (before and after the event) is insufficient space to handle the crowd of fans that would like to shop. Pro teams frequently employ workers to

---

[19]If you have ever wondered whether or not people are misguided and obsessed with auto minutiae such as the fact that only 1,150 Maserati Ghibli coupes and 125 Spyders were built between 1967 and 1973, please go to www.thecarnut.com. They are.

Ready for a Rumble or Not

The fan I have in mind never changes his favorite cap between the first preseason game in Ft. Myers and the last drizzly cold game in the last series in October. Drives a vintage pick-up that puts a GMC Sierra to shame. Resides in a brick house with a newly hewn cedar deck—38 steps from the grill (outside) to the kitchen refrigerator (inside). Roughly the equivalent of walking to first base at Fenway Park.

Doesn't go anywhere without his Red Sox cap.

Strong, tough, smooth, comfortable (could just as easily be speaking of the fan). For taking friends to the game, taking long walks with the retriever, meeting the guys down at the local watering hole on the other side of town.

The Boston Red Sox #9 Garment Washed Adjustable Cap (№. 1997365). Distinguished wool skull, cotton's more rugged cousin. Front crown features ole N° 9. Adjustable, comfortable rear strap, properly designed to avoid catching the last few hairs remaining on his head. Price: $29.

Men's sizes: One size fits all, and One size larger than one size fits all for the larger fan.

Color: Blue, Mustard (Colman's, of course).[20]

monitor and control the number of people that are allowed into the shop. This obviously creates an inconvenience for fans, reduces sales

---

[20]The J. Peterman catalog (http://www.jpeterman.com/) was the inspiration for this fresh product description. For those who have yet to catch on, this is supposed to represent an attempt at humor.

due to space constraints, and loses sales of those that aren't willing to stand in line just to get in the store—let alone brave the long check-out lines that promise to result in missing action on the floor or field.

Electronic kiosks can alleviate some of this pressure by increasing the speed at which shoppers can evaluate merchandise and make purchases. Merchandise kiosks can also provide those waiting in line (or elsewhere in the venue) the ability to virtual shop the store and make purchases that are either shipped or packaged for pick-up at the venue.

Self-service check-out kiosks can provide an easy way for the majority of shoppers who just want to purchase one or two items to check out quickly. The prevalence of such kiosks at Wal-Mart and other major grocery chains has educated consumers on how to use the systems. Pro sports teams that want to be ahead of the technology curve can overcome the pressing need to make better use of limited selling space and time by the use of such kiosks.

12. Scout Empty Retail Space

Opportunistic teams can take advantage of nearby temporary retail space by making a minimal offer to the lessor until a permanent tenant is secured. Sam's Clubs in Ohio, for instance, introduced a promotion they entitled "Traveling Roadshow" that leased out nearby vacant retail space to offer merchandise that couldn't normally be housed in their current facilities.[21] Similarly, teams can expand space during the season to other retail space under the guise of a special promotion, such as an All-Star Celebration centered around the all-star game break. The temporary use of the facility may also give the team the option to consider a long-term lease if the outlook is favorable based on early results.

Increasing Impulse Buying

Merchandise purchased in sports venues is frequently an impulse purchase. Impulse purchases can be partially or completely unplanned. Partially planned impulse purchases occur when the individual plans to buy some merchandise at the event, but has not determined what particular item will be purchased. Completely unplanned impulse

---

[21]Troy, Mike. 2000. Ultimate Roadshow latest Sam's Club innovation. *DSN Retailing Today* 39 (November 6): 3–4.

purchases occur when the individual had no intention of buying any merchandise prior to attending the event.

Two potential barriers limit the likelihood of impulse merchandise purchases at sporting events. From the fan's perspective, the first barrier is a function of an external structural problem related to the flow of traffic in and around the venue and the fan's actions that lead to time pressure in the sports venue. The second barrier is more specifically an internal dilemma for the fan related to spending money on impulse purchases that may have negative post-purchase repercussions. Each barrier is discussed below.

Time pressure. The prime time for impulse purchases is limited in sports venues. Figure 10.2 demonstrates the time pressure and related stress that fans experience as they attend a sporting event. Fans forced to spend too much time parking and entering the venue reduces the amount of time available for shopping and otherwise exploring the venue. Anything that the organization can do to speed up the parking and entry process will likely have a direct effect on fans' ability and willingness to buy merchandise—as any minute outside the gates is a minute not inside exploring. The longer it takes before arriving at an interior checkpoint—where the fan gets oriented to the venue and estimates how much time he or she has until the event starts—the higher the stress level that fans experience. The higher the stress, the less likely it will be that fans are going to be in the mood to shop once they get past the time checkpoint.

The best opportunity to prompt impulse merchandise sales is shortly after the fan gets his or her bearings after entering the gates. Between

Figure 10.2

Sports Venue Fan Stress. *Source:* Model adapted from Scholvinck, J. (2000). *The Travel Stress Curve*, Market Square Consulting, Amsterdam.

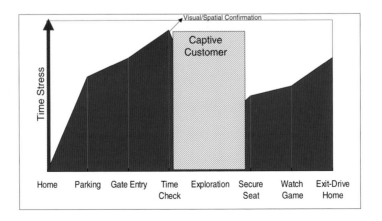

the time checkpoint and when the fan decides to sit and stay in the seats, he or she is a captive consumer subject to the environment and entertainment options available in the venue. This suggests that venue layouts should include merchandise shops or displays that are immediately available after the fan enters the venue, preferably in an open layout that allows a view of the entire venue. Failing that, clear signage to merchandise shops can facilitate exploration.

A problem faced at many venues is limited entry points and the presence of only one high quality, fully stocked merchandise shop. Worse yet, in older venues, the merchandise shop is apt to have been something of an afterthought—poorly configured and largely inaccessible.

In future sports venues, teams can facilitate shopping and the likelihood of impulse purchases by designing more entry points using self-service gates (viz., ticket-swipe technology) and locating shops (or carts) in close proximity to each side of the venue that encourage fans to explore the entire venue.[22] Another remedy to resolving the time pressure issue is to provide fans with the ability to purchase merchandise from their seats via order forms or interactive devices such as cell phones or wi-fi PDAs.

Internal pressure. The purchase of team merchandise is similar to purchases made by tourists at souvenir shops or travelers at airports.[23] In such situations a shopper may be reluctant to indulge in an impulse purchase. Since team merchandise is not exactly a necessity of life—as most sane[24] people perceive life—buyers may feel some guilt if the purchase is viewed merely in economic terms. An adult male fan may believe that an impulse purchase will be viewed negatively by others, namely the fan's wife. In such cases, the excitement or pleasure that accompanies the impulse purchase may be offset by the post-purchase evaluation that the money was not well spent.

---

[22]Teams might experiment with locating unique boutiques in various locations in the venue that would encourage fans to explore the venue to the different kinds of shops. For instance, shops could be segmented by product category: Caps/hats on the west side; jerseys/shirts/jackets on the east side; souvenirs on the south side; collectibles on the north side. We've never seen this done, but it sounds interesting. The downside is that this increases the effort of fans that want multiple items.

[23]The substantive portion of this discussion is drawn largely from Crawford, Gerry, and Melewar, T. C. 2003. The importance of impulse purchasing behaviour in the international airport environment. *Journal of Consumer Behaviour* 3 (September): 85–98.

[24]We assume that most readers of this text are not in this sane group. In fact, odds are that you wear team-related merchandise as part of your daily apparel . . . and that you would do so even if you were homeless.

Solutions to reducing the cognitive dissonance that occurs when making impulse purchases revolve around appealing to (a) the value offered or (b) the hedonic benefits of the purchase.

The first solution, increasing the value of the offer, may be accomplished by advertising displays that indicate that the fan is saving money by buying now. Price discounts on select merchandise will appeal to the fan that is price sensitive (or the fan that has other household members that want the fan to be price sensitive). Some merchandise will inevitably have to be discounted to move the inventory. These items can be used to improve impulse sales to price-sensitive shoppers.

Strategically, however, one must keep in mind that sale and regular priced inventory does not have to be sold through the same distribution channel. Off-site stores or online clearance outlets (or only specific stores) can be used to sell discounted items—for those willing to search for discounted merchandise—without affecting the image of the on-site or primary stores.

As we've discussed earlier in the text, you would rather not get fans thinking about purchases on merely an economic or rational level. If your answer for increasing sales is to lower the price, you're missing the point of most of this book, assuming you've been reading it. You would rather motivate impulse purchases by appealing to hedonic motives, which leads us to the second solution to dealing with fans' misgivings about impulse purchases.

Most fans don't come to games to shop for bargains.[25] They come to have fun, excitement, and to socialize. The way to take advantage of the emotional state of fans at the sports venue is for advertising, displays, and salespeople to emphasize themes along the following lines:

1. Guilt: Fans can compensate for the fact that they didn't bring family or other friends along with them by buying them a gift.

---

[25]However, you know you're a redneck if this doesn't apply to you and you only come on $1 hot dog and beer night. You also might be a redneck if you bring your snacks and cold drinks in your girlfriend's purse; or if you consider finishing off that half-full container of popcorn another fan leaves sitting in the seats; or if you're one of those people who go around the stadium collecting all the souvenir cups to give to your mom for Mother's Day. Finally, you might be a redneck if you go to the game and use words like the following: bo•lo•gna (b_ lo′n_), v. 1. to be amazed, impressed. As in, "That team is good! I'm tellin' you man, I was bologna way!" See: Foxworthy, Jeff (2005), *Jeff Foxworthy's Redneck Dictionary: Words You Thought You Knew the Meaning Of.* Villard Books.

- Salesperson: "Did you bring your family with you to the game today?"

2. Reward: Fans may believe that they should purchase because they deserve a break today or because they are worth it or for some other self-indulgent reason.
   - Salesperson: "You look like the kind of person who deserves to have a cool jersey like this."

3. Information overload: The cognitive processing and mental accounting of fans can become confused or distracted in highly entertaining or interesting store designs. Why else would anyone buy merchandise in the shops contained in a Rainforest Café?
   - Store interior design: Provide a variety of interesting graphics, colors, lights, sounds, smells, and even tastes to generate excitement—which leads to higher purchases.[26]

4. Exclusivity: Fans are more willing to make purchases if they believe there is a scarcity of a desirable product. Offering exclusive items only available at the sporting event can attract those who were considering buying merchandise at some point, but not today.
   - Advertising/Salesperson: "Only sold here. Not available outside of Fenway Park."

5. Forgetting: Fans sometimes forget things they actually need at the sporting event, such as sunglasses, visors/caps, rain ponchos, sunblock, seat cushions, team diapers, etc.
   - Store advertising (visually display frequently forgotten items): "Forget Something?"

Now that you are supplied with plenty of good ideas to keep your merchandise manager busy for the next five years, we now turn to how teams can more effectively control the entire merchandising process through closed-loop management.

Closed-Loop Management

Teams can enhance the brand equity of their merchandise through long-term and short-term decisions. Long-term decisions include the distribution and positioning strategy that enables the team to build and maintain brand equity in the minds of fans. Short-term efforts

---

[26]Wakefield, Kirk, and Baker, Julie. 1998. Excitement at the Mall: Determinants and effects on shopping response. *Journal of Retailing* 74 (Fall): 515–540.

include creative merchandising tactics and increasing impulse purchases through well-defined approaches employed in their advertising, displays, and sales methods.

Team management responsible for merchandising may develop excellent long-term strategies and short-term creative tactics; yet, the initiatives can fail in the field due to untimely or incomplete execution. To prevent, recognize, and remedy implementation failures and to assure successful implementation, management must undertake a circular process known as closed-loop management.[27] The closed-loop approach means that for each strategic initiative management assigns responsibilities and tasks and requires accountability downstream to complete those responsibilities and tasks. The basic closed-loop process of merchandise management is:

$$\text{design} \rightarrow \text{implement} \rightarrow \text{execute} \rightarrow \text{evaluate} \rightarrow \text{redesign}$$

Management of closed-loop processes in merchandising is not just supply chain management, where the primary concern is with logistics, inventory, and distribution timelines and fulfillment. Effective supply chain management is necessary just to be able to play the game. To excel, closed-loop management in merchandising must monitor each store's or unit's tasks associated with a given project to guarantee that plans are executed in a coherent manner. Projects could include any of the creative merchandising initiatives previously discussed in this chapter, such as occasion-based promotional events, a new launch of a limited-edition jersey, or some other advertising/display roll-out.

As the San Francisco Giants roll out a new merchandise campaign around Barry Bonds assault on the all-time homerun record, each team store and licensee should have specific responsibilities. Stores will need to receive and put up signage; additional salespeople may need to be scheduled; product space/displays removed, rearranged, and replaced; and stock made available and priced according to plan. Failure to complete these tasks on the appropriate timeline will result in suboptimization of the merchandising strategy, as customers may see advertising campaigns for the merchandise but are unable to easily find the merchandise in stores because of poor execution of end-of-aisle or entrance displays.

For organizations with only one or two outlets, checking off the task list to execute the plan is important, but may not require very

---

[27]For application of this process in fashion design see Baker, Stacy. 2004. Next trends in apparel retail, manufacturing, fashion & merchandising—Management briefing: Retail. *Just—Style*. December: 2–11.

sophisticated means to complete. However, for larger operations and multiple outlets and licensees, organizations should use software solutions that allow for an integrated response and score sheet regarding the actions of all relevant parties. With such software, each unit or store marks off each task in "to-do" lists associated with each project that are electronically communicated between management and those selling merchandise at the point of customer contact. Those units that complete all of the tasks by the assigned times are considered in compliance. Units not in compliance are subject to remedial actions (e.g., licensees may not be renewed or may not be included in certain projects). This also implies that team management will need to conduct field audits of units to confirm compliance of larger organizations.

Whether it is pencil/paper or advanced software solutions, effective control is necessary to ensure successful merchandising strategies.

Create Technological Advantages

11

Technology Adoption

How can technology change the way you do business? Consider the experience of Major League Baseball[1] over the last five years. What would have happened if MLB had sat on their collective hands during this time?

- In the 12 hours following the last pitch of the 2004 World Series, the league's Web site, MLB.com, sold $3 million worth of Sox gear. In 24 hours, the site sold $5 million of Red Sox merchandise.

- One week earlier, MLB.com set a site-record mark for single-day traffic when more than 8 million fans viewed approximately 11 pages each to, among other things,
  - look at news and stats,
  - listen to or watch a game,
  - buy merchandise, and
  - play online games.

- For the 2004 season, more than 1 billion visits to MLB.com generated a reported $120 million to $140 million in revenue (including 11.2 million tickets). All this despite the fact that critics

[1]Surmacz, Jon. 2005. In a league of its own: Major League Baseball used CRM to succeed with a venture that many thought would strike out. *CIO* 18 (April 15): 1.

figured that MLB.com would never amount to much for Major League Baseball.

- Major League Baseball Advanced Media (MLBAM) has been profitable since 2002, deriving revenue from paid content, advertising, sponsorships, and e-commerce—notwithstanding a checkered beginning with audio and video glitches and an initial poorly designed homepage.

- MLBAM negotiated seven-figure sponsorship deals with Real-Networks, MasterCard and Marriott Vacation Club to bolster its market offerings.

- A key segment attracted to MLB.com were "displaced fans" who live too far away to go to games and can't catch them on TV, and will pay for Web content (currently $79.95 for a season pass).

- MLB.com has gone through two major renovations (after the 2001 and 2003 seasons) to accommodate strategy.

- During peak in-season hours, the Web site updates every six seconds.

- MLB.com uses SAS (www.sas.com) to collect and manage customer data to be used in understanding its customers and designing services they want. Most of the data is collected through subscriptions and e-commerce transactions, and is supplemented by emails collected via sweepstakes, online newsletters, and other offers. Web-tracking tools allow for knowing which customers go to what pages.

- In four years, MLB.com has collected 10 million email addresses—half of which opt in to receive offers from the site.

- AOL and other instant message services partner with MLBAM to feed MLB content to customers who sign up for an MLB Buddy on their Buddy Lists.

- MLBAM is aggressively moving toward wireless devices to be accessible to the next generation of sports fans who want content on the go. For instance, Mets fans who express an interest may receive a text message with something like: "Good afternoon, Mr. Smith. It's a sunny 71 degrees outside. There are still seats available for the Mets game at 1:10 p.m. today against the Reds at Shea Stadium. Press '1' if you'd like to purchase tickets." If the offer is accepted, the fan receives a bar code that will be accepted at the gate.

- In the wireless market, MLBAM sold over 1 million cell phone wallpapers, ring tones, and other downloads. Future wireless efforts will focus on expanding fantasy baseball league content to wireless to the five to eight million people in the United States who participate in online fantasy leagues.

From this example, it is clear that MLB is an innovator or early adopter in the use of technology in marketing to its fans. MLB identified a primary target audience (displaced fans and rabid stats fiends), key needs of fans (highlights, stats, fantasy games), appropriate product and distribution (video, frequently updated pitch-by-pitch coverage of games, personalized downloads), appropriate communication media (online, wireless, emails), and delivered it at a high perceived value to the targeted fans who were willing to pay.

Importantly, MLB found corporate partners (RealNetworks, Master-Card, and Marriott Vacation Club) who share the same customer footprint. This is a critical element in sports marketing, as teams can avoid footing the entire bill for new technology that has a direct interface and interchange with fans. If that new technology enables the team to better communicate with fans, it also enables sponsors to better communicate with fans or to be associated with a service that fans appreciate. When AT&T provides the San Francisco Giants with universal wireless service at AT&T Park, fans are able to associate this service with its sponsor (AT&T) while the Giants are able to better meet the needs of its technologically savvy market.

> **AT&T Park** became the first professional sports venue to provide continuous universal wireless access to fans in all concourses and seating areas. Working in conjunction with AT&T, the Giants have installed 123,802.11b/g WiFi access points, creating one of the largest public wireless hotspots in the world. Fans who bring their PDA, tablet PC, laptop, or other WiFi-enabled device to the ballpark will gain free access to the Internet and the Giants Digital Dugout. To learn more, go to http://www.pervasiveservices.com/

When it comes to technology adoption, where are you personally? Are you an innovator? An early adopter? A laggard? If you are working for a sports organization, how quickly is your organization likely to adopt and adapt to new technology? While most teams have adopted the use of ticket scan technology, some have been slower in moving in this direction despite the obvious benefits to customers (easily replaced and electronically transferred) and the venue (controls fraud, provides real-time attendance tracking, improved database customer tracking, etc.). The speed at which technology is adopted varies across teams and leagues. While we may appreciate the uniqueness of changing the line scores literally by hand at Wrigley Field, we aren't likely to classify the Cubs organization as innovators in technology.

In contrast to the Cubs, the major sports leagues such as MLB, NFL, NBA, and NHL in the United States have moved quickly to adopt the newest technologies that are used to serve the needs of customers and to generate revenue. Individual teams, such as the San Francisco Giants, are at the forefront of new technology, paving the way for others. The Giants were the first sports team to provide universal wireless service to the entire facility at AT&T Park. Anyone with a mobile wireless device in AT&T Park can connect online to find the food they want in the stadium, play interactive games, check real-time stats and scores, watch highlight videos and replays, or even watch other live MLB games on their mobile devices.

Interestingly, according to research from www.forrester.com:[2] "NFL, MLB, and NBA fans are more likely than the average consumer to own video game consoles, receive cable TV, and shop online. NHL fans are ahead of the technology adoption curve, including online and broadband penetration."

Consequently, it is imperative that sports teams stay ahead of the curve in the use of technology so that they can keep up with their fans.

RFID Enters the Sports Arena[3]

Two NFL stadiums are leading the way in one company's efforts to use RFID to speed payments, increase customer insight and boost consumer spending.

Having run trials of its PowerPay cashless *RFID* payment system at limited locations at two National Football League stadiums— the Seattle Seahawks' Qwest Field and the Philadelphia Eagles' Lincoln Financial Field—during the past football season, *Smart System Technologies (SST)* is now fully deploying its RFID payment system across both stadiums in time for next season.

The system works by linking PowerPay RFID readers to point-of-sale (POS) terminals. To make purchases, consumers can opt to use a personal PowerPay key fob fitted with an *RFID tag.* That

---

[2]Charron, Chris. 2006. "Business View Research Documents," www.forester.com, April 6.

[3]Reprinted from Jonathan Collins, *RFID Journal*, July 30, 2004.

tag carries a unique *license plate* number and no personal data. By putting the tag within an inch and a half of the reader the consumer can make the purchase. The company says it has initially targeted football stadiums for its payment system, but it says that is just the first part of a push to see its RFID payment systems installed throughout a range of arenas and retail outlets.

"Football is a good place for us to start. Football teams consistently sell out so they have to look for new ways to raise incremental revenues beyond selling seats," says Michael Richardson, chief technology officer at SST, which is based in New York City. For SST, partnering with NFL teams to promote its cashless payments system to their fans creates a way to tie cashless payments into targeted marketing promotions. So far, promotional offers have allowed fans to enter sweepstakes and earn points for dollars spent with PowerPay that could be redeemed for merchandise and rewards.

Assume, if necessary, that you have the responsibility to determine whether or not your organization will adopt a new technology such as radio frequency identification (RFID) tracking systems for merchandise purchases and management.[4] You are asked, "When is your organization going to invest in that technology?"[5] What would your response be?

Attitude	Stage
We want to be the first one to have that technology.	Innovator
We keep tabs on what the innovators are doing and we're usually one step behind them.	Early adopter
When we've seen the system prove itself and there are plenty of others invested in the technology, we'll join in.	Early majority
We won't invest until most teams have made the switch and it becomes really inconvenient to do what we've been doing.	Late majority
Not until the Cubs win the World Series. Twice.	Laggard

[4]See Box on RFID use in the NFL or http://www.rfidjournal.com/ for more general information.
[5]The table is a paraphrase of Everett Roger's Diffusion of Innovations and is adapted from Moore, Geoffrey A., and McKenna, Regis. (2002). *Crossing the chasm: Marketing and selling high-tech products to mainstream customers.* New York: HarperCollins.

If sports leagues are like any other industry, the teams that invest in advanced technology are more likely to gain market share.[6] Organizations that increase their strategic decision-making speed to act on shifts in technology use will grow faster and be more profitable than competitors.[7] So, you're welcome to be a laggard when it comes to technology, but odds are high that you'll be chasing the other teams in the league in terms of profitability and growth. Ultimately, this leads back to being able to afford the payrolls to put a good product on the field.

Some might argue that their teams (or owners) simply don't have the money to invest in new technology. However, organizations choose how to invest their monies, whether it is on facilities improvements, player personnel, executive salaries, or technology. Hence, it is an issue of priorities. If the technology investment results in greater internal efficiency that enables better service and ultimately increases fan satisfaction and consumption, the costs of being a technology laggard are high.

The reason individual decision makers in organizations fail to adopt new, useful technologies has more to do with their own personal risk aversion and inability to deal with change[8]—which may be compounded by the fact that they have surrounded themselves with other technology-cautious individuals who still picture a hot smash over the third-baseman's head when someone talks about a "hard drive."[9] Consequently, if you are in a position that allows you an opportunity to embrace new technology and you find yourself blaming the organization or others for being behind the times in a technological sense, then (a) you are deceiving yourself, or (b) you really are in a backward organization and have not been able to find a better job elsewhere. Thankfully, after having read this section of the chapter, you will be

[6]Baldwin, John R., and Sabourin, David. 2002. Advanced technology use and firm performance in Canadian manufacturing in the 1990s. *Industrial and Corporate Change* 11 (August): 761–789.

[7]Smith, Robert H. and Wally, Stefan. 2003. Strategic decision speed and firm performance. *Strategic Management Journal* 24 (August): 1107–1129.

[8]See Brennan, Linda L., Miller, John R., and Moniotte, Susan M. 2001. Herding cats to water: Benchmarking the use of computers in business education. *Journal of Education for Business* 76 (July/Aug.): 345–352. Also see Chan-Olmsted, Sylvia M., Li, Jack C., and Jung, Jaemin. 2005. The profiling of cable modem broadband consumers: Characteristics, perceptions and satisfaction. *Journal of Targeting, Measurement and Analysis for Marketing* 13 (August): 327–345.

[9]Yes, we know this isn't hilarious. But, it's hard to make a chapter on technology very funny.

a new convert to technology advancement and will promptly make www.zdnet.com your homepage and attach your new RIM Crackberry to your belt.[10]

Technology Acceptance

Now that we are all on the same page, technologically speaking, we can turn our attention to understanding those factors that determine when individuals (fans or employees) will generally be willing to accept and use new technology.

The two basic determinants of technology acceptance[11] are perceived usefulness (PU) and perceived ease of use of the technology (PEOU). Perceived usefulness is the degree to which someone believes that using the technology will improve performance. Perceived ease of use refers to the extent to which someone believes that the technology would be easy to use. When Sony introduced its new Sony PSP (Playstation Portable), it sold more than 500,000 units in two days, as consumers apparently believed that it was easy to use and would improve their ability to play games online via wireless networks.

The benefits to using the Sony PSP were easy to understand by its target market, primarily because it was based on existing technologies. The PSP uses the same wide-aspect ratio as HDTV units and incorporates a CD/DVD-like device that is small but capable of storing an entire movie, and it communicates with other systems via existing wi-fi networks. The PSP was a component innovation that used new parts or materials within an existing technological platform. The Universal Media Disk (which is a CD/DVD device of a size small enough to fit into the system to load games, yet large enough to hold large amounts of data) introduced a different component—but still relies upon the same technological platform as other digital storage devices.

---

[10]Assuming you are not wearing *Sansabelt®* brand slacks. To the uninformed: *Crackberry* is the street name for RIM's Blackberry, because the use of the product becomes so addicting that people check their email no matter where they are (e.g., driving, restroom, church, operating table, etc.). For more information, go to www.blackberry.com

[11]Davis, F. D. 1989. Perceived usefulness, perceived ease of use, and user acceptance. *MIS Quarterly* 13 (3): 319–340. Also see Ma, Qingxiong, and Liu, Liping. 2004. The technology acceptance model: A meta-analysis of empirical findings. *Journal of Organizational and End User Computing* 16 (January): 59–62.

A radical innovation is based on scientific principles that are manifestly different from existing technologies.[12] A compact disk was radically different from the use of cassettes or floppy disks to record and play music and other data, as it relied on a different technology (laser optics) than the old technology (magnetic recording). Variations on this laser optic technology have since occurred that are simply design innovations, which is rearranging or reconfiguring the layout or relationships between components within the same technological platform. Most of what Apple has introduced with the iPod and other pc's are design innovations featuring plastic coverings that are aesthetically more pleasing than other pc's.

Radical innovations typically take longer for consumers to understand than do component or design innovations. As consumers learn about the technology, their perceptions regarding its ease-of-use improve, which in turn enhances the perceived benefits of using the technology. The more that consumers believe it is easy to use and that it will work better (i.e., improve performance) than the old technology, they will have a positive attitude toward the technology and will begin using it.

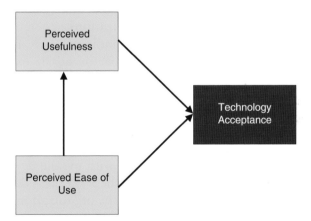

Being the astute learner that you are, you are now beginning to ask the question, "So, what does this have to do with sports marketing?" It is at this point that we must carefully consider all aspects of the issue and admit that we have no idea. No, seriously, as sports marketers, you must be able to assess the technological environment and

---

[12]See Sood, Ashish, and Tellis, Gerard J. 2005. Technological evolution and radical innovation. *Journal of Marketing* 69 (July): 152–168.

estimate the future impact of technology on your business. To do so, you must understand what constitutes radical innovations and how quickly (if at all) such innovations are likely to be accepted by consumers.

As this is being written, professional sports teams are uncertain as to the growth in the use of mobile communication devices. Team business executives are not willing to invest in wireless technology applications in their venues because the current number of fans who are using mobile devices to transmit and receive rich media is limited. However, one doesn't have to be a fortune teller to know what will happen next in this market. A scan of related business news stories—or even occasionally picking up a *Wall Street Journal*—will tell you that 3G mobile devices (capable of high-speed, high-quality wireless video transmission) are already widely used in Europe, indicating that the devices are easy to use and are useful and that acceptance of the technology will be swift. While other parts of the world, including the United States, have been slower to invest in the appropriate technology infrastructure and provide appropriate commercial content guidelines, it is a foregone conclusion that the market penetration for 3G devices will begin to be saturated in developed countries by 2010.[13] Hence, we return to two questions: When it comes to technology adoption, where are you personally? Where is your organization?

Organizations that choose to be technology innovators or early adopters are likely to have at least one person at the executive level that engages in technology assessment to make strategic decisions. Strategic technology assessment is a process to determine if emerging technologies are appropriate for broad-based applications within the sports arena. An assessment of the G3 technology we've been discussing should make it clear that it is not a question of whether or not fans will be walking into sports facilities with mobile devices in hand and electronically communicating with others via these devices during the game. The only question is when will the organization be prepared to communicate with their fans via these devices in ways that fans value. As the strategic-type thinker that you are, you would opt for the more proactive stance (innovator, early adopter, early majority) than for the reactive stance of the late majority or laggard.

---

[13]If I am wrong on this, it is someone else's fault. Industry estimates now are that the wireless content market will grow from worldwide revenues of around $17 billion in 2005 to $78 billion by 2007. That's a pretty robust growth rate, which we would calculate if we were finance majors.

Doing Business Online

Now that you are convinced of the need to assess innovations and to be ahead of the technology curve, we turn to the management of the most critical technology component for sports marketers: online retail stores.

The process fans go through to make a purchase decision online is no different than for any other consumer purchase. Table 11.1 outlines the five stages in the consumer decision-making process adapted to the information-rich online environment:

Need recognition $\rightarrow$ Information search $\rightarrow$ Information evaluation $\rightarrow$ Purchase decision $\rightarrow$ Post-purchase behavior

Table 11.1 includes practical checkpoints for online store management to facilitate the fan's ability to progress through each stage. We discuss each stage in turn and what your organization needs to do to be successful with online retail sales.

Need Recognition

For fans to consider buying merchandise online, they must first recognize an unsatisfied need or want. Dynamic Web sites can help motivate a fan to recognize a substantive difference between the fan's current state (lack of a particular product) and his or her desired state (ownership of a particular product), thereby prompting the initiation of the decision process. The wider the perceived gap between the current state and the desired state, the greater the likelihood of eventual purchase.

Appetizers and banner ads. Effective Web sites offer well-designed attention-getters that prompt the initial consideration of the current-desired state with respect to a given product or product category. Attention-getting devices can be classified as nonproduct-related and product-related appetizers that work together to produce sales. Nonproduct-related appetizers attract and involve site visitors to play games or read articles that lead to or incorporate product-related appetizers, which are promotions for products. Once the fan engages in the interactive game or reads the article, the fan may be exposed to banner ads or other forms of Web ads for a specific product (e.g., a special edition cap) or category (team caps).

Frequent-buyer incentives. One way to get the attention of loyal site visitors is to offer premiums on purchases for frequent purchases. The Jacksonville Jaguars have an "Extra Points Loyalty Card" that allows season ticket holders to receive merchandise discounts (10% on

Table 11.1

Online Stone Checkpoints	
Stage in Decision-Making Process	**Checkpoint**
Need recognition	**Does the online store**
1 Product-related appetizers	Provide product-related appetizers such as sales items, hot products, or product recommendations?
2 Nonproduct-related appetizers	Provide nonproduct-related appetizers such as magazines, games, etc.?
3 Banner ads on the pages	Put banner ads for itself?
4 Frequent-buyer incentives	Give discounts or premiums to frequent buyers?
5 Extra questions to collect customer information	Ask additional personal questions on the order form?
Information search	
6 FAQ	Provide an FAQ on product and service-related information?
7 Site index	Provide an overview of the entire site?
8 Product/store index	Provide lists of all products? All brick-and-mortar stores?
9 Product search function	Provide its own product search function?
10 Freshness	Offer new information on a systematic, regular basis?
Information evaluation	
11 Link between related product pages	Provide links between related products (e.g., caps, hats, other headgear)?
12 Help on product selection	Provide tables or figures to help customers evaluate alternatives?
13 Phone/email	Provide 1-800 number or email address for customers to contact a sales representative?
14 Endorsement	Provide links to locations that have endorsements from other customers?
15 Colors	Have pictures that demonstrate the true colors of the merchandise?
Purchase decision	
16 Shopping in different modes	Allow customers to shop in different mode (brand, price, or department)?

Table 11.1 *Continued*

Stage in Decision-Making Process		Checkpoint
Purchase decision		**Does the online store**
17	Order by phone	Allow customer to order the product by phone?
18	Money-back guarantee	Provide some form of money-back guarantee?
19	Order tracking	Have a mechanism for customers to track their orders?
20	Privacy/Security	Contain statements regarding security and at least one consumer privacy/security seals (e.g., Verisign)?
Post-purchase behavior		
21	Online user group/chat room	Provide a way for customers to communicate with other customers who have similar interests?
22	Online support	Provide online support (e.g., chat with service operator)?
23	Return customer recognition	Recognize return customers ("Hello Bubba") with stored shopper data (shipping address, etc.)?

Source: Framework adapted from Huarng, Adam S., and Christopher, Doris (2003). Planning an effective Internet retail store. *Marketing Intelligence & Planning* 21 (4/5): 230–238.
Other sources: Nitse, Philip S., Parker, Kevin R., Krumwiede, Dennis, and Ottaway, Thomas. The impact of color in the e-commerce marketing of fashions: An exploratory study. *European Journal of Marketing* 38 (7): 898–915.
Waite, Kathryn, and Harrison, Tina. (2002). Consumer expectations of online information provided by bank websites. *Journal of Financial Services Marketing* 6 (June): 309–323.
Wakefield, Robin L., Stocks, Morris H., and Wilder, W. Mark. The role of web site characteristics in initial trust formation. *The Journal of Computer Information Systems* 45 (Fall): 94–103.
Yuan-shu, Lii, Lim, Hyung J., and Tseng, L.P. Douglas (2004). The effects of web operational factors on marketing performance. *Journal of American Academy of Business* 5 (September): 486–494.

items $8 and over). Such offers not only get the fan's attention, prompting the decision process (by informing or reminding them of the bonus offer), but also make the decision easier by reducing the perceived (financial) risk of purchasing the item (stages 3 and 4, information evaluation and purchase decision, respectively) and rewards loyal customers (stage 5, post-purchase behavior).

Information collection. Another way to prompt the decision-making process is by collecting pertinent information on sign-up or order forms so that specific offers best suited to the fan's needs are generated in future visits. For instance, if a data query indicates that the fan attended the majority of the home games, an offer could pop up for a special edition team jersey. Conversely, if the fan lives out-of-state and is a frequent site visitor, an offer to receive video-on-demand or live Web game broadcasts may be more appropriate. Such offers can be designed and activated according to the cookies stored on the recipient's pc.

Information Search

The primary purpose of Web site visits is to gather information.[14] If pertinent information is not available, interested site visitors may terminate the process or opt to search elsewhere. The quality of the information on the site directly represents the usefulness of the site to the user.

Just as you accommodate first-time visitors to the stadium by providing attendants, information desks, and other service people to provide directions, care must be taken to provide appropriate information and directions for online sites. Sites that provide live chats with service people are attempting to remedy the lack of personal interaction that is available at bricks-and-mortar venues or stores. Other ways to facilitate information search are listed in Table 11.1.

FAQ's. Since site visitors may be using the Web site to gather information before making a purchase at a physical store, the team Web site should provide locations and directions to all store outlets. Since team employees may have difficulty understanding the perspective of uninformed or new customers, focus groups can be employed to develop a list of frequently asked questions.

Site index and search engines. Since team Web sites cover a wide range of topics and product information, a thorough, searchable site index, including a list of all products, should be provided. Technically poor search functions can easily frustrate site visitors, leading to premature site exits. The choice of the type of search engine used on the Web site determines the quality of the search. Crawler-based search engines, such as Google, are more likely to return good matches for

---

[14]Waite, Kathryn, and Harrison, Tina. 2002. Consumer expectations of online information provided by bank Web sites. *Journal of Financial Services Marketing* 6 (4): 309–322.

obscure searches. Human-based search engines based upon listings put together by employees are more apt to miss such requests. Site visitors frequently use search functions because they can't find what they're looking for in the obvious places (i.e., links available on primary pages). Consequently, human-based search engines may turn up "zero" results for something that visitors know is there somewhere, perhaps because they ran across it on previous visits. The result is frustration and likely exit from the site.

How Search Engines Work

The term "search engine" is often used generically to describe both crawler-based search engines and human-powered directories. These two types of search engines gather their listings in radically different ways. Crawler-based search engines, such as Google, create their listings automatically. They "crawl" or "spider" the Web, then people search through what they have found. If we change our Web pages, crawler-based search engines eventually find these changes, and that can affect how we are listed. Page titles, body copy, and other elements all play a role.

Crawler-based search engines have three major elements. First is the spider, also called the crawler. The spider visits a Web page, reads it, and then follows links to other pages within the site. This is what it means when someone refers to a site being "spidered" or "crawled." The spider returns to the site on a regular basis, such as every month or two, to look for changes.

The second part of the crawler-based search engine is the index. The index, sometimes called the catalog, is like a giant book containing a copy of every Web page that the spider finds. If a Web page changes, the book is updated with the new information.

Search engine software is the third part of a crawler-based search engine. This is the program that sifts through the millions of pages recorded in the index to find matches to a search and rank them in order of what it believes is most relevant.[15]

A human-powered directory, such as the Open Directory, depends on humans for its listings. When directories have enough Web sites for a category and it is "full," more categories and

---

[15]Sullivan, Danny. 2002. How search engines work. http://searchenginewatch.com

subcategories are created. There are thousands of directories on the Web today and many of them specialize in particular subject areas. When you submit a Web site to a directory it is usually accompanied with a short description of the Web site and some keywords that best describe the Web site's content. The directory editors then review the site by visiting it on the Web and then adding it to their category. In some cases they may even create a new category or subcategory. Usually listings appear in alphabetical order but you may possibly also have to pay a small subscription fee to be listed at the top.

Changing the Web page has no effect on its listing. Things that are useful for improving a listing with a search engine have nothing to do with improving a listing in a directory. The only exception is that a good site, with good content, might be more likely to get reviewed for free than a poor site. Usually a hybrid search engine will favor one type of listing over another. For example, MSN Search is more likely to present human-powered listings from LookSmart. However, it does also present crawler-based results (as provided by Inktomi), especially for more obscure queries.

Source: Raisinghani, Mahesh S. (2005). Search engine technology: A closer look at its future. *Information Resources Management Journal* 18 (April–June): 1–7.

Freshness. A key objective in site maintenance is keeping fresh content. The nature of sports Web sites is to provide immediate updates regarding team performance and related information. To drive business through a Web site, however, new product information and offers must also be made available to generate interest among frequent visitors. If visitors always see the same offers in the same format, they grow accustomed to the information and screen it out. While some consistency is recommended to accommodate frequent shoppers, some variation in offers and product information is necessary to generate fan interest that may lead to purchases.

Information Evaluation

Product selection. In order to drive repeat business, Web site designs should facilitate consumer search and evaluation to help site visitors make good purchase decisions. Interactive shopping aids (ISAs) or shopbots help shoppers compare products based on criteria important to the shopper. For instance, when you go to www.circuitcity.com

searching for a new computer, you can select models to compare with respect to price, brand, and features. Models selected are placed side by side in a comparison matrix so that the shopper can determine which model has the best mix of desired features.[16] The ISA simulates what we do when we go to a store and compare multiple products. In the same way, team Web sites can facilitate consumer decision making by providing similar shopbots that might allow a fan to compare products—or just to keep track of the products they are considering buying.

Contact information. Team Web sites should have clear and obvious contact information to facilitate product evaluation. If you visit www. mavsgear.com, the official online store of the Dallas Mavericks, you will find their phone number, email, mailing address, and fax under the first FAQ and in the About Us sections. Of course, a 1-800 number would also be appropriate.

Some teams have allowed the league to host the team retail site. An advantage to this approach is a coherent and consistent team site design. A problem with this approach is that such sites may not provide the personal attention from the home team and their employees. Guess where you find the contact information on www.nbastore.com? You don't. As of this writing, no phone number or email is readily available on that site for individual teams, stores, or anyone else for that matter.

Endorsements. Individuals visiting a team Web site are likely to differ with respect to the kinds of information they use to evaluate products. That is, some people will want to read detailed information about products and services and judge for themselves whether or not the product is suitable. Others, however, look elsewhere to confirm that a product is good or that the service provider is trustworthy. In the latter case, customer endorsements and expert opinions are likely to influence their evaluations.[17]

For instance, the Web site http://shopfootball.co.uk has a wide variety of football jerseys from teams around the world. When evaluating whether or not you want to pay £39.99 for Sweden's home jersey, you can find information regarding the fact that you can get jerseys with the official name and numbers of stars like Larsson, Ibrahimovic,

---

[16]You might also go to www.bestbuy.com to inspect their ISA. Do a search for pc's and determine which ISA is more informative. We'd tell you what we think, but we don't want to get such large companies mad at us.

[17]Li, Dahui, and Browne, Glenn J. 2006. The role of the need for cognition and mood in online flow experience. *The Journal of Computer Information Systems* 46 (Spring): 11–18.

and Ljungberg. Providing the stars' names provides some credibility. However, even better would be endorsements from satisfied customers: "I was in Norway for vacation and wanted to go to Oslo to buy some football gear. As I was driving along the interstate highway listening to the radio, I was interrupted by a warning message that said that there was a car driving the wrong way on the highway. 'One!' I yelled to my friend Ollie, 'There are hundreds of them out there!' Later, while I was staying at the Rikshospitalet, I went to shopfootball.co.uk and found that they had the best selection of football kits anywhere."

Colors. Inaccurate colors displayed on merchandise Web sites leads to loss of sales, increased complaints, and returns (estimated at 11–12% of online purchases), and customer defections.[18] It may seem obvious that true colors should be displayed online, but as you may have experienced, that's easier said than done. Colors may be misrepresented for at least four reasons:

1. *Colors are affected by adjacent colors.* Perception of a color will change, depending on the colors around it, an effect called simultaneous contrast. If a small square of green is placed on a blue background, the green will have a yellowish tinge. Change the background to yellow, and the green will have a blue tinge.
2. *The human eye is different from a scanner or camera.* As a result, the sensors in scanners and cameras are sensitive to specific frequencies of light in different proportions than the color sensitive cones in the human eye.
3. *Different devices have different color gamuts.* Monitors can show colors that printers can't print, and printers can print colors that monitors can't show. Cameras and scanner sensors can register colors that neither monitors nor printers can produce.
4. *Different devices use different color models.* A color model is simply a mathematical way to represent colors. When different devices use different color models they have to translate colors from one model to another, which often introduces errors. This is a particular problem for device-dependent models, meaning models defined strictly in terms of a specific printer, monitor, scanner, or camera (see footnote 17 on page 241).

Since color does matter when buying apparel and related team merchandise, customers can be assured with purchase guarantees (see next

---

[18]Nitse, Philip S., Parker, Kevin R., Krumwiede, Dennis, and Ottaway, Thomas. 2004. The impact of color in the e-commerce marketing of fashions: An exploratory study. *European Journal of Marketing* 38 (7): 898–915.

section) and information that reassures them of the color accuracy (e.g., "All colors are identical to authentic apparel worn by players.").

Purchase Decision

The objective at the purchase stage is to facilitate purchase by reducing any perceived risks. As depicted in Table 11.2, consumers evaluate seven aspects of risk when making a purchase.[19] Online retailing has suffered from high perceived risk and trust issues, so a primary task for those involved in selling merchandise, tickets, or other services online is to reduce perceived risk. Compared to men, women are more likely to perceive risk in online shopping, even if they are frequent

Table 11.2

Perceived Purchase Risks		
Perceived risk	**Description**	**What the customer thinks**
Financial	Loss due to hidden costs, inadequate information or warranty, fraudulent behavior, loss of privacy	Will I lose money?
Performance	The product is faulty or isn't the same as depicted online	Will the product work right?
Physical	The product might cause physical harm[a]	Can I get hurt?
Psychological	The product may not match the buyer's internal self-image	Will I like this?
Social	The product may not match the buyer's desired external social image	Will other people like this?
Convenience	The purchase may result in lost time due to shipping, returns, or customization	How long will this take?
Overall	The general satisfaction with all aspects of the purchase	Is this the right choice?

[a]For instance, the sale of lawn darts has been banned in the United States since 1988 despite the manufacturer's warnings on labels: Should not be played at night. Game is not intended for use while operating heavy machinery, motorcycles, or lawn equipment. Wear appropriate protective headgear in competitive matches.

---

[19]See Pires, Guilherme, Stanton, John, and Eckford, Andrew. 2004. Influences on the perceived risk of purchasing online. *Journal of Consumer Behavior* 4 (December): 118–131.

online shoppers. One of the most effective means of overcoming such risks is for the site to be recommended by a friend.[20] In this case, the sports marketer can't directly control such recommendations. However, third-party endorsements, from similar customers (e.g., Mary Smith, mother of three, reports, "I loved going online to get my tickets. It saved time not standing in line with my kids at the stadium.") or online verification agencies (e.g., Verisign) can reduce the perceived financial risk.

Perceived psychological and social risk can also be reduced by endorsements by appropriate celebrities and players, as well as customers. Guarantees that cover all circumstances ("100% satisfaction guaranteed. You may return this product for any reason within 30 days.") can reduce perceived performance, physical, psychological, and social risks. Providing clear shipping directions, order tracking and shipping times can reduce perceived convenience risks. Online retailers frequently track consumers' perceptions of this important risk factor. Immediately following an online purchase, the buyer is asked via an online survey, "When do you expect this shipment to be delivered?" In this way, the online retailer can determine if this information is being effectively communicated.

Providing ISA's, as discussed before, can help reduce the cognitive dissonance shoppers may have when they assess the overall efficacy of the purchase. Some shoppers may want to shop primarily based on price, so having the ability to sort product choices by price would be important to such shoppers. Similarly, others are looking for specific brands (e.g., Adidas) or products (football socks) and will want to search and sort accordingly.

Some teams are beginning to use new streaming video technology to simulate a social influence in the online shopping experience. The San Antonio Spurs have had cheerleaders appear online to introduce visitors to season ticket packages. The NBA has used Julius Irving to promote the playoffs on NBA.com (visit http://www.rovion.com/Showcase/DRJ_demo.htm). The New York Rangers have star players appear online to promote attendance (see http://www.rovion.com/Showcase/NYrangers_demo.htm). Employing these technologies stimulates shoppers' interest, provides a pleasant online experience, and can lead shoppers directly to making a purchase decision.

---

[20]Garbarino, Ellen, and Strahilevitz, Michal. 2004. Gender differences in the perceived risk of buying online and the effects of receiving a site recommendation. *Journal of Business Research* 57 (July): 768–775.

Post-Purchase Behavior

Providing a way for fans to interact with each other about the team, players, or transactional issues (tickets, merchandise, etc.) generally adds value to buyers after they have purchased merchandise, tickets, or other services. Assuming that the team has a relatively positive brand image among fans, message boards and chat rooms should have positive effects, even if some of the messages are negative.[21] Message boards and chat rooms facilitate consumer problem solving, as well as offer opportunities to reinforce team-related experiences and purchases. These fan interactive devices also help keep the team accountable for their actions, as they know that fans are likely to transmit messages to other fans regarding unfair business practices through chat rooms or fan forums.[22]

As noted earlier, sports teams often fail to provide appropriate contact information on team Web sites. Offering online support, either via live chat with a service operator or simply providing a phone number, can help customers deal with issues they have after they've already decided to make or have made a purchase. Some Web sites initiate a live-chat pop-up box available as customers get further along in the purchase process. For instance, after customers have placed items in the shopping cart and begin to check out (but prior to actually concluding the transaction), online chat with a service agent could help assure that the purchase is completed.

Web sites that personalize and customize the site for return visits by the customer are likely to lead to increased future visits and sales.[23] People shop online for time savings. Web sites that track and store vital customer data to facilitate future purchase decisions and purchasing are likely to be seen as more convenient and efficient. For instance, if you are a frequent traveler, you would like to have all of your personal data stored so you don't have to reenter it every time you make a flight reservation. In the same way, fans appreciate the personalization when they return to the site ("Hello, Sven") and the time saved when making repeat purchases after signing in.

---

[21]Chiou, Jyh-Shen, and Cheng, Cathy. 2003. Should a company have a message board on its web sites? *Journal of Interactive Marketing* 17 (Summer): 50–61.

[22]For an interesting take on the downside effects of targeting switchers versus loyal customers, see Feinberg, Fred M., Krishna, Aradhna, and Zhang, Z. John. Do we care what others get? A behaviorist approach to targeted promotions. *Journal of Marketing Research* 39 (August): 277–291.

[23]Boyer, Kenneth K., and Hult, G. Tomas M. 2005. Customer behavior in an online ordering application: A decision scoring model. *Decision Sciences* 36 (December): 569–598.

Conclusion

Teams that effectively employ technology as innovators in the sports world will likely be the most profitable in the long run. However, in addition to following the guidelines for online stores already discussed, three important back-office issues must be monitored and effectively resolved:

1. Do software/technology processes prevent lost orders, shipment delays, or incomplete orders?
2. Will large waves of orders (e.g., Christmas) overload processing capacities causing system failures?
3. Does the software/technology system track inventory and update the online store, shipping, and supply in a timely fashion?[24]

The best designed Web sites are only as good as the technology and supply chain systems that support them. If you have a very cool Web site with attractive merchandise or ticket offers, but the site crashes during the mad rush, you may end up with more dissatisfied customers than before the promotion. Marketing and sales personnel are often the cause of such crashes, because they forget to mention planned online promotions to the IT personnel responsible for handling the resulting orders. As many as 73 percent of company Web site crashes occur during marketing campaigns—and as many as 26 percent of marketers never communicate promotion plans to IT.[25] So, a word to the wise, keep the IT folks in the loop on all promotion plans.

---

[24]Phan, Dien D., Chen, Jim Q., and Ahmad, Sohel. 2005. Lessons learned from an initial e-commerce failure by a catalog retailer. *Information Systems Management* 22 (Summer): 8–13.

[25]Sherriff, Lucy. 2005. Marketing dept to blame for website crashes: Official. www.theregister.com, August 4: http://www.theregister.com/2005/08/04/marketing_to_blame/.

Build Community
Kirk Wakefield and
Madison Clark

12

Value in brand communities is interactively co-created by companies and consumers, rather than merely exchanged between them.[1] Brand communities are participants in the brand's larger social construction and play a vital role in the brand's ultimate legacy.[2] Due to the high level of fan identification with the team (brand), sports teams can build fan communities in ways that few other brands can.

Building community is important to sports teams. Repeat customers generate over twice as much gross income as new customers.[3] Bridging the gap between a customer who attends a single game or two and becoming a loyal fan is where community begins. The concept of community means an open partnership between management and customers where the customers feel a sense of belonging to the organization. Being part of a community also gives fans a feeling of belonging with other fans with similar interests. Joining a community suggests an interdependence of giving and doing for others as expected of them and produces a feeling that one is part of a dependable and stable social structure.[4]

[1]Leavy, Brian. 2004. Partnering with the customer. *Strategy & Leadership* 32.3: 10–14.

[2]Muniz Jr., Albert M., and O'Quinn, Thomas C. 2001. Brand community. *Journal of Consumer Research* 27.4: 412–432.

[3]Winer, Russell S. 2001. A framework for customer relationship management. *California Management Review* 43.4: 89–109.

[4]Sarason, S. B. *The Psychological Sense of Community*. London: Jossey-Bass, 1977.

Manchester United does an excellent job of building community by including fans at every point possible—making fans feel like their input and opinions matter. After signing up to be a part of the "Talking Reds" community, fans can go to the team's Fanzone to have a chance to win tickets, signed jerseys, books, and pictures or other merchandise (plasma TV's, DVD recorders, etc.) or chat with other team fans.

Once customers become members in a community, switching costs dramatically increase due to the social bonds, personal rapport, and the trust that has been built. Sports teams are capable of building psychological exit barriers by building solid communities where fans will identify with not only the players on the team (who may come and go), but with the entire organization.[5]

For the team, a community allows the firm to effectively serve its fans at a level where retention and reputation will be high. Well-managed customer relationships provide for a high tolerance or "goodwill," opening a larger communication channel and allowing the firm to attend to service problems, without losing a customer.[6]

Building communities starts with building one-to-one relationships through customer relationship management (CRM). Satisfying brand community experiences are a function of six factors (see Figure 12.1).[7]

1. Reactive and Proactive Customer Service
2. Membership Reward Programs
3. Membership Value
4. Customization
5. Website Community
6. Management Partnering

We discuss each of the factors in turn, explaining how teams can effectively build satisfying communities.

---

[5]See Caruana, Albert. 2004. The impact of switching costs on customer loyalty: A study among corporate customers of mobile telephony. *Journal of Targeting, Measurement and Analysis for Marketing* 12.3: 256–268.

[6]Parasuraman, A. 1991. Understanding customer expectations of service. *Sloan Management Review* 32.3: 39–49.

[7]See footnote 3 on page 247.

Figure 12.1

The Community Model

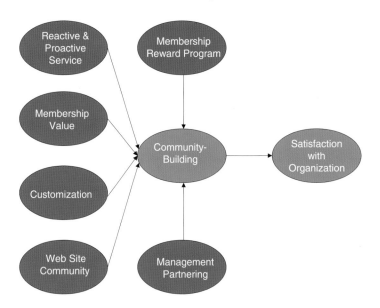

Customer Service

Customer service is critical to any business. Not too many folks want to be part of a community where no one cleans things up, no one helps others when things go wrong, or members find it difficult to get anyone to return their calls.[8] Are there still organizations out there that just don't get it? In a word: Yes. A Google search for "worst customer service" turned up 204,000 separate entries, with thousands of Web sites and blogs nominating well-known corporate brands as worthy recipients of "worst ever." Some specifically reference professional sports teams (e.g., Yankees concessions). My guess is that you can think of someplace that's given you terrible service within the past week.[9]

---

[8]An exception would apparently be those of us who continue to use Microsoft Windows.

[9]My nomination goes to the Yellow Cabs of NYC, if you call it bad service when the cab driver lets you off at LaGuardia without letting you get your luggage out of the trunk before speeding out of the terminal at roughly 120 mph. FYI, you must be personally in NYC to file a police report—which makes it convenient for cab drivers to pull this off on people who have to catch an immediate flight.

What kind of customer service must teams provide to help build community? Community building as it relates to customer service quality is not limited to only reactive services that respond to service failure or deficiencies. Any contact that a fan has with a team is a customer service encounter, and has the potential to either gain or lose repeat business.[10] In addition to providing extraordinary reactive service, firms must practice proactive customer service. Proactive customer service entails anticipating and meeting customers' needs before they occur. Effective reactive and proactive service creates a level of customer service that enhances the community environment.

Reactive Service

Reactive service initiates when the customer has a problem and contacts the organization to resolve it. To develop a healthy community, teams must reach beyond merely providing adequate service to reach fans' desired service level. Responsive service quality[11] can be characterized in terms of what fans expect employees to do. Employees are expected to:

- always be available when a customer needs them,
- never be too busy or distracted to respond to customer requests,
- always be willing to help customers,
- provide prompt service, and
- perform their jobs in a timely manner.

Reliable customer service is critical because of the deleterious effects of poor service. A fan's expectation for good customer service actually increases when he or she experiences poor service.[12] After the fan has a negative experience, the next interaction with the organization must not only meet original expectations, but make up for the last letdown. The poor service fans receive in the parking lot now alerts them to be more attentive to customer service issues, as they search to (dis)confirm the initial impression that the organization provides poor service.

---

[10]See footnote 3 on page 247.

[11]See Parasuraman, A., Berry, Leonard, and Zeithaml, Valerie. 1991a. Refinement and reassessment of the SERVQUAL scale. *Journal of Retailing* Winter: 420–450.

[12]See Parasuraman, A., Berry, Leonard L., and Zeithaml, Valerie A. 1991b. Perceived service quality as a customer-based performance measure: An empirical examination of organizational barriers using an extended service model. *Human Resource Management* 30.3: 335–364.

Developing community requires a higher standard than simply providing parking, concessions, and entertainment on the field. A positive community experience requires that employees be available at the point of the customer's need. To be able to react with good customer service, teams must show a willingness to (a) add employees where understaffed, (b) schedule employees according to demand, (c) train employees on the frequency and types of customer service issues, (d) hold employees accountable for excellent service, and then, ultimately, to (e) to incur labor costs to ensure service. It is difficult to have any kind of customer service if no one is available to help.

The majority of service failures are related to employees' unwillingness to effectively address the situation.[13] So, the key is in management allowing employees to make decisions. Rather than micromanaging through rules and requirements for all contingencies, management and customers benefit when management loosens the grip to empower employees. Employees are able to identify root causes of problems more quickly. Employee empowerment requires effective and satisfactory internal exchange between contact employees and the organization, which in turn engages the contact employee and allows the organization to have a successful external exchange with the fans in the community.[14]

Providing prompt service challenges the organization's system of problem solving. The service must be available at the time the customer's need arises. If employees can't solve a problem for members of the community, a service delay ensues as they must turn to a superior for answers. As customer service becomes more customized and requirements more difficult to predict, it is more likely that employees will be called to interpret customer needs.[15] Employee empowerment is the mark of a true community where the needs of employees and customers are valued.

Proactive Service

An organization practicing proactive service anticipates and provides for customers' needs before they happen instead of waiting for the customer to initiate contact. Acting proactively requires a deep

---

[13]See footnote 12 on page 250.

[14]Yoon, Mahn Hee, Seo, Jai Hyun, and Yoon, Tae Seog. 2004. Effects of contact employee supports on critical employee responses and customer service evaluation. *The Journal of Services Marketing* 18.5: 395–412.

[15]Lashley, Conrad. 1999. Employee empowerment in services: A framework for analysis. *Personnel Review* 28.3: 169.

customer focus and necessitates new ways of doing things rather than just listening to customers and reacting.[16] Proactive service can pleasantly surprise customers by consistently exceeding expectations. Fans are accustomed to and even expect long service lines when stadiums are filled to capacity. But, what would happen if management surprised fans by offering speedy service through technology (self-service lines or kiosks), adding employees to handle the crowd, or in a cosmic other-earthly turn of events provide enough service space in concessions areas to accommodate quality service? Fans would be pleasantly surprised at the prompt service and ultimately be more satisfied and committed to the community.

Proactive service can be characterized in terms of four related tasks (AAAA):

1. Anticipate the customers' needs
2. Accept responsibility for solving problems before they happen
3. Act to prevent problems
4. Ante-up before being asked.

When a team anticipates fans' needs, it builds community because the team establishes interdependence between the fan and the team.[17] In order to anticipate needs, the team must know its fans. In addition to effective CRM and database management, organizations can initiate employee teams to analyze customer activities to determine service gaps (see footnote 15 on page 251). Trying to understand each other's needs helps strengthen any relationship. When team management and employees are committed to understanding fans and their needs, fans will grow in their commitment to the community.

Beyond understanding the customer, knowing the process of the transaction and the points at which customer needs arise will help the firm map out the potential service needs. This means that management must consider possible problems at each stage in the service delivery process experienced by fans.

1. Information search
2. Purchase
3. Travel
4. Parking

---

[16]Vandermerwe, Sandra. 2004. Achieving deep customer focus. *Sloan Management Review* 45.3: 26–37.

[17]See Wiesenfeld, Esther. 1996. The concept of "We": A community social psychology myth? *Journal of Community Psychology* 24.4: 337–345.

5. Gate entry
6. Finding seat
7. Watching event
8. Finding and consuming services
9. Property exit

What can go wrong at each stage for infrequent fans, season ticket holders, groups, parties, or suite owners? Are employees prepared and empowered to prevent those problems from occurring? The notion of proactive service is fundamentally different from reactive service. The goal is to not have any problems to solve because the organization has committed itself to anticipate and prevent them from happening. In the realm of customer service, we can personally think of few things that chap our posteriors more than to see organizations not fix things until the customer complains. When fans see broken toilets, spills in hallways, or obnoxious fans, they know that employees are also seeing these things and deciding to do nothing about it. This is not what people look for in a good community. On the other hand, individuals highly committed to the community are likely to report such deficiencies to employees because they want the best for the community. Some highly committed fans may even opt to help clean up by picking up trash or "fixing" the obnoxious fan on the behalf of the rest of the community.

A good example of effective anticipation comes from Proflowers, an online flower company.[18] Proflowers analyzed potential customer issues that allowed them to take preemptive measures. Flower companies frequently receive calls from customers wondering if the order was successfully delivered. Proflowers automatically emails the customer upon delivery of each order. Such proactive activities make customers realize the company cares enough to keep them informed, thus strengthening community. Proflowers *anticipated* customer needs, *accepted* responsibility for solving the problem before their customers had to deal with it, took *action* to prevent the problem, and was willing to *ante-up* or invest in the CRM program that emails customers when orders are delivered.

Membership Reward Program

Membership reward programs are promotional activities that reward repeat purchases in an attempt to add value for the fan and to help

---

[18]Greco, Susan. 2001. Fanatics! *Inc*. Apr: 36.

create loyalty to the community. The design of reward programs should accentuate the psychological benefits of:

1. Providing a feeling of participation and interaction
2. Anticipation of future awards
3. A sense of belonging.[19]

When a fan commits to being a member of the Talking Reds community of Manchester United's football team, that fan is differentiating himself from nonmembers. Enrollment in a reward program is a means of self-selection and identification with the organization. Joining reward programs can be the fan's first statement of involvement with the team. Once a fan has entered, reward programs also create exit barriers because the fan will not be able to collect rewards if community membership is not maintained. Accordingly, members must be provided with real benefits that make them feel valued, not targeted.[20] If the fan sees the membership as a means for the team to advertise more instead of allowing the fan to contribute and belong to the community, the team is less likely to achieve its goals.

A crucial issue in the relationship between community and reward programs is that the rewards given are seen as highly desirable by the "true" fans who are already heavily vested in the program.[21] These true fans believe they are already loyal; so, they should receive extra attention. Most often this can be seen in the differences in the benefits afforded to season ticket holders (club vs. tickets-only) versus mini-plan buyers. The difference should be noticeable so that the high volume fan feels appropriately appreciated. When the reward and structure is appropriate, the loyal fan places a higher value in being part of the community.

In order to maximize loyalty and profitability, a team must give its best value to its best fans.[22] Teams may be so oriented toward getting new business that they reward new fans for coming in while neglecting the season ticket holders or club-level suite owners. Well-designed reward programs can target and attract valuable customers while

[19]Dowling Grahame R., and Uncles, Mark. 1997. Do customer loyalty programs really work? *Sloan Management Review* 38.4: 71–83.

[20]Wansink, Brian. 2003. Developing a cost-effective brand loyalty program. *Journal of Advertising Research* 43.3: 301–309.

[21]Id.

[22]O'Brian, Louise, and Jones, Charles. 1995. Do rewards really create loyalty? *Harvard Business Review* 73.3: 75.

discouraging less profitable customers. When the Frisco Roughriders (www.ridersbaseball.com) decided to provide promotional items only to season ticket holders, they were recognizing the importance of building value for being part of the community. If you aren't a part of the community, you don't get a reward just for showing up once on a promo night. Instead, the occasional fan sees the benefits of joining and is motivated to gain the benefits only available through membership.

Membership Value

Membership value is the additional attributes added to a service for those who have extended relationships with the firm. As we just discussed, initiating and designing reward structure is critical to building community, such that there are clear differentiating features that separate members and nonmembers, as well as low-volume versus high-volume members. In this way, the emphasis is on the internal structure of the reward program. Beyond that, however, membership in the community must represent clear value from an external perspective relative to competition and relative to nonmembers.

Consumers perceive the value of their membership in terms of: (1) the membership value in relation to competitors and alternatives, (2) membership value in relation to nonmembership, and (3) the benefits received for what they must give up to be a member. Community can be enhanced when the team provides the best membership deal compared to competitors. An individual selecting membership in a community (e.g., online communities, social clubs, Harley bike clubs, etc.) will evaluate the relative trade-offs in joining one association over another. Within the realm of sports, fans will only commit the resources—time, money, and effort—to those communities that offer the best value. A sports fan in Chicago, for instance, is not going to be a season ticket holder for all the major league teams (Bears, White Sox, Cubs, Blackhawks, and Fire), let alone all the other minor league and collegiate sports teams that compete in the Chicago area. Fans will choose to join those communities that offer the best psychological, social, and economic benefits.

The organization striving to bridge the gap between value and perception must pay attention to the nonmonetary factors the customer legitimately considers a cost.[23] Within the sports and leisure space in

---

[23]Zeithaml, Valerie A. 1988. Consumer perceptions of price, quality, and value: A means-end model and synthesis of evidence. *Journal of Marketing* 52: 2–22.

people's lives, the key consideration is the time and effort spent by the fan in community-related activities. Time and effort are not a cost, but an attribute, to the Harley motorcycle owners and community members who spend their entire Saturday afternoon cooking hot dogs at the local Harley-Davidson dealership. In the same way, fans who spend hours tailgating and attending an event are investing the time and effort in the community. Consequently, teams should make every effort possible to facilitate such activities. The Houston Texans invest heavily in accommodating the 35,000+ tailgaters that show up on game day with special music and band, fan recreation areas, and dedicated parking areas for tailgating. The Texans even offer a tailgaters contest (sponsored, of course; see below). Conversely, other organizations do less to accommodate fans, placing difficult or costly restrictions on tailgating (see http://www.bearshistory.com/tailgating/).

Source: Courtesy of Houston Texans.

Offering visible differences for members provides membership legitimacy.[24] Whatever value is added for members must be at a level to distinguish between members and nonmembers. If there is no noticeable difference there is no need for nonmembers to switch. In the football tailgating context, community members may receive preferential treatment (best spots, early entry, etc.) over nonmembers.

---

[24]Muniz Jr., Albert M., and O'Quinn, Thomas C. 2001. Brand Community. *Journal of Consumer Research* 27.4: 412–432.

Visibility adds value for those who want to join and/or are part of the community because these people are important to the organization and they want everyone else to know just how important they are. So, the question is, "What is the team doing to offer visible benefits that differentiate between members and nonmembers of the community?"

Switching costs. Another important component is creating a level of benefits that makes it difficult to discontinue membership in the form of switching costs. Two types of switching costs influence fans' decisions to remain or exit the community.[25]

Relational switching costs are the intangible benefits received through relational connections to individuals, the group, or the organization as a whole such that defection would cause a personal/emotional loss. Fans become emotionally attached with other fans who are highly identified with the team. Ideally, fans develop personal contact and relationships with their customer service or account representative, team management, as well as limited contact with players. The greater the degree of contact and relationship building, the more difficult it will be for the individual to leave the community.

Informational switching costs relate to the time and money put into a value exchange, which is relevant in membership programs. For example, a member of Southwest Airline's Rapid Reward program who has flown five times with Southwest will be motivated to continue to patronize knowing the eighth flight is free. Similarly, teams should develop loyalty programs and membership value that builds over time and commitment. The San Antonio Spurs rewards program does this by increasing the value of the rewards as members attend more events at the AT&T center (see Chapter 3). Programs which increase benefits and—importantly—recognition to long-time members create significant switching costs. Bill Sutton, consultant for the NBA, makes a relevant suggestion that is low cost to the team, but outstanding value to long-standing members of the community. Teams can honor long-time season ticket holders (e.g., 20 years or more) with their names listed on banners hanging from the ceiling alongside their championship banners. Special ceremonies could be held each year honoring 5, 10, 15, and 20+ year season ticket holders. Other privileges could also be provided that add value and increase switching costs as members anticipate future rewards.

---

[25]Caruana, Albert. 2004. The impact of switching costs on customer loyalty: A study among corporate customers of mobile telephony. *Journal of Targeting, Measurement and Analysis for Marketing* 12.3: 256–268.

Customization (Flexibility)

What is important to one fan may be unimportant to another. To integrate fans into the community requires a dynamic approach to adding value. Customization implies the creation of products and services for individual customers.[26] Fans do not want to feel as though they have no control over what role they can take in the community or are limited in some way to take only what is offered when other feasible alternatives exist. Specifically, some teams offer little flexibility in ticket packages or hospitality services, basically operating with a one-size-fits-all attitude. You can tell when a team has a lousy community concept when the response fans get to special requests is something along the lines of "we don't do it that way." You can see the problem. The team doesn't see itself as part of an integrated community. It sees itself as dictating policy and "allowing fans the opportunity" to purchase tickets.[27]

Organizations would do well to remember to not "pigeonhole your customers by forcing them to interact with you in only one way."[28] For instance, some fans may prefer a specific channel of communication (email, phone, fax, ticket office, etc.) at a certain time or location (morning/evening; work/home). An account representative needs to know each customer's preferred method (which is attainable at sign-up) and customize accordingly. Teams that do not interact with their customers in their preferred method will find themselves not communicating at all.

Corporate sponsors and suite owners may make a request to use the facility in a way that the team has not offered previously. Season ticket holders may prefer to pay for their tickets in a way currently not available. Mini-plan buyers may want more choices of game packages. What will the team do? The concept of community means that the team will work with the customer to find a solution that works for both parties. This will require flexibility on all parties involved in the community, but the focal issue is that it should not always be the fan who has to be flexible. Providing choices builds community because it recognizes the unique needs of customers. The quantity of choices is important to serve the array of customers and their varying desires. Numerous choices also allow for a more personalized experience

---

[26]See footnote 3 on page 247.

[27]Yes, there are teams like this, mostly in the NFL.

[28]Mollison, Caitlin. 2001. Driving customer service. *Internet World* 7.17: 28–35.

between the team and the fan and places the team in a unique position in the community—and puts them at a competitive advantage over other entertainment communities that do not customize offerings to the needs of customers.

Web Site Community

With the introduction of mass media via the Internet, geographic boundaries on a community hold less meaning than in the past. Major League Baseball has taken advantage of this fact by offering members access to every game anywhere during the season, allowing faithful Red Sox fans in California to watch all of Boston's home games. Members of the Red Sox Nation do not have to live in Boston to be a part of the community. Clearly, the Web is a critical element in building a network of customers for exchanging product-related information and to create relationships between customers and the company.[29] The goal of the Web site is to enable the fan to be a part of the organization, providing information and input as well as receiving it.

Maintaining freshness by continuously updating, making it easier to use, and improving the physical appeal of the firm's Web site is an effective part of developing community.[30] The Web site, in most cases, will be the first source of information for the potential customer, the curious customer, or the customer with a question, so it is crucial that the Web site make a good first impression and meet the specific needs of its various users and potential members. The adage that "Content is King" holds true for all Web sites, but particularly those designed for community building. In contrast to transaction-designed Web sites, community Web sites are designed for users that come and go frequently, but not necessarily to transact economic business. Activities like discussion boards, surveys, and subcommunities on certain topics allow for personalization and interaction.

A firm's Web site can act as the forum for the community to make customers feel a part of the whole.[31] The Phoenix Suns send streaming video messages from its players promoting new ticket packages. The Web site offers times when the customers can chat with important

---

[29]See footnote 3 on page 247.

[30]Ansari, Asim, and Mela, Carl F. 2003. E-Customization. *Journal of Marketing Research* XL: 131–145.

[31]See footnote 3 on page 247.

members of the organization, view live feeds of events, take surveys, have chances to express opinions, purchase customized goods and services, read reviews of reward program points with chances to redeem points, and have the chance to read special recognition of individual customers. Again, in our opinion, the best team Web site in the world is Manchester United (www.manutd.com). If you need new ideas for Web site community building, just keep checking back to their site to see the latest advances in Web site development geared to building its worldwide community.

Management Partnering

Management Partnering means that value is interactively co-created by management and fans who together are united in their goal to serve the welfare of the community. The more that fans and management interact, the higher the likelihood of forming a strong relationship or bond.[32] High levels of fan-management interaction can build a relationship that can be used to add and create value through cooperation. To implement management partnering, management must communicate the idea of community with the fans and then maintain open communication lines between the team and fans.

The team must assume the role of community initiator. Management is charged with creating the connection because customers are less likely to perceive a relationship if they always have to initiate communications.[33] The notion of a social constellation represents a successful community.[34] The constellation is a link between the fan, the team, and other fans that provides the fan with a consciousness that each belongs. In that sense, it is similar to our concept of identification with the team, but in this case the fan reaches the point where he or she believes that everyone—including the players and management—are in the group together. The team must demonstrate good faith within the community such that members perceive that they are on relatively equal footing, rather than worshipers and the worshiped.

The concept of management partnering in pro sports may be seen as anathema to old school professionals. However, management part-

[32]McMillan, D. W., and Chavis, D. M. 1986. Sense of community: A definition and theory. *American Journal of Psychology* 14.1: 6–23.

[33]See footnote 12 on page 250.

[34]Muniz Jr., Albert M., and O'Quinn, Thomas C. 2001. Brand community. *Journal of Consumer Research* 27.4: 412–432.

nering is not abdicating decision-making responsibility. Instead, management seeks to place proper value on fans' opinions and to make decisions that seek the welfare of all involved—including management. By helping others, you are helping yourself, as fans become more committed to the community when their viewpoints are appreciated.

Four tasks must be completed in order for effective management partnering to lead to satisfying community experiences.

First, management must create an atmosphere that makes fans feel that the organization and fans all work together. The fan's level of participation during the exchange determines the level of the fan's satisfaction with the service and the community.[35] As discussed elsewhere in the text, this means that management decisions regarding ticket increases, changes in game day policies, and the like should be open to community discussion prior to implementation. This can be done with online or offline focus groups and forums.

Second, management must do all it can to make the customer feel a "part of the family." Members of a family give to others without necessarily receiving benefits in return. In fact, that's mostly what family is about. In business terms, this translates into operational benevolence. Operational benevolence reflects an "underlying motivation to place the consumer's interest ahead of self-interest . . . that is operationalized in visible behaviors that unambiguously favor the consumer's interest, even if a cost is incurred in the process."[36] This means that team employees seek to surprise fans with extra service, support, or products—just like you would do if you were really trying to impress someone. As a practical example, some Starbucks will add whipped cream on top of my decaf with a shot of Toffee Nut syrup without charging, while others don't. The benevolence of the front line employees at the former positively influences my feelings about being part of the Starbucks community, while the latter makes me want to crumble my cinnamon scone into little pieces and donate them to the tip jar. The point is that just giving a little extra can add positive karma to the community.

Third, communications with fans should iterate, "We're partners." Current standard business practices include references to customers as "targets" that are "managed." Within the community concept, teams should be more production-focused (viz., the product is a strong

---

[35]Yoon, Mahn Hee, Seo, Jai Hyun, and Yoon, Tae Seog. 2004. Effects of contact employee supports on critical employee responses and customer service evaluation. *The Journal of Services Marketing* 18.5: 395–412.

[36]Sirdeshmukh, Deepak, Singh, Jagdip, and Sabol, Barry. 2002. Consumer trust, value, and loyalty in relational exchanges. *Journal of Marketing* 66.1: 15–23.

community) with fans as actors in the co-creation of value.[37] The aim is to break down the physical, psychological, and social separation between fans and management. Teams can develop creative advertising campaigns and promotions that lead to exciting community experiences (viz., for some good examples go to http://www.nba.com/mavericks/entertainment/entertainment_index.html). All pro teams engage in community service activities to communicate the partnership idea. As discussed elsewhere in the text, these efforts should be coordinated and integrated with a central purpose and theme so that fans make a clear connection between the activities and the team.

Finally, management can develop a community level partnership by facilitating open lines of communication between fans. Online forums and chat rooms will reveal problems that might not be sent directly to management, but are communicated between fans—with knowledge that management has access to the conversations. Sharing information, whether positive or negative, if conducted in good faith will build a bond between the fan and the team that is advantageous to both parties, especially in the exchange of value over the long haul.[38]

Conclusion

Teams that grasp the community concept will be the ones that prosper in the twenty-first century. Marketing has moved to one-to-one communications and mass media is dying in the process. Customer relationship management must focus on building communities where fans and management co-create value, partnering together to seek the welfare of the community.

---

[37]Prahaland, C. K., and Ramaswamy, Venkat. 2004. Co-creation experiences: The next practice in value creation. *Journal of Interactive Marketing* 18.3: 5.

[38]Zinkhan, George M. 2002. Relationship marketing: Theory and implementation. *Journal of Market-Focused Management* 5: 83–89.

Index